McDONNELL DOUGLAS

McDONNELL DOUGLAS
A TALE OF TWO GIANTS

BILL YENNE

Crescent Books
A Division of Crown Publishers, Inc.
 A Bison Book

This edition published 1985 by
Crescent Books, distributed by
Crown Publishers Inc.

Produced by
Bison Books Corp.,
15 Sherwood Place,
Greenwich, CT. 06830,
USA.

British Library Cataloguing in Publication Data

Yenne, Bill
McDonnell Douglas Airplane — History
629.133'34 TL686.M25

ISBN 0-517-442876

Printed in Hong Kong

h g f e d c

Acknowledgements

The author wishes to thank the following people for helping to supply the
information to make this book possible: Bob Foster at the McDonnell
component of McDonnell Douglas; Dave Eastman, Don Hanson and Audrey
Corrigan at the Douglas component of McDonnell Douglas; Carleen Bentley
and Garrison Leatch at the Donald Douglas Museum; and Susan Flowers at
McDonnell Douglas Astronautics. For helping to supply the photos, thanks are
due Bob Foster, Marion Pyles and all the people listed in the photo credits. I
would especially like to thank Harry Gann at McDonnell Douglas Long Beach,
whose help was indispensible and who took many, and supplied most, of the
photos of Douglas aircraft included here. Finally, I'd like to thank Rod Baird and
Kathleen Jaeger for their research help and Carol Yenne for typing the
manuscript.

All production close-ups, charts, graphs and maps were compiled, designed
and produced by the author.
Edited by Susan Garratt and Thomas G Aylesworth

Picture Credits

All photos are official McDonnell Douglas photos except as noted below.
American Airlines Museum via Paul F. Kent: 92 top, 108 top.
J. Roger Bentley: 150-51.
Phil Brooks: 110 top, 130-131, 148 top.
Langford Brown: 15 third from bottom right, 21 bottom right, 22 second from
top left, 24 bottom left, 42 bottom, 96 bottom.
Howard J. Chaloner: 158-159.
Collect-Air Photos via Mike Sparkman: 92-93, 94-95, 108 top, 112 top and
bottom, 114-115 (AeroGem Slide).
Continental Airlines via John D. Clayton: 161 top.
Harry Gann (McDonnell Douglas Corp, Douglas Aircraft component): 2-3,
55 top right, 58-59, 62 top and bottom, 117 top, 149 top, 224 top.
E William Helmer: 135 top.
McDonnell Douglas via George Gayuski: 134-135.
McDonnell Douglas via Harry Miller: 199 both.
Michael M. McGown: 142-143, 150 left.
Harry Miller collection: 16 bottom, 22 top left, 23 top left, 26 bottom left and
top right, 46 bottom, 109 second from top.
NASA: 205, 206, 207.
Richard Neyland: 170-171.
Pan American World Airways via George Gayuski: 109 bottom, 128.
Terry Panopalis: 78-79, 122 second from top left, 224-225.
Bryant Petitt Jr.: 146-147, 174-175
© Marion Pyles: 139 top left, 148-149, 152-153.
Norbert G. Raith: 110-111, 126-127.
Erik Simonsen: 157 top.
TWA via George Gayuski: 98-99.
United States Air Force: 21 top left, 26 center left, 37 bottom, 38 top, 53 top, 76
top left and right, 83 top right, 101 top, 111 top right, 113 both, 166 top left, 176,
177 top, 180-181, 214 bottom, 215 top, 216-217, 217 top, 218 top, 219 top, 230
top, 233 both, 236-237, 238-239, 240.
United States Marine Corps: 242 bottom, 246 bottom, 248 top.
United States Navy: 45 second from top right, 49, 56-57, 61 top, 63 bottom, 65
top, 69 top right, 72 top right, 73 top, 75 top, 125 top, 214 top, 220-221, 243,
246-247, 247 bottom, 251 top.
© Bill Yenne: 7, 14 bottom, 20 bottom, 30-31, 31 top, 32, 36 top, 40, 48, 56 top
right and left, 58 top left and bottom, 68 top left, 71 bottom right, 111 top left,
154, 155, 187 bottom, 218-219, 222-223, 232, 242 top, 252, 253.

Page One: A Douglas AD-4Q Skyraider (*foreground*) and McDonnell F2H
Banshees on the deck of a US Navy carrier after a snowfall off the coast of Korea
in 1953. Douglas and McDonnell aircraft in service together.

Page 2-3: A McDonnell Douglas KC-10 aerial refueling tanker tops off the tanks
of the Skyhawks of the US Navy's aerobatic team, the Blue Angels.

Below: The Long Beach, California offices of McDonnell Douglas were a major
Douglas Aircraft Company facility for 25 years before the 1967 merger.

TABLE OF CONTENTS

A TALE OF TWO GIANTS

The McDonnell Douglas story is the story of two men, the aircraft companies they started and the aircraft company that resulted from their April 1967 merger. The two men were both of Scottish ancestry, both graduates of the Massachusetts Institute of Technology (MIT), and both built airplanes. Beyond this they had little in common, following dissimilar paths that ultimately resulted in their becoming two of the true giants of American aviation.

Donald Wills Douglas was born on 6 April 1892, the son of Bill and Dorothy Douglas of Brooklyn, New York. Young Douglas, the future airplane builder, was fascinated by ships and, like his older brother, enrolled in the US Naval Academy at Annapolis, Maryland. While at the Academy, Douglas, like so many others of the era, discovered the wonders of this newfangled invention called the 'aeroplane.' He had heard through the grapevine about an aeronautical engineering course offered at MIT and decided to pursue it. In 1912, after two years at the Academy, he resigned and changed schools. He completed the four-year engineering course in half the allotted time and was immediately hired as an assistant aeronautical engineer by MIT, where he stayed for a year. Douglas had just left MIT and gone to work for Connecticut Aircraft in 1915 when he got a job offer from Glenn Martin, proprietor of the Glenn Martin Company, which was at the time one of the leading manufacturers of aircraft in California. Except for a brief stint on the payroll of the US Army Signal Corps Aviation Section in Washington DC just before the United States entered World War I, Douglas was with Martin for five years. During this time, he served as chief designer for Martin's most important project of the era – the MB-1.

On 17 January 1918 the US Army issued a contract for a twin-engined four-place observation/bombing aircraft. When the United States had entered World War I nearly a year earlier, it had no domestically designed first-line combat aircraft and was depending on foreign-built (primarily French and British) or foreign-designed/American-built aircraft. The airplane that the Army had in mind was to replace the British Handley Page and Italian Caproni aircraft that were used by the Army Air Service. Given the provisional designation GMB (Glenn Martin Bomber), the Donald Douglas-designed bird first took to the air on 15 August 1918. By the time that the war ended three months later, nine of the aircraft had been completed under the designation MB-1 (Martin Bomber, First). Donald Douglas had designed the Army's first bomber and the largest plane yet designed in the

Above: Donald Wills Douglas (*left foreground*) with his family on the front steps of their Brooklyn brownstone, circa 1899.

Right: These two men, captured by enthusiasm for flying when aviation had just been born, were to become captains of an industry whose development they helped direct. Neither forgot his Scottish ancestry, which is represented here in the tartan ties of their respective clans.

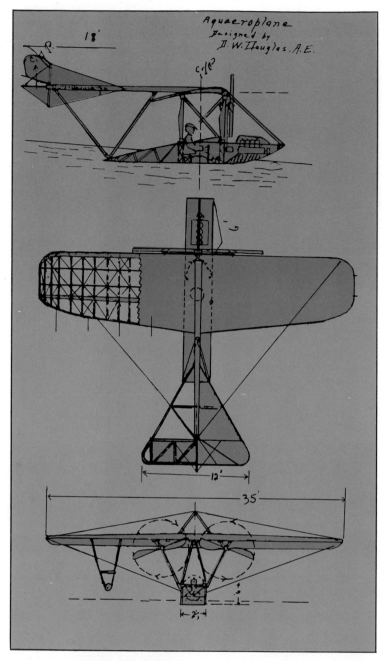

Left: The Aquaeroplane was designed by Donald Douglas when he was still at Annapolis, making it the first Douglas airplane, though it was never built.

Below left: Don Douglas at his desk in the drafting room at the Glenn Martin Company. He was soon to be chief designer for one of Martin's most important projects, the MB-1 bomber.

Below right: The Martin MB-1, the US Army's first multiengined bomber, was designed by Donald Douglas.

United States. It is ironic that he designed the plane for Martin after having had all his drawings rejected while he was an in-house designer with the Army Signal Corps Aviation Section in 1916. In 1918 the Martin Company moved to Ohio, then the center of the nation's aviation industry, and in June 1920 got a contract for 20 improved bombers designated MB-2. By that time, however, Donald Douglas was heading back to California, a state that he was destined to help transform into the next center of the nation's aviation industry.

James Smith McDonnell Jr was born on 9 April 1899, the third son of James and Susie McDonnell of Denver, Colorado. (The family surname had been changed from MacDonald when their ancestors arrived from Scotland about five generations before.) The McDonnells moved to Altheimer, Arkansas where James Sr established a general store and where young James, his two brothers and sister grew up. James McDonnell turned 18 just a week before the United States entered World War I, but his marginal eyesight kept him from realizing his dream of being an Army flier. He finally succeeded. Five years after the end of the war, after earning a degree from Princeton and studying aeronautical engineering at MIT, he earned his wings as an Army Air Service Reserve second lieutenant in 1923. Two years later he received a Masters in Aeronautical Engineering from MIT. In the postwar United States, with a huge surplus of war-era airplanes on the market, there was little need for new aircraft. Manufacturers found it hard to get orders, and newly graduated engineers like James McDonnell found it hard to get jobs. Nevertheless, he managed to pick up a few odd jobs in the Northeast, at Huff Daland in Ogdensburg and Consolidated in Buffalo, in New York. His first big break came with a job offer from the Stout Airplane Company in Detroit. William Bushnell ('Jackknife') Stout had developed a series of aircraft, including the ST-1 Bat, a torpedo bomber for the US Navy, and the single-engined Air Pullman, of which Henry Ford bought several for his Ford Air Transport Service. What really caught the eye of the eccentric elder Ford was a three-engined transport loosely based on the Air Pullman. Ford disliked the actual plane, but he loved Bill Stout's idea so much that he bought the company. Ford promptly put to work a group of former Stout designers, including James McDonnell, redesigning the three-motored Stout. The result was the Ford Trimotor, the famous 'Tin Goose,' an aircraft that became renowned among pilots and aircraft buffs as one of the most durable aircraft of the next 50 years.

Douglas and McDonnell left the employ of others to start their own firms in 1920 and 1926, respectively. By 1926 the Douglas Company was well on its way to becoming one of the giants of the industry, but it was not until 1939, on the eve of World War II, that James McDonnell accepted his last pay envelope from a company that did not bear his name. He had left Ford in 1924 to join the Hamilton Company as chief engineer. He remained there for two years, and in 1926 established James McDonnell and Associates. McDonnell meanwhile had been inspired with an idea that he'd gotten from Henry Ford. Ford's original idea a quarter century earlier had been to mass market automobiles so that virtually anyone in the country could own one; in 1924 he was toying with the idea of doing the same with airplanes. Ford dropped the idea of a 'flying Flivver,' but James McDonnell and Associates were resolved to pick it up and run with it. The result was McDonnell's 'Doodlebug,' which made its first flight on 15 November 1929. A two-place monoplane powered by a single radial engine, it was entered in the Daniel and Harry Guggenheim Safe Aircraft Competition, where it did well until a broken stabilizer nearly killed McDonnell, who was in the cockpit at the time, and dashed all hopes of winning the contest. With the onset of the Great Depression, all hopes had also been dashed for the idea of getting every family in the country into a personal plane. Families couldn't even afford cars then. McDonnell dissolved his firm and went to work for a Chicago consulting firm as a pilot and consulting engineer while continuing to demonstrate his Doodlebug. In 1931 he went to work for Great Lakes Aircraft Corporation of Cleveland and in 1933 he moved to the Glenn Martin Company, headquartered in Baltimore. Thirteen years after Donald Douglas had left his job as chief engineer for the division of the company concerned with Army bombers, James McDonnell stepped into the same slot. He stayed with Martin for half a decade, where he worked on the B-10 and B-12 programs, but around Christmas 1938 he decided to go his own way. He selected Lambert Field near St Louis as the headquarters of the new McDonnell Company because it was a major airline hub and there was a lot of aircraft repair business there. That seemed a good place to start.

The next few years, the World War II years, were to change the landscape of the American aircraft industry profoundly. McDonnell's company did well during that period, but really blossomed only in the postwar era. The Douglas Company was at its apogee during the 1940s, doing 18 times the amount of business McDonnell did during the war. After the war, Douglas stayed at the top for a decade until it began to lose ground to Boeing in the all-important jetliner market in the late 1950s. McDonnell began producing high-performance combat aircraft for both the Air Force and Navy in the postwar years, and by the time the paths of the two companies finally crossed in April 1967, it was an industry leader with few equals.

Above: Mr Mac in his younger years. A 1923 ROTC graduate, Mac took his flight training at Brooks Field, Texas, in the same class as Hoyt Vandenberg and Nate Twining. They went on to command the Ninth USAAF and Thirteenth USAAF, respectively, during World War II, and to serve as USAF chief of staff after the war.

James Smith McDonnell took an early interest in both the world of aviation and the world of the supernatural. Had his father not disagreed, young Mac would have gone to England to work for the Society for Psychical Research instead of embarking on the career that took him to the pinnacle of the aviation industry. Eventually the two interests became intertwined, as evidenced in names like Phantom, Banshee and Voodoo that he gave his postwar fighters.

THE PLANES OF DONALD DOUGLAS

Starting Out

Donald Douglas arrived at Union Station in Los Angeles in April 1920 with a family, a few hundred dollars, a letter of recommendation from the great Glenn Martin and the desire to start an airplane company. He opened an office in the back room of a Pico Boulevard barbershop and set about trying to find a client for a Douglas-designed airplane. Through a friend he knew from his days with Martin in Los Angeles before the war, Douglas met David Davis, a well-heeled Southern Californian with an idea for sponsoring the first-ever nonstop coast-to-coast flight. Endurance flights were customary in those days, but nobody had yet flown coast to coast without a stop, and Davis wanted his name associated with a winner. Davis also wanted to know whether this young engineer could build an airplane to accomplish the task. Douglas 'allowed as how he could build the plane' and Davis 'allowed as how he'd bet $40,000 on Douglas.' A Davis-Douglas Company was formed to design and build what was to be the first of the long line of Douglas aircraft, the Cloudster.

The partners rented a warehouse near the center of Los Angeles for construction of subassemblies, and Douglas began hiring a staff of engineers and draftsman. It took more than half a year to design and build the Cloudster, which was finally trucked out to the Army's March Field near Riverside on 24 February 1921 for

its maiden flight. Douglas's chief test pilot, Eric Springer (formerly a Martin test pilot), nearly cracked up on his first attempt to get the plane airborne, but on the second try he got aloft for nearly an hour. By the end of June, with four months of test flights behind them, Douglas and Davis decided that the time was right to send their Liberty-engined biplane aloft to capture the transcontinental record. With Springer at the controls and Davis in the passenger's seat, they set out for New York on the morning of 27 June 1921. By mid-afternoon they had made it as far as El Paso, where engine failure forced them down at Fort

Below left: The famous Pico Boulevard barber shop as it appeared in the 1930s, 12 years after Don Douglas had left.

Below: The Cloudster, shown here with Eric Springer at the controls, was the only Davis-Douglas airplane, but it launched a long series of Douglas airplanes.

Above: Posing before the Cloudster's wooden hull at the Wilshire plant in 1921 are Bill Henry, a *Los Angeles Times* writer who had helped arrange financing; Eric Springer, the Douglas chief test pilot who first flew the Cloudster; a US Navy officer in California to discuss buying Cloudster derivatives; David Davis; Donald Douglas and Jim Goodyear, who helped in the assembly of Douglas airplanes.

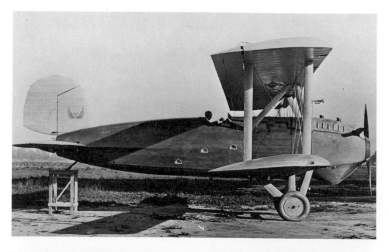

	Cloudster	DT-1	DT-2	O-2
Wingspan	56'	50'	50'	39' 8"
Length	36' 9"	37' 8"	37' 8"	29' 7"
Height	12'	15' 1"	15' 1"	11'
Ceiling	19,160'	8,700'	7,400'	12,275'
Range (mi)	440 (normal) 2,800 (nonstop)	232	274	400
Weight (lb)	9,600	6,895	7,293	4,985
Engine type	Liberty	Liberty	Liberty	Liberty
Engine hp	400	400	420	433
Speed (mph)	120	101	101	130

Top row and far right: The civil predecessor and military derivatives: the Cloudster, the US Navy DT-1, a US Navy DT-2 dropping a torpedo, a US Army O-2A and a US Army O-2B.

Lower right: The Douglas plant on Wilshire Boulevard in 1923 before the eucalyptus trees were cut down. A pair of O-2s can be seen on the right.

Bliss. Before they could try again, Davis's dream evaporated like a shimmering mirage on the Texas prairie. On 3 May 1923 two Army pilots put the wheels of a Fokker monoplane down on the runway at Rockwell Field in San Diego, completing their nonstop flight from New York that had begun the day before. His bid for glory dashed, Davis sold his interest in the company and left Douglas alone at the helm.

The First Government Contracts

Meanwhile, Donald Douglas had interested the US Navy in the idea of a military version of the Cloudster, and in 1921 it had ordered three of them configured as torpedo bombers and designated DT-1 (Douglas Torpedo, First). The DT-1 was designed with folding wings and twin pontoons for operation as a seaplane. Provision was also made for the pontoons to be replaced with wheels for operating the plane from land. A single 1800-lb torpedo could be mounted under the plane's center fuselage between the pontoons or wheels. During 1922 tests the DT-1 proved itself to be the best torpedo bomber available, and the Navy ordered 93 production versions under the designation DT-2. Douglas built 38 of the planes itself; 31 were produced by contract manufacturers and 24 were built by the Navy in its own aircraft factory. The DT-2 version was similar to the DT-1, but it had a redesigned tail and its radiator was moved from the side of the cowling to the front. The engine was a 420-hp Liberty, rated slightly higher than the 400-hp Liberty that had powered the Cloudster and DT-1. In April 1923 the Navy produced five DT-4 versions with a 525-hp Wright T-2 engine, and the following year two DT-2s were experimentally converted to one DT-5 with a 450-hp Wright cyclone radial and one DT-6 with a 750-hp Packard inline. The DT program marked the real beginning for Douglas. The design gave him credibility in the industry and the production contract gave the company the necessary cash flow to get rolling. At the same time the Post Office Department and the US Army ordered a few Cloudster/DT derivatives for use as mailplanes and observation planes under the respective designations M-1 and O-2. One of the latter was converted experimentally to attack-plane configuration by the Army under the designation XA-2. It was the first of a long series of single-engine attack planes that the Army was to buy from various manufacturers throughout the interwar period. (The A-1 designation had been assigned to the Cox-Klemin air ambulance.)

The XA-2 was powered by a 433-hp air-cooled Liberty—air-cooled to rid the overall system of the highly vulnerable radiator. There were six forward-firing Browning machine guns and the radiator. There were six forward-firing Browning machine guns and the rear seat was occupied by a gunner with a pair of Lewis machine guns in a flexible turret.

The Army Air Service (AAS) also bought five DT-2s from Douglas's Navy production run for a secret project under which they were designated DWC, for Douglas World Cruiser. The project was the first round-the-world flight by aircraft of any nation. Testing of the first DWC took place at the AAS's Langley Field, Virginia beginning in December 1923, and on 17 March 1924 the project was ready to go. The starting point was Clover Field at Santa Monica, California, adjacent to the Douglas factory. Four DWCs were flown up to Seattle, from where they

DOUGLAS WORLD CRUISER FIRST ROUND-THE-WORLD FLIGHT

September 5, prototype **Boston II** joins flight

April 6 from Seattle as seaplanes

August 3, flight is terminated for plane 3, **Boston**

July 30, from Brough as seaplanes

April 30, flight is terminated for plane 1, **Seattle**

September 8, from Boston as landplanes

July 1, from Calcutta as landplanes

The Douglas World Cruiser (DWC).

Dates and destinations:

1. March 17, 1924, departed Santa Monica, California
2. March 17, Sacramento, California
   (The aircraft which was to become the **New Orleans** first flew to San Diego from Santa Monica, joining the other planes later in Seattle.
3. March 20, Seattle, Washington
4. April 6, Prince Rupert, British Columbia (Canada)
5. April 13, Seward, Alaska
6. May 9, Attu, Aleutian Is (U S A)
7. May 15-16, Komandorskie, Russia
8. May 22, Kasumigaura, Japan (air base of Tokyo)
9. June 4, Shanghai, China
10. June 10, Haiphong, French Indo-China

11. June 16, Saigon, French Indo-China
12. June 18, Bangkok (Krung Thep), Siam
13. June 20, Rangoon, Burma
14. June 26, Calcutta, India
15. July 4, Karachi, India (Pakistan)
16. July 7, Bandar Abbas, Persia
17. July 8, Bagdad, Mesopotamia (Iraq)
18. July 9, Aleppo (Haleb), Syria
19. July 10, Constantinople (Istanbul), Turkey
20. July 12, Bucharest, Rumania
21. July 13, Vienna Austria
22. July 14, Paris, France
23. July 16, London, England

24. July 30, Kirkwall, Orkney Is., Scotland
25. Aug. 5, Reykjavik, Iceland
26. Aug. 21, Frederiksdal, Greenland
27. Aug. 31, Icy Tickle Bay, Labrador
28. Sept. 3, Pictou, Nova Scotia
29. Sept. 6, Boston, Massachusetts
30. Sept. 9, Washington, DC
31. Sept. 15, Chicago, Illinois
32. Sept. 18, Muskogee, Oklahoma
33. Sept. 20, El Paso, Texas
34. Sept. 23, Santa Monica, California
35. Sept. 25, San Francisco, California
36. Sept. 28, Seattle, Washington

PRODUCTION CLOSE-UP
CHILDREN OF THE CLOUDSTER
DOUGLAS SINGLE-ENGINED MILITARY BIPLANES* (1921-1930)

	0	100	200	300

US Navy

DT-1 (1921)
1

DT-2 (1922)
45 (an additional 55 were built by other contractors)

T2D (XTN) (P2D) (1927)
12

T3D (1933)
1

P2D (1932)
18

US Army

A-2 (1925)
1

BT-2 (1930)
196

C-1 (1925)
26

0-2 (1923) 25 converted to 0-7/0-8/0-9; 59 converted to BT-1; 2 converted to 0-32/0-34
246

0-5 Douglas World Cruiser (DWC) (1923)
5

0-14 (1928)
1

0-22 (1929)
3

0-25 (1930)
83

0-32 (1930)
30

0-38 (1930)
162

*In addition to the military biplanes, 59 mailplanes were built between 1925 and 1926 for the US Post Office Department.

departed during the first week of April, flying into a vicious North Pacific storm in which one of the planes, ironically the one christened *Seattle*, was lost at Dutch Harbor in the Aleutian Islands off Alaska. Fortunately, no one was killed in the crash and the remaining aircraft—*Boston, Chicago* and *New Orleans*—continued around the world. *Boston* was lost in the North Atlantic, but the other two arrived back at Clover Field on 23 September and returned to Seattle five days later. Two aircraft had circled the globe on a 27,000-mile route in just over 371 hours of actual flying time.

As the supplier of the aircraft for the first round-the-world flight, Douglas was very much in the world aviation spotlight. Norway purchased a couple of DTs, along with a license to produce the torpedo bomber abroad. The Army ordered 27 six-to-seven-passenger transport versions of the DWC under the designation C-1, and four Douglas observation seaplane (DOS) versions that it designated O-6. In addition to the DWC variants, a large number of developments of the basic O-2 were produced, ranging from the O-7, O-8 and O-9, which were simply re-engined O-2s, to the O-22 and O-34, which involved airframe redesign.

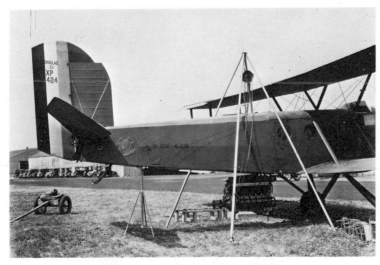

Above: The Douglas C-1 was the US Army's first designated transport. The C-1 was designed to be able to carry a second Liberty engine as freight.

Above from top: The DWC *New Orleans* being refueled, an M-2 mailplane, an O-2M for the Mexican Air Force and a Peruvian O-38P.

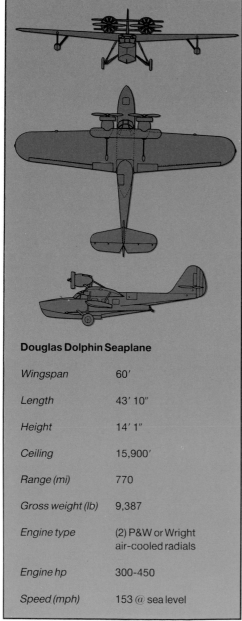

Douglas Dolphin Seaplane

Wingspan	60'
Length	43' 10"
Height	14' 1"
Ceiling	15,900'
Range (mi)	770
Gross weight (lb)	9,387
Engine type	(2) P&W or Wright air-cooled radials
Engine hp	300-450
Speed (mph)	153 @ sea level

Above from top: An RD Dolphin in US Coast Guard markings, the US Army's Y1C-26 Dolphin over San Francisco Bay on 24 June 1932 and a US Coast Guard Dolphin on Santa Catalina Island.

The Douglas Dolphin

The 1920s was a period of expansion for not only the Douglas Aircraft Company but for the whole American economy. On the heels of successful Navy contracts, Donald Douglas in 1929 decided to expand the company product line to include a small, commercial flying boat. Initially called *Sinbad*, the plane was designed by Douglas himself. It was a twin-engined, cantilever-winged, monoplane amphibian with clean lines and a yacht-like duraluminum hull. There was an exceptionally quiet and roomy passenger compartment with large picture windows that afforded the six to eight passengers a clear view of the outside. There was a lavatory and a 30-cubic-foot rear baggage compartment.

Douglas had high hopes for the *Sinbad* when he first dreamed of her in 1929. But the sudden crash of the stock market in October (and the onset of the Great Depression by the time *Sinbad* first flew in 1930) kicked the guts out of the commercial airplane market. All but 11 of the 58 production aircraft (all called Dolphin) that followed the *Sinbad* prototype were purchased by the US military. The prototype itself was sold to the US Coast Guard in 1931, and by 1934 the Coast Guard and Navy took delivery of 23 Dolphins under the designation RD (Transport, Douglas). There were three RD-1s and one RD-2 for the Coast Guard (including the *Sinbad*), three RD-2s and six RD-3s for the Navy (including three transferred to the Marine Corps) and finally 10 RD-4s for the Coast Guard.

The US Army, not particularly well known for its amphibious aircraft, actually took 24 Dolphins, one more than the Navy and Coast Guard combined. There were eight Dolphin Is procured as C-21s (becoming OA-3s in 1933), 14 Dolphin IIIs procured as C-26s (becoming OA-4s in 1933) and two nine-passenger Dolphin IIIs (ordered as C-26Bs) that were procured as C-29s. There is a story that one of the military Dolphins was converted to a luxurious executive transport for President Franklin Roosevelt, but it is not known if he actually used it. A single Dolphin purchased by the Argentine Navy was the forty-eighth military sale of a Dolphin and the only one that Douglas sold to a customer based outside the United States.

Above: This Douglas civil Dolphin was originally ordered as an executive transport for Boeing Company founder William Boeing in 1934.

During the 1930s, just about the best place for a plane spotter to observe a Dolphin was the Catalina Air Terminal on Santa Catalina Island in the Pacific, just west of Los Angeles. Not only did the Coast Guard have several based there, but it was the terminus of the Wilmington–Catalina Airline, which operated Dolphins. Aside from the military, Wilmington–Catalina bought more Dolphins (three) than any other customer. The airline made 39,295 flights between Catalina during the 1930s, carrying 213,000 passengers. The Vanderbilt family bought a pair of Dolphins, as did Pan American Airways for its Chinese subsidiary, China National Aviation Corporation. Crosley Radio of Cincinnati, Ohio, bought the fourth Dolphin produced and another went to Standard Oil of New Jersey. A single luxuriously appointed, bar-equipped Dolphin went to Armand Esders of France, who wrote Donald Douglas a personal check for $57,000 in advance.

The most interesting Dolphin story of all, though, involved the one nicknamed *Rover*. It was ordered as a personal executive transport by none other than William Edward Boeing, founder of the Boeing Airplane Company, chief rival of the Douglas Aircraft Company! It is interesting to note that this Dolphin was delivered in January 1934 before Bill Boeing sold his interest in the company that still bears his name. In a further irony, Boeing returned to Douglas in 1940 to trade his Dolphin in for a Douglas DC-5. In yet another twist of fate, *Rover* later served for a few years during the mid 1960s with the Catalina Channel Air Service. Today *Rover* is owned by Colgate Darden III of Columbia, South Carolina, who has restored his plane, the only Dolphin still in existence, to mint condition.

A New Generation for the Navy

The US Navy also commissioned Douglas to build a follow-on to the successful DT series. It was to be a torpedo bomber similar in size to the DTs and, like them, was to be convertible from seaplane to land plane. However, power was to be provided by two engines, a pair of 525-hp Wright R-1750

Above (both): The Douglas XT3D-1 photographed at the Wilshire plant with its wings folded as they would be for storage aboard an aircraft carrier.

Left: The Douglas PD-1 was the company's first US Navy patrol bomber and among the company's earliest twin-engined aircraft. As a patrol bomber, it was not noted for speed, so crewmen could stand on its foredeck without being whipped too severely by the airflow.

	T2D-1	P2D-1	T3D-1	T3D-2
Wingspan	57'	57'	50'	50'
Length	42'	43' 11"	35' 4"	35' 6"
Height	16' 11"	17' 6"	14' 8"	14'
Ceiling	13,830'	11,700'	17,300'	13,800'
Range (mi)	454	1,010	N/A	748
Weight (lb)	9,986	12,791	7,744	8,543
Engine type	Wright Radial	Wright Radial	1860 P&W	1860 P&W
Engine hp	525	575	575	800
Speed (mph)	124	135	134	142

Above: The cumbersome XT3D-2 was similar to the XT3D-1 on the facing page, except for its enclosed cockpit and rear-firing machine gun.

Below: The P2D-1 floatplane was a successor to the PD shown at the left. Defensive armament consisted of open turrets both fore and aft of the open cockpit.

Below: The enclosed-cockpit O-46 series, including this P-46A, was the most successful US Army program that Douglas had had since the O-2.

PRODUCTION CLOSE-UP
THE SECOND GENERATION
DOUGLAS MILITARY MONOPLANES (1930-1935)

| 0 | 25 | 50 | 75 | 100 |

US Army

B-7 (1930)
8

B-11 (1930) Us Army version of P3D/DF
1 (later became 0-44)

C-21 Dolphin (1932)
8 (later OA-3

C-26 Dolphin (1932)
14 (later OA-4)

C-29 Dolphin (1933)
2

0-31 (1930)
13

0-35 (1930)
6

0-36 (1930)
1 (later became B-7)

0-43 (1932)
25 (including one former 0-31)

1 (formerly B-11, later OA-5)

0-46 (1935)
91 (including one former 0-43)

0-48
0 (0-46 conversion project that never took place)

US Navy

P3D (1930)
5 (including 4 sold to Russia as Douglas DF)

RD Dolphin (1932) (Same as US Army C-21/OA-3)
22 (Including 2 RD-3 for the US Marine Corps and 10 RD-4 for the US Coast Guard.)

radials. The new plane was also to carry a second gunner for a three-man crew. The design originated with the Navy's Bureau of Aeronautics (BuAer) and the plans called for production to be divided between the Naval Aircraft factory, which would produce the planes under the designation TN-1, and Douglas, which which would produce them as T2D-1 (Second Douglas Torpedo, First Version). The first two experimental planes, XTN-1 and XT2D-1, were completed in May and July 1926, respectively, and Douglas got the go-ahead for nine production T2D-1s that were completed over the course of the next two years. In 1930 a second batch of 18 was ordered under the designation P2D-1. The T was changed to P because shore-based bombers were being classed as patrol planes; the T designation was applied to torpedo bombers designed to operate from aircraft carriers. The P2D-1 was coincidentally a bit different from the T2D-1 in that it had an enclosed cockpit, twin rudders and was powered by a pair of 575-hp Wright R-1820 radials.

Now that the Navy had a pair of carriers, the USS *Lexington* and *Saratoga*, it set about commissioning aircraft designs for possible use aboard these new floating bases. Among the torpedo bomber designs submitted was the Douglas XT3D-1, powered by a single 575-hp Pratt & Whitney R-1860 engine, which underwent Navy testing in October 1931. The Navy found the plane lacking and sent it back to the Douglas drawing board the following May. The single prototype was returned in February 1933, greatly streamlined and with a more powerful, 800-hp Pratt & Whitney R-1830-54 engine. Redesignated XT3D-2, Douglas's third Navy bomber was rejected a second time and was never seen on a production line.

Heavy Bombers for the Army

Meanwhile several companies were submitting designs to the Army to break the virtual monopoly on the big multiengined US Army bombers enjoyed by the Keystone Aircraft Company. The Martin MB-1 that Donald Douglas

had designed back in 1918 was one of only a handful of such bombers not designed and produced by Keystone, and Douglas wanted to get back into the field. Both the Douglas XO-35 and Fokker XO-27 were experimental monoplane observation aircraft on order from the US Army Air Corps (it had changed from the US Army Air Service in 1926) when the decision was made in February 1929 to modify as bombers one of each of the two prototypes being prepared. Thus, in 1930, the Air Corps received a Fokker XO-27 and XB-8 and a Douglas XO-35 and XB-7. No production B-8s were ever produced, but Douglas did get the nod for seven B-7s as well as five O-35s. The gull-winged aircraft were powered by a pair of 675-hp Curtiss Conqueror V-1570 engines, manned by four crewmen, and carried a 1200-lb bomb load. Faster than the earlier Keystones, the planes were also bigger than anything Douglas had yet built for the Navy. It was not an enormous order, this dozen planes, but it did press the Douglas company down the road a little farther toward twin-engined monoplane transports, on whose wings the company would ride to immortality.

Top and right: The B-18 Bolo (Douglas Model DB-1), the first Douglas heavy bomber, was based on the DC-3. Some, like the one at the right over the orange groves of Southern California, were equipped with ventral gun turrets.

Above: The B-18A was similar to the B-18, but had an extensively redesigned nose and bombardier's station.

Insets: B-23 Dragons as originally delivered to the US Army Air Corps, and, in color, as restored in 1983 after many years as a civilian transport.

The B-7 program also put the company in line for other twin-engined Air Corps bombers. The B-7 and B-8, along with Boeing's similarly designed B-9, marked a transition in first-line heavy bombers from the World War I-influenced biplanes of Keystone to the closed-cockpit bombers that were to follow. While revolutionary when they were designed, these three open-cockpit monoplanes were obsolete by the mid-1930s when they appeared. Aviation technology was moving at a rapid pace by that time, and the future was represented by the 200-mph Martin B-10, which first flew in 1932. The B-10 was followed by successively improved Martin bombers, including the B-12 and B-14, which had speeds comfortably above 200 mph.

In August 1934 the Army announced a competition for a new, 'multiengined' strategic bomber that it hoped would represent the kind of technological leap the Martin bombers had achieved over the Keystones. In 1934 multiengined no longer meant only two; Boeing had tested its four-engined behemoth, the XB-15, and Martin had a four-engined XB-16 on paper. Nevertheless, two of the three participants in the competition, Douglas and Martin, presented twin-engined aircraft. Boeing entered its four-engined Model 299, which was destined to become, under the Air Corps designation B-17, one of the greatest American aircraft ever produced. In the short term, however, Douglas was the winner when production contracts were issued at the beginning of 1936. The unit price of the Douglas Model DB-1, which was based on the highly successful DC-3, was about half that of the larger Boeing bomber and 133 were ordered under the designation B-18 against an order for 65 B-17s. For the Martin Model 146, another B-10 derivative, there would be no production contract.

The production version of the B-18 Bolo differed slightly from the prototype and, with the addition of a powered nose turret in 1937, the Douglas model number became DB-2. An additional

Left: The Royal Canadian Air Force purchased 20 B-18As from Douglas under the designation DB-280 Digby. This Digby was photographed in December 1939 at the time of delivery.

Inset, lower left: A silver B-23 Dragon in the hangar at March Field, California about 1939. Note the flat black antiglare panel on the inside of the engine nacelle.

Below: Another B-23, photographed at March Field in December 1939, having just arrived after a long flight. Note the pillow in the bombardier's station.

Right: A flight of US Army Air Corps B-18As over the Statue of Liberty in New York Harbor at 6:45 pm on 2 August 1939. World War II was just 30 days away.

177 DB-2/B-18As were ordered in 1937 and in 1938 an order was placed for another 78. Of the Bolos ordered in 1938, 38 were drastically redesigned with a more streamlined fuselage and a taller (B-17-type) tail. The initial plan called for the B-18As to be simply re-engined with 1600-hp Wright R-2600-1 engines and designated XB-22. In November 1938 the specifications were further changed, resulting in a plane with a new fuselage and tail, a pair of Wright R-2600-3 Cyclones and the first tail turret to be built in an Air Corps bomber. The resulting prototype aircraft, the B-23 Dragon, was first flown in July 1939 and the last of the B-23s were delivered 14 months later.

Douglas produced a total of 371 Bolos (including 20 delivered to the Royal Canadian Air Force) and 38 Dragons. Though officially classified as obsolete in 1942, 122 modified Bolos were in service with the US Army Air Force (the USAAF superseded the Air Corps in 1941) on antisubmarine duty in the Caribbean area throughout the Second World War, patrolling shipping lanes and sinking German U-boats. The handful of Dragons also served in the Caribbean, and after the war many of them became C-67 executive transports.

In 1935, with the preponderance of Air Corps thinking tending toward large numbers of twin-engined bombers instead of the more radical four-engined types, Douglas had followed conventional wisdom in developing the Bolo; indeed, an order totalling over 300 units was a good one for the era. Nevertheless, the more farsighted Air Corps officers and their counterparts at Douglas still doggedly predicted the need for the power and range of four-engined bombers. In July 1935 the Air Corps Matériel Division requested designs for huge bombers under the designation XBLR (Experimental Bomber, Long Range). The XBLR-1 was assigned to Boeing, XBLR-2 to Douglas and XBLR-3 to Sikorsky. The Sikorsky proposal was rejected. (Igor Sikorsky, founder of the company, had designed the world's first four-engined bomber, the *Ilya Mourometz*, for Tsar Nicholas II of Russia in 1913.) Boeing's XLRB-1 was redesignated XB-15 and the single prototype served as the grandfather to the B-17, which was being developed concurrently. Douglas received an order on 29 September 1936 for a prototype XLRB-2, which was redesignated XB-19 in March 1938. Despite the company's own assertion that the plane would be obsolete before it was built, the Air Corps pressed for its completion. The resulting aircraft, which first lifted off the field at Santa Monica on 27 June 1941, was then the largest American bomber ever flown and remained so until after the war. The wingspan of the huge B-19 was twice that of the B-17 and half again as large as that of Boeing's B-29 Super-

	B-18 Bolo	B-23 Dragon	XB-19
Wingspan	89′ 6″	92′	212′
Length	56′ 8″	58′ 4″	132′ 12″
Height	15′ 2″	18′ 6″	42′ 9″
Ceiling	25,850′	31,600′	39,000′
Range w/ payload (mi)	1,200	1,455	7,300
Gross weight (lb)	21,130	26,500	140,000
Engine type	Wright R-1820-45	Wright R-2600-3	Wright R-3350-5
Engine hp	930	1,600	2,000
Speed (mph)	217 @ 10,000′	282 @ 12,000′	224 @ 15,700′

DOUGLAS B-19. Super Bomber Landing Wheel 96 in.diameter weight over 2400 lbs.Largest Airplane ever built,82 tons.

fortress. The big plane, with its provision for a crew of 18, never saw a production run, but it proved to be an invaluable aid in the design of the B-35 and B-36 that appeared after the war. Originally built with four Wright 2000-hp engines, it was re-engined with four Allison inline V-3420s in 1943 and redesignated XB-19A. Designed and built before the United States entered World War II, the B-19 was the last venture Douglas made into the world of heavy or strategic bombers. It continued in the USAAF and USAF inventory until June 1949, when it was unceremoniously cut up for scrap.

While Douglas was at work designing America's largest-ever bomber and building the more 'practical' twin-engined Bolos, the company was pressing forward with its efforts toward a completely different type of combat aircraft.

Far left, from top: The maiden flight of the B-19 with the Douglas Santa Monica workers looking on; the B-19 after being re-engined and redesignated B-19A and the enormous tire of the B-19.

Left: This contemporary postcard used the B-19 as a symbol for American airpower.

Right: The B-19 after rollout at Santa Monica. Note the DC-3s, A-20s and Bostons on the apron in the background.

Below: As security guards stand by, crews prepare the B-19 prototype for her first flight.

Below: Walter Hamilton and Ed Heinemann with a Northrop 8A at the El Segundo plant, which was 51 percent Douglas-owned even before it became Douglas El Segundo in 1936. Hamilton was plant manager and Heinemann was perhaps the greatest aircraft designer ever to work at Douglas.

Attack Bombers for the Army

While it enjoyed modest success in the immediate prewar years with its B-18 Bolo strategic bomber, the Douglas Company's wartime efforts in the area of combat aircraft were almost entirely in the field of light tactical bombers, twin-engined aircraft for the Army and single-engined carrier-based aircraft for the Navy. The lineage of Douglas Army attack planes can be traced back to a single A-2 version of the O-2 of 1925, but there had been a 10-year hiatus in which the company's efforts for the Army were concentrated on heavy bombers and noncombat planes. In 1938, as the war clouds were gathering in the skies over Europe and the Far East, Douglas absorbed the Northrop facility at El Segundo, south of Santa Monica, that was building the Northrop Model 8 attack plane. Jack Northrop, who was himself one day recognized as one of the giants of American aviation, had worked as draftsman for Donald Douglas on the O-2 and Navy T-2D programs back in the early 1920s. After a brief stint with Lockheed, he started his own shop in Burbank in 1929 and two years later moved to El Segundo. Donald Douglas bankrolled the Northrop El Segundo operation and got 51 percent of the stock in return.

The Northrop Model 8, powered by a single 750-hp Pratt and Whitney R-1535, had been given the Army designation A-17, but was designed principally for export. Northrop had sold a pair of aircraft and a manufacturing license to Sweden and 30 aircraft to Argentina. Douglas redesigned the aircraft for the export trade and upgraded the engine to a 1200-hp Wright R-1820. Twenty

Douglas-built A-17s went to Peru in 1939 and 15 to Iraq the following year. At the time of the German invasion of Holland in 1940, the Royal Netherlands Air Force (Koninklijk Luchtmacht Nederland, KLN) had 20 of the Douglas-built birds in its hopelessly outnumbered inventory. In the year and a half following the fall of continental Europe, 35 of the Model 8s went to the Norwegian Air Force in exile in Canada, 31 to the USAAF, and several to Britain's RAF under the designation Nomad I.

Even as the company's new plant was turning out the stepchild Northrop-originated A-17s, Douglas was gearing up for a major effort in the field of twin-engined attack aircraft. The project had originated with Jack Northrop, and starting in 1936 was developed by Ed Heinemann, whose name was to be associated with many of the most successful Douglas-built aircraft over the next 20 years. The company designation for this new major effort was DB-7 (Douglas Bomber, Seven). Jack Northrop was officially general manager and chief engineer of the Douglas bomber program and Ed Heinemann was the project engineer for the Model 7 program. Heinemann had originally joined Douglas in 1926 as a draftsman but he quit the same year to work for the Moreland Aircraft Company. He joined Jack Northrop in 1932 and stayed on as a project engineer when the company became the El Segundo Division of Douglas. He was made chief engineer of that division in 1936. He stayed with Douglas until 1960, designing all of the major Douglas combat aircraft of the World War II and postwar years.

The Model 7, on which Ed Heinemann held the patent, was a fast, sleek ship with tricycle landing gear, and like the Northrop 8,

Above: General Hap Arnold with Jack Northrop at El Segundo in August 1936. Arnold became USAAF commanding general shortly thereafter, and Northrop struck out on his own after concluding his association with Douglas.

Above and below: Northrop A-17As in flight with US Army Air Corps markings, and in Iraqi colors with Major Al Hindi in the cockpit.

Above: A US Army Air Force A-20A in prewar markings. The red was later deleted from US insignia to avoid confusion with Japanese markings.

Above right: The A-20K, such as this one photographed on the flight line at Douglas Santa Monica in 1944, was the last A-20 model and sported a one-piece plexiglass nose.

Below and right: The Douglas Intruder began and ended its service as A-26 but was designated B-26 for most of its career. This one, preserved at Beale AFB in California, was painted gloss black with red for low visibility during night operations.

PRODUCTION CLOSE-UP
DB-7/A-20 BOSTON/HAVOC

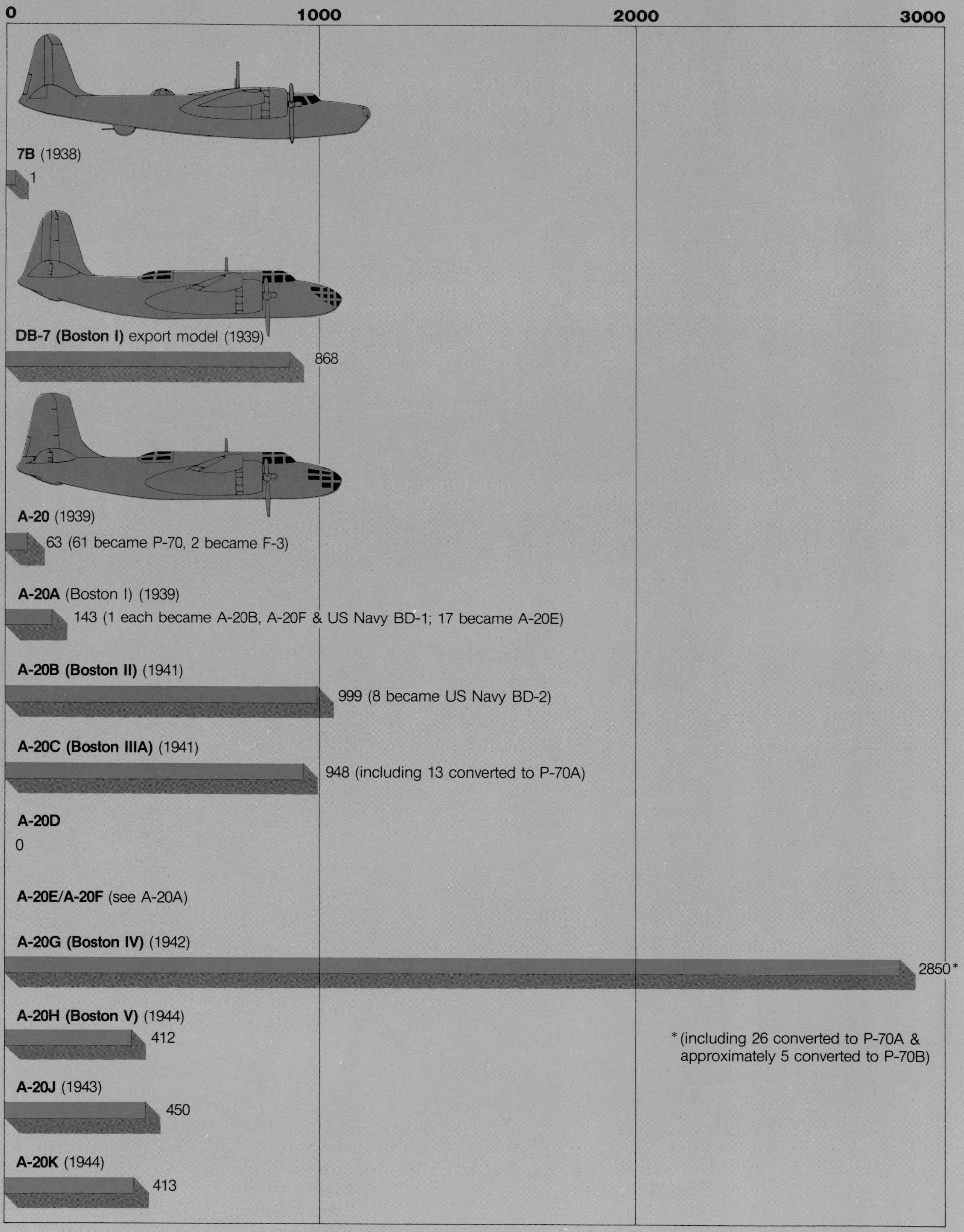

0	1000	2000	3000

7B (1938)

1

DB-7 (Boston I) export model (1939)

868

A-20 (1939)

63 (61 became P-70, 2 became F-3)

A-20A (Boston I) (1939)

143 (1 each became A-20B, A-20F & US Navy BD-1; 17 became A-20E)

A-20B (Boston II) (1941)

999 (8 became US Navy BD-2)

A-20C (Boston IIIA) (1941)

948 (including 13 converted to P-70A)

A-20D

0

A-20E/A-20F (see A-20A)

A-20G (Boston IV) (1942)

2850*

A-20H (Boston V) (1944)

412

* (including 26 converted to P-70A &
approximately 5 converted to P-70B)

A-20J (1943)

450

A-20K (1944)

413

the first sales were in the export market. Despite official neutrality, there was little doubt in the United States that the country should provide at least tacit support to its old allies, Britain and France, over Germany if push came to shove in a European war. Thus, when France's Armée de l'Air came to the United States shopping for a tactical bomber in 1938, there should have been little surprise when the US Government allowed it to view the then secret DB-7 project at the Douglas Santa Monica facility. The first 105 DB-7s to be built were delivered to France on 17 August 1939, two weeks before the outbreak of World War II. Two months later, with the German Blitzkrieg thundering across Poland, the French ordered another 270 DB-7s and DB-7As, which were delivered the following spring as the German war machine turned its attention westward. The planes first went into action against the Germans at the end of May, near St Quentin, by which time a handful had also been in service with Belgium's Air Force. By the end of June both Belgium and France were overwhelmed by the Germans, and 162 of the French DB-7s were yet to be delivered. These were transferred to the British Royal Air Force (RAF) as 15 Boston I tricycle landing gear trainers and 147 Boston II (later Havoc I) night fighters. Britain also became the beneficiary of 100 DB-7As that the French had ordered but which had not been built. These were delivered to the RAF in November 1940 under the designation Havoc II. The Royal Netherlands Navy had meanwhile ordered 48 DB-7C torpedo bombers for use in defending the Netherlands East Indies. Six were delivered before the Japanese overran the islands.

The USAAC had also ordered 143 DB-7s, under the designation A-20A, which were delivered beginning in December 1940. Another batch of 63 A-20s were ordered with two 1700-hp Wright R-2600 Cyclone turbo-supercharged engines, but these engines were determined to be unsuitable for low-level attack operations and the aircraft were converted to 60 P-70 (including one XP-70) night fighters and three F-3 photoreconnaissance aircraft. With national defense suddenly an objective of highest priority, in October 1940 the Air Corps ordered 999 A-20Bs to

Above: A Douglas DB-7 Boston in RAF colors approaches the coast of North Africa during a mission circa 1942.

Below: The original Douglas Model 7 bomber prototype was a sleek, handsome airplane with clean lines and a promising future.

be built at the newly completed Douglas facility at Long Beach and delivered over a 13-month period beginning in December 1941.

In March 1941 Congress passed the Lend-Lease Act, permitting the still-neutral United States to lease 'any defense article' to any nation whose defense the president 'deems vital to the defense of the United States.' This action paved the way for transfer of matériel to Britain by the US Government, which bought it from American manufacturers. It also marked the de facto end of American neutrality and the beginning of the US role as the arsenal of democracy. Eventually 38 countries benefited from Lend-Lease.

The British had earlier ordered 541 DB-7Bs under the RAF designation Boston III, so the first actual Lend-Lease order for these planes was 665 of the 999 USAAC (by now USAAF) A-20Bs, which were transferred to Soviet Russia after the German invasion in June 1941. While these aircraft were being produced at the new Long Beach factory, the main Douglas plant at Santa

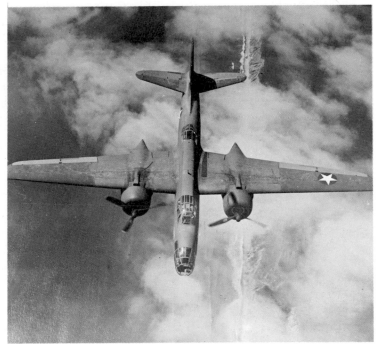

Above: An unarmed early Model A-20 photographed in 1942 over the rugged California coast north of Los Angeles.

Left: Acres of A-20 noses on the factory floor. All but a handful of the DB-7/A-20 Boston/Havoc series were built at Santa Monica.

Monica was tooling up for 808 A-20Cs, all of them Lend-Lease aircraft. (Boeing had been licensed to build an additional 140.)

By the time the United States was plunged into the war at the end of 1941, British Havocs and Bostons had already been turning in a good performance against German targets in North Africa and southern Europe for most of the year. The first encounter of American A-20s with the enemy came at the hands of the Japanese at Pearl Harbor, when several were destroyed on the ground. It was not until August 1942 that they would have a chance to strike back at the Japanese, but in Europe the A-20s were the first USAAF bombers to strike an enemy target. These A-20s were part of the 15th Bomb Squadron, an advanced echelon of the Eighth Air Force that arrived in England in May 1942. On the Fourth of July this squadron made a successful raid on a German air base in occupied Holland. Night operations were an important part of the Havoc's repertoire. The P-70 was the only USAAF night fighter when the war began, and A-20s were frequently used as night intruders. In one modification, 36 of them were configured with a yard-wide searchlight called a 'Turbin light' driven by 2000 lb of batteries that could illuminate a 150-yard swath a mile away. While the Turbin light lit up the target, other aircraft, such as P-70s, could attack it.

Of the 7385 Havocs of all models that were built, 2850 were A-20Gs. First introduced in February 1943, the A-20G was both better armed and better armored than its predecessors. The glass bombardier's station in the nose was replaced with a solid nose containing a variety of 20-mm cannons and .50-caliber machine guns. The first 250 A-20Gs, which were lend-leased to the Soviet Air Force, had four cannons and a pair of machine guns, whereas the remainder of the production run had six machine guns. A glass-nosed A-20G was developed and 450 of them were built under the designation A-20J. Of this total, 169 were lend-leased to the RAF as Boston IVs.

The DB-7 program was Douglas's most successful combat aircraft program in terms of numbers. Douglas produced 7098 of them at the company's Southern California facilities, and Boeing produced 380 license-built aircraft in Seattle. The program was

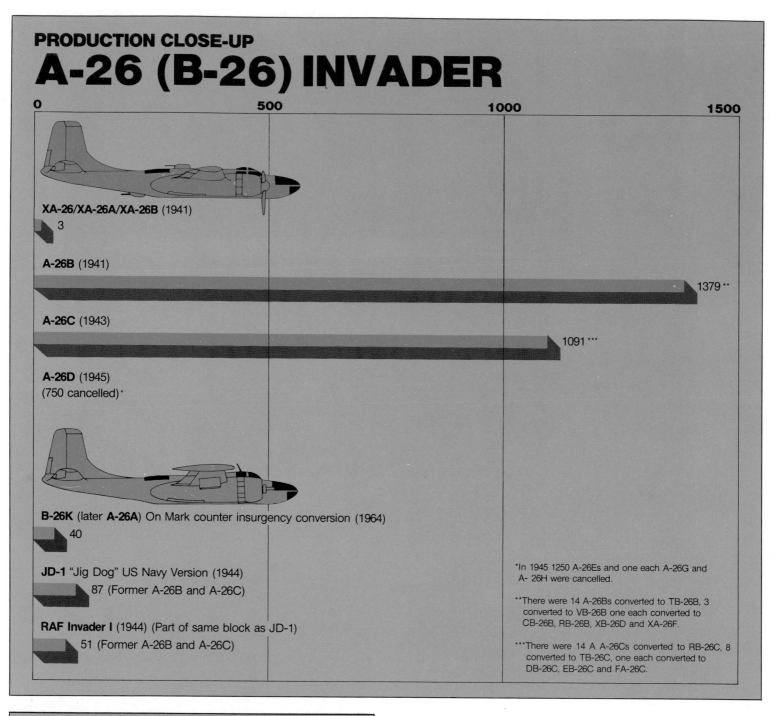

PRODUCTION CLOSE-UP
A-26 (B-26) INVADER

| | 0 | 500 | 1000 | 1500 |

XA-26/XA-26A/XA-26B (1941)
3

A-26B (1941)
1379 **

A-26C (1943)
1091 ***

A-26D (1945)
(750 cancelled) *

B-26K (later **A-26A**) On Mark counter insurgency conversion (1964)
40

JD-1 "Jig Dog" US Navy Version (1944)
87 (Former A-26B and A-26C)

RAF Invader I (1944) (Part of same block as JD-1)
51 (Former A-26B and A-26C)

*In 1945 1250 A-26Es and one each A-26G and A-26H were cancelled.

**There were 14 A-26Bs converted to TB-26B, 3 converted to VB-26B one each converted to CB-26B, RB-26B, XB-26D and XA-26F.

***There were 14 A A-26Cs converted to RB-26C, 8 converted to TB-26C, one each converted to DB-26C, EB-26C and FA-26C.

	A-20A Havoc	A-20G Havoc	A-26B Invader
Wingspan	61' 4"	61' 4"	70'
Length	47' 7"	48'	50'
Height	17' 7"	17' 7"	18' 6"
Ceiling	28,175'	25,800'	22,100'
Range w/payload (mi)	675	1,090	1,400
Gross weight (lb)	19,750	21,971	35,000
Engine type	Wright R-2600-3	Wright R-2600-23	P&W R-2800-27
Engine hp	1,600	1,600	2,000
Speed (mph)	347 @ 12,400'	339 @ 12,400'	355 @ 15,000'

also important to Lend-Lease because over half the production run went into foreign service; 2125 of them, or 42 percent of the total, went to Russia alone.

Even as the A-20s were streaming off the Douglas assembly lines in peak numbers, Ed Heinemann and his team were hard at work on a successor to the popular Havoc. The idea had been to upgrade the armament of the A-20 to include a 75-mm cannon. Frank Collbohn, an assistant to Douglas Santa Monica vice-president A E Raymond, felt that it was possible. Collbohn, who later headed the Rand Corporation when it was still a Douglas subsidiary, took the idea to his boss, Donald Douglas. Ed Heinemann, who had designed the A-20, insisted that the specs called for an entirely new aircraft. Heinemann went into a huddle with his El Segundo design team and returned two weeks later with a design for a sleeker, slightly larger, twin-engined attack bomber with more than double the payload of the A-20. A contract was issued to Douglas in June 1941 and the prototype A-26 Invader first took to the air on 10 July of the following year. The first production models were designated A-26B and were first delivered in August 1943 with six .50-caliber machine guns (re-

placing the notion of a 75-mm gun) in a solid (A-20G-type) nose. In addition to these guns there was a pair of guns in the dorsal and ventral turrets. By then the Douglas plant at Tulsa, Oklahoma was functional and it produced exactly one quarter of the 820 A-26Bs, with the rest coming from the Long Beach plant. Production of the A-26C with the plexiglass bombardier's station in the nose shifted almost entirely to Tulsa, with only five of the 1091 ships being built at Long Beach. USAF Invaders flew the first of 11,567 sorties over Europe in November 1944 with the USAAF Ninth (tactical) Air Force. Though it was in action for less than a year during World War II, the A-26 so impressed Army Air Force planners that it was chosen as the standard light bomber for the postwar US Air Force.

By 1948 the A-26 was one of few wartime aircraft types in service with the greatly stripped-down postwar US Air Force. With the retirement of the famous Martin B-26 Marauder and the deletion from Air Force nomenclature of the A for attack category, the A-26 attack bomber became the B-26 light bomber. The Marauder was Martin's last successful Air Force combat aircraft, and the transfer of the B-26 designation marked a final irony between Donald Douglas and Martin, the company where he had first cut his teeth three decades before.

Not only did the Invader survive postwar demobilization, it went on to serve as a first-line aircraft during the Korean War and as an important part of the USAF arsenal in Southeast Asia 20 years after it first went after German targets in occupied Europe. It earned the distinction of being the only American combat aircraft to fly missions in three wars.

The A-26 had reached the Pacific Front just after the end of World War II in Europe, so it had only a couple of months of

Above: Unlike the A-26B, the Douglas A-26C had a plexiglass, not a solid, nose.

Below: USAF Invaders attack a North Korean railroad yard circa 1950.

combat until the capitulation of the Japanese Empire. When the Korean War broke out, the 72 remaining active-duty Invaders (there were an additional 982 in reserve) were all assigned to Light Bombardment and Tactical Reconnaissance wings in Japan, and thus became the first US bombers to strike back at North Korea. They flew their first mission two days after the initial North Korean invasion and their last mission was the last bombing mission of the war, which took place on the same day the armistice was signed in July 1953. There were 72,040 missions flown by over 400 B-26s in Korea, six times the number of Invader sorties flown in Europe during World War II. Of these, just over 80 percent were bombing missions; the rest were reconnaissance missions flown by RB-26s.

The Invader's war record was not restricted to service with the United States. The first customer for its predecessor, the A-20, had been the prewar French Government, and by the time the USAAF was flying its first A-26 sorties, the Free French Air Force had its eyes on the Invader. After the war, with the Germans

Above: A B-26K (A-26A) Counter-Invader photographed at Korat AB in Thailand in 1967 (*top*), compared with a modified A-26B Invader photographed at Santa Monica circa 1944 (*bottom*).

Lower left: A solid-nosed A-20G, photographed under the camouflage netting at Santa Monica in October 1943.

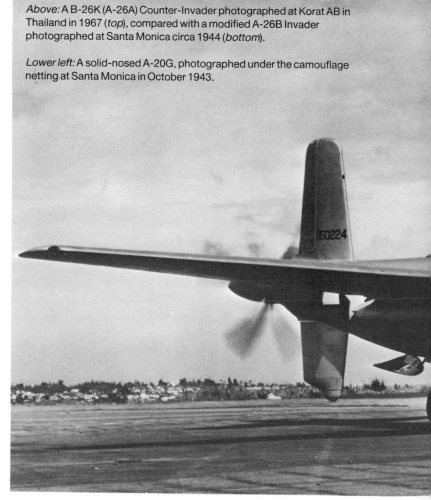

removed from their homeland, the French turned their military attention to a colonial war in far-off French Indochina. The Japanese had occupied the French colony during the war, and the populace was up in arms at the idea of throwing out the Japanese only to have the French return again to set up colonial domination. During the eight years of off-and-on armed struggle the French provided their troops with B-26s for air support. The first 25 Invaders were introduced into Indochina in January 1951. By the time the French cut their losses and submitted to a cease-fire in July 1954, 111 Invaders had seen service against the Viet Minh, with the last ones being supplied out of US stocks during the latter years of the war. After Indochina the French used their

Top: A stark head-on view of the original B-42 Mixmaster with plexiglass bombardier's nose and unified cockpit.

Below: This view of a jet-augmented XB-42A Mixmaster shows the divided cockpit in which both pilot and copilot had a separate canopy.

Douglas aircraft in the war in Algeria during the early 1960s, before the last bomber was retired.

Meanwhile the US Government was peddling surplus B-26s to six Latin American countries under the Military Assistance Program. Of the 119 Invaders thus disposed, 30 went to Brazil and 34 to Chile, beginning in 1955. A number of the durable little bombers were also brokered to anti-Castro Cubans and, ironically, the Invader found itself being used by both sides during the ill-fated 1961 Bay of Pigs invasion of Cuba.

The A-26/B-26 had been conceived before the United States entered World War II, and over 20 years later it was one of the first American combat aircraft to go to war in Southeast Asia. On 11 October 1961 President John F Kennedy authorized deployment of the USAF 1st Air Commando Group to South Vietnam. Its mission was to assist the South Vietnamese Government in the war against Communist Viet Cong guerrillas. Of the 16 propeller-driven aircraft in South Vietnamese markings that were deployed with the 1st Air Commando Group, four were RB-26s. By the end of 1962 there were eight RB-26s in Southeast Asia, and by the end of 1963, 13 of the 18 that had been deployed to the theater were in service. By February 1964, however, metal fatigue in the wings of the old warbirds had caused a rash of structural failures that in turn resulted in severe restrictions on their operation. The grounding of the entire B-26 fleet took place on 11 February after a wing crumpled on a mission. The last original US Air Force B-26 was flown out to Clark Air Base (AB) in the Philippines on 1 April, marking the end of an odyssey that had begun three wars earlier over occupied Europe. It was not so much an end of the Invader's story as it was an end simply to a major chapter in its career. The epilogue was being drafted as early as 1962 as the B-26s were still droning over the jungles and rice paddies of Vietnam.

A firm called On Mark Engineering, known for its conversions of B-26s to executive aircraft, was contracted by the Air Force to rebuild 41 B-26s for counterinsurgency operations in Southeast Asia. The prototype of the new aircraft, designated YB-26K, first flew on 28 January 1963 and the first production version B-26K followed on 26 May 1964. In June 1966 eight of the On Mark Invaders, their designation changed back to A-26, arrived at Nakhon Phanom Air Base in Thailand to begin a 120-day combat trial period with the US Air Force. In January 1967, the A-26s, nicknamed Counter-Invaders to reflect their counterinsurgency mission, were transferred to the 606th Air Commando Squadron (later the 609th Special Operations Squadron), their trial period over. The Counter-Invaders continued to serve until November

PRODUCTION CLOSE-UP
DOUGLAS USAAF BOMBERS
(1936-1944)

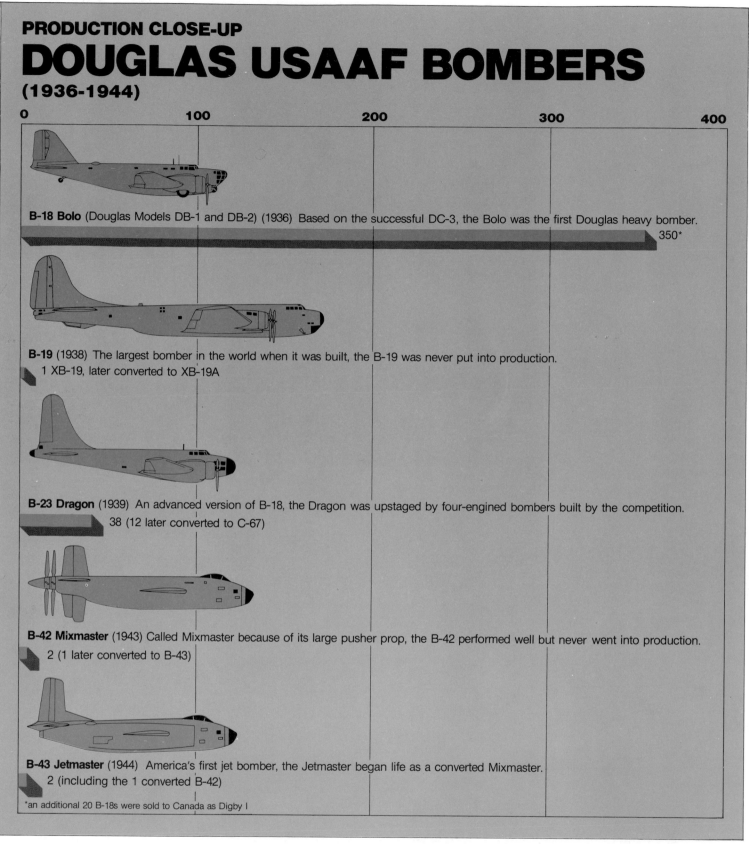

0   100   200   300   400

B-18 Bolo (Douglas Models DB-1 and DB-2) (1936) Based on the successful DC-3, the Bolo was the first Douglas heavy bomber.
350*

B-19 (1938) The largest bomber in the world when it was built, the B-19 was never put into production.
1 XB-19, later converted to XB-19A

B-23 Dragon (1939) An advanced version of B-18, the Dragon was upstaged by four-engined bombers built by the competition.
38 (12 later converted to C-67)

B-42 Mixmaster (1943) Called Mixmaster because of its large pusher prop, the B-42 performed well but never went into production.
2 (1 later converted to B-43)

B-43 Jetmaster (1944) America's first jet bomber, the Jetmaster began life as a converted Mixmaster.
2 (including the 1 converted B-42)

*an additional 20 B-18s were sold to Canada as Digby I

1969, when the 609th was deactivated and the aircraft flown to Clark AB. By the end of the year, the last of the A-26s were out of combat and out of service, bringing down the curtain on a career spanning a quarter of a century and three major wars.

The Last Air Force Bombers

Midway through World War II, Douglas Long Beach was producing the most important light attack bomber in the USAAF arsenal, the A-26. On the other end of the scale the Douglas heavy bombers of the prewar era, the B-18

and B-23, were rendered obsolete by advancing technology. The medium bomber scene was dominated almost entirely by the North American B-25 and the Martin B-26. In 1943 Douglas proposed a unique twin-engined attack plane in the same size and weight class as the A-26 and B-26. Unlike these aircraft and the other conventional bombers of the day, the Douglas Santa Monica design had both of its 1800-hp Allison B-1710 engines enclosed within the fuselage behind the bomb bay. The engines drove a pair of tail-mounted coaxial propellers, with the result being an extremely clean aircraft. The USAAF took an interest in this plane, called the Mixmaster (because of its huge pusher

Below: The XB-43 Jetmaster retained the two-part cockpit, disliked by the aircrews, that had been introduced on the XB-42A.

prop) and issued an experimental contract on 25 June 1943 under the designation XA-42. As originally designed the Mixmaster carried eight machine guns in a solid nose to fulfill its attack bomber role.

By November 1943, however, it became evident that with a 4-ton bomb capacity (twice that of the A-26) the XA-42 was more of a medium bomber than a light bomber and the designation became XB-42. The first prototype, which flew on 6 May 1944, had a top speed of over 400 mph, better than any existing USAAF light or medium bomber, and a maximum range equivalent to some heavy bombers. The second prototype was flown on the first of August, but by then the emphasis was on perfecting and building large quantities of proven bombers, and no production contract was forthcoming for the promising Mixmaster.

Even before the first flight of the Mixmaster, Douglas Santa Monica engineers were at work on a follow-on utilizing jet engines. The USAAF issued on contract for the updated Mixmaster, called Jetmaster, on 31 March 1944. This historic contract was the first issued in the United States for a jet bomber. Designated XB-43 and powered by two General Electric J35 turbojets, the Jetmaster did not make its first flight until 17 May

Above: Lieutenant Colonel Warden and Captain Edwards with the Douglas XB-42 at Muroc Army Air Field in 1945, just before their record-breaking transcontinental flight. Three years later Glen Edwards was killed in the crash of a Northrop YB-49 at Muroc, and the base was renamed Edwards AFB.

Below: This view from behind shows the huge contrarotating propellers that gave the Douglas B-42 Mixmaster its nickname.

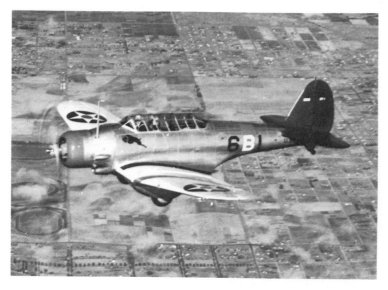

Above: The Northrop BT-1, designed by Ed Heinemann, was the direct ancestor of the Douglas SBD Dauntless.

Below: The Douglas TBD-1 Devastator, shown here in flight and on the ground with wings folded. The folding wings were for aircraft carrier storage.

1946. Though it had a top speed in excess of 500 mph, the B-43 tested out with a much shorter range than the B-42, owing to the primitive state of jet engine technology in 1946. Like the B-42, the new B-43 had a three-man crew and a 4-ton bomb capacity. Also like the B-42, the program was considered only experimental and there was no production contract.

Attack Bombers for the Navy

It had been two years since the Douglas XT3D was rejected by the Navy and a decade since the heyday of the DT series, when the XTBD-1 (Experimental Torpedo Bomber, Douglas) first lifted off Clover Field at Santa Monica on 15 April 1935. The new plane marked not only the return of Douglas to the Navy bomber business, but a technological leap as well. It was a low-wing monoplane in an era of biplane carrier aircraft, and it was the first monoplane ordered for carrier service. The Navy placed its first order for 114 production TBD-1s on 3 February 1936. The designation for torpedo bomber had changed from T to TB in 1934, otherwise the TBD would have been designated T4D to succeed the T3D.

The new bomber was powered by a 900-hp Pratt & Whitney R-1830 engine that gave it a top speed in excess of 200 mph. By the end of 1941, all the torpedo squadrons of the Pacific Fleet were equipped with TBDs. Of the 130 TBDs, including the prototype that had been built by Douglas at Santa Monica, 100 were in service when Pearl Harbor was attacked, and these were thrown into the first frantic actions against the Japanese.

The TBD, nicknamed Devastator, saw action against the Japanese beginning in February 1942 and later in the Battle of the Coral Sea during the first week of May. Devastators based on the carriers *Yorktown* and *Lexington*, augmented by Douglas SBD Dauntless dive bombers from the same carriers, attacked a Japanese task force consisting of three carriers and 10 cruisers. On 7 May they succeeded in sinking the carrier *Shoho*, the first carrier lost in the Pacific war. The following day, however, Japanese torpedo bombers located the American task force and so severely damaged the *Lexington* that she had to be scuttled.

Overall losses on the two sides were roughly equal, with the United States Navy losing 66 aircraft, including a number of Devastators. Against the heavily defended Japanese fleet, several key weaknesses in the TBD became evident. Both the slow speed and low altitude that were required for the TBD's attack run were costly, as was the need for the plane to close to 1000 yards before launching its torpedo. Many Devastators were chewed to bits by Japanese guns at relatively close range in the battle.

Less than a month later, the swan song of the TBD came in a battle that was to mark the turning point in the naval war in the Pacific. A Japanese armada with four carriers was intent on capturing the island of Midway at the north end of the Hawaiian Archipelago. On 4 June 1942 the enemy carriers were located by aircraft from an American task force and at about 9:20 am, 15 Devastators from the USS *Hornet*'s Torpedo Squadron 8 (VT-8) attacked. Only one of the TBDs survived the fusillade of fire from the Japanese ships and carrier planes, and none of the torpedos launched by the American bombers scored a hit. A dozen Devastators from the carrier *Yorktown* then attacked, with the loss of 10 of their number.

The three American carriers at Midway, *Hornet, Yorktown* and *Enterprise*, had gone into the battle with 41 TBDs and at the end only five remained. As naval historian Rodney Baird pointed out later, the Devastator at Midway had become a devastatee. Meanwhile, dive bombers from the American carriers succeeded in sinking all four Japanese carriers and routing the Japanese task force. The battle was the turning point in the Pacific war, but it was also the end of the TBD. Of the 100 Devastators on the rolls at the start of the war, only 69 were operational. Attrition and the Coral Sea battle picked away at this number, but with 60 percent of the prewar operational total shot down at Midway alone, it was clearly a plane of the past.

The Diving Dauntless

While the TBD was being devastated at Midway as it made low-level runs on the Japanese carriers, the aircraft that was saving the day and sinking the Japanese flattops was its cousin, the SBD (Scout Bomber, Douglas). Nicknamed Dauntless, the SBD became one of the greatest carrier-based bombers of the war. The Dauntless began life, not in the Douglas plant at Santa Monica, but at Northrop in El Segundo, a facility whose ownership was shared by Donald Douglas and Jack Northrop. It was a product of the fertile mind of aircraft designer Ed Heinemann. Destined to become one of America's greatest designers, Heinemann had joined Douglas when the company absorbed the El Segundo and stayed with it for 25 years, designing all the important Douglas warbirds of the wartime and postwar eras.

The immediate ancestor of the Dauntless was the Navy's Northrop BT-1 (Bomber, Northrop, First). First flying in August 1935, this was an Ed Heinemann creation, a contemporary of the Douglas TBD-1 torpedo bomber, and was, like the TBD-1, a low-wing monoplane. It was based on the A-17 (Northrop Model 8) attack bomber which was developed for both the Army and the export market.

A major difference between the Army and Navy aircraft, despite their common origins, was the designation of the Navy's plane as a dive bomber. While other bombers release their ordnance in level flight, a dive bomber is designed to achieve pinpoint accuracy by diving straight down on a target, dropping the bomb and then pulling out of the near vertical dive. To pull out of such dives routinely requires an aircraft of better than average stability. Heinemann overcame his initial problems with

Above: An SBD-3 Dauntless dropping a 500-lb bomb on its target. The holes in its dive brakes, known as 'Swiss-cheese flaps,' are clearly visible.

	TBD-1 Devastator	SBD-1 Dauntless	SBD-3 Dauntless	SBD-5 Dauntless
Wingspan	50'	41' 6"	41' 6"	41' 6"
Length	35'	32' 2"	32' 8"	33'
Height	15' 1"	13' 7"	13' 7"	12' 11"
Ceiling	20,800'	29,600'	27,100'	24,300'
Range (mi)	435	860	1,205	1,115
Gross weight (lb)	9,862	8,138	9,407	9,353
Engine type	Pratt & Whitney R-1830-64	Wright R-1820-32	Wright R-1820-52	Wright R-1820-60
Engine hp	900	1,000	1,000	1,000
Speed (mph)	206 @ 8000'	253 @ 16,000'	252 @ 16,000'	252 @ 16,000'

the BT-1's stability by punching the plane's dive brakes full of 3-inch holes. The 'Swiss-cheese flaps' were unusual in appearance, but they solved the problem and became an integral part of the subsequent SBD program. The first BT-1s were put into operational service in May 1938 with the Navy's Bomber Squadrons VB-6 and VB-5 aboard the USS *Yorktown*. Including the prototype (XBT-1) there were 55 of the bombers built, including one that was experimentally fitted with tricycle landing gear (and which later was sold by Douglas to the Imperial Japanese Navy) and one that was retrofitted with fully retractable landing gear. The latter was redesignated XBT-2 and rebuilt with upgraded

Above: An SBD-5 Dauntless during an attack on Wake Island, an American possession captured by the Japanese in December 1941.

systems throughout, and the 700-hp Pratt & Whitney R-1535 was exchanged for a more powerful Wright R-1820. While Ed Heinemann was in the midst of the XBT-2 conversion, Northrop El Segundo became Douglas El Segundo and the XBT-2 became the prototype for the SBD Dauntless.

The XBT-2 became the XSBD-1 in 1938 and in April 1939 Douglas received a contract for 144 SBDs. These included 57 SBD-1s for the US Marine Corps and 87 SBD-2s with greater fuel capacity for use by the Navy aboard its carriers. The new birds first flew on 1 May 1940 and in September the Navy ordered the first of 584 SBD-3s—the first Dauntlesses to carry two nose-mounted .50-caliber machine guns and a pair of rear-firing .30-caliber guns at the aft end of the cockpit. The USAAF received 168 of the SBD-3 under the designation A-24, which were to see service in the Pacific alongside Navy and Marine Corps SBDs. The SBD-4s (USAAF equivalent A-24A) were virtually identical to the SBD-3/A-24 but incorporated the Hamilton Standard Hydromatic propeller. The SBD-5 (USAAF equivalent A-24B) with its Wright R-1820 was the archetypical Dauntless. There were almost 300 of them built and they saw service in the forefront of the Navy's carrier operations.

The SBD chalked up an impressive record. The first enemy ship sunk by the Navy in World War II (the Japanese sub I-70) fell to a Dauntless from the USS *Enterprise* 3 days after the Pearl Harbor attack. Dauntless went on to sink 18 major enemy warships including a battleship and 6 carriers.

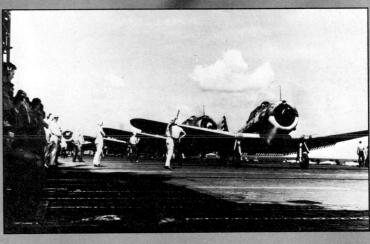

Top: SBD-5s, with wing-mounted 250-lb bombs, en route to action against Japanese shipping in the western Pacific.

Above: Dauntlesses prepare for takeoff from the USS *Yorktown* in April 1942. Less than two months later, the *Yorktown* was sunk at Midway.

Below: A USAAF A-24 and a virtually identical US Navy SBD-3 await delivery at Douglas El Segundo on 20 June 1941. Both planes carried a life raft but only the SBD was equipped with an arrestor hook (under the tail) for carrier operations.

Attack bombers are always vulnerable to attack from the rear by enemy aircraft during their bomb run, but the rear-firing machine guns that were wisely introduced with the SBD-3 took out 138 of the would-be attackers. In addition to service with the US Navy, Marine Corps and the USAAF, 68 SBDs were transferred to New Zealand beginning in July 1943, and 32 were supplied to the French Navy in November 1944. By the end of 1944, however, the career of the 'Speedy D,' or 'Barge,' as it was known to the US Navy airmen, was in decline.

Heinemann had designed the Dauntless without folding wings. This resulted in a lighter, faster aircraft with higher performance, but it prevented the Navy from using it aboard its new series of light or 'jeep' carriers where storage was limited and where aircraft with folding wings were a must. Thus the plane, which had played a central role in the carrier war from 1942 through early 1944, began to take a back seat to newer aircraft in the naval battles of the war's final year.

After the war the USAAF (USAF after 1947) reconnaissance version of the Dauntless, the RA-24 (F-24 after 1948) survived in small numbers until 1950.

Three Turkeys

The SBD series, like the DT series two decades before, was an immensely successful program for the airplane company of Donald Douglas. Like the DT two decades earlier, the SBD was followed by a series of aircraft that were designed to upgrade its technology, but which were less successful than the original. As the Dauntless began to recede from its first-line role in 1943–44, its place was gradually being taken by the Curtiss SB2C Helldiver, whose career had followed the Dauntless by roughly a year. Ultimately the Helldiver was to be the Navy's premier dive bomber in the last year of the war. As early as 1941, before either aircraft had made its mark, the two companies were at work on successors, which would of course be designated SB2D and SB3C.

The Douglas XSB2D, first flown on 8 April 1943, was an airplane of compromise. It was a ton over the required specs because of systems required by the Navy. Because of the required internal bomb bay, the landing gear had to fold into the wings, whose size was limited by the requirement that the span (with wings folded) be less than 26 feet. The latter requirement was

	SB2D	BTD	TB2D
Wingspan	45'	45,9	70'
Length	38'7₀	38'7"	46'
Height	16'11"	13'7"	22'7"
Ceiling	24,400'	23,600'	24,500'
Range w/payload (mi)	1,480	1,480	1,250
Gross Weight (lb)	16,273	18,140	28,525
Engine type	Wright R-3350-14	Wright R-3350-14	P & W XR-4360-8
Engine hp	2,300	2,300	3,000
Speed (mph)	346 @ 16,100'	344 @ 16,100'	340 @ 15,600'

Above: The SB2D (*top*) and BTD (*bottom*) were planes of compromise and represented obsolescent technology.

Below: The TB2D, shown here in March 1945 with its huge contrarotating propellers, looked modern but fell short of what was required.

because the Navy's small jeep carriers had room on their hangar decks for planes to pass one another only if their spans were less than 26 feet. Even Ed Heinemann, who designed the plane, recognized its failings. 'Although it demonstrated reasonably good high-speed characteristics,' he wrote, 'we were instinctively aware that we didn't have an overwhelming winner on our hands.'

When the gull-winged XSB2D was axed after the construction of a second prototype in 1944, Heinemann reflected, 'we learned a bitter lesson. If the plane was not a failure it was most certainly, in today's vernacular, a turkey.'

The lessons learned in the SB2D fiasco were quickly put to work in the gull-winged attack bomber/torpedo bomber designated BTD and nicknamed Destroyer. Like its gull-winged predecessor, the BTD had tricycle landing gear and no provision for a rear gunner, the necessity for which had been obviated by this time by the advent of American air superiority over the battlefronts of the western Pacific. The prototype first flew on 5 March 1944 and, although 28 (of 358 ordered) were built by VJ day, the plane was still not on the leading edge of the technology boom that came with the war.

The BTD designation implied that the aircraft was primarily an attack bomber, with its role as a torpedo bomber being secondary. The Devastator, primarily a torpedo bomber, had carried the TBD designation. Late in the war the Douglas El Segundo shop produced a short-lived design for another torpedo bomber, which was, of course, designated TB2D. It was similar to both the SB2D and the BTD, but was much larger; it had two four-bladed contrarotating propellers and the gull wings were set at a less acute angle. Designed for the new, larger *Midway* class carriers the Navy was planning, the TB2D first rolled out of the factory in March 1945. Nicknamed Skypirate, the TB2D came too late to play a part in the war, and like its two predecessors it fell through the cracks of the rapidly expanding world of aviation technology. Like many aircraft developed in 1944–45, the SB2D, BTD and TB2D were light years ahead of Pearl Harbor-era technology but failed to incorporate all the lessons learned during the war. Hence they fell on the scrap heap of aviation history, just mileposts on the road to the jet age.

Below: The prototype BT2D would soon become the AD, an Able Dog far superior to its brothers that are pictured on the facing page.

The Skyraider

Ed Heinemann asked the Navy directly to consider rejecting the BTD. In a meeting between top Navy brass and Douglas engineers in Washington in June 1944, he predicted things to come and asked them for 'permission to use the unexpended (BTD) funds to build an entirely new bomber, one that I am convinced will do the job for you.' He asked for 30 days to prepare the new design and was given less than 30 hours. Heinemann phoned Donald Douglas to obtain his blessing for this rash departure. He then retired to the Statler Hotel, where, along with Douglas engineers Leo Devlin and Gene Root, he worked up the basic drawings in a marathon session that lasted until the wee hours of the following morning. Both Douglas and Heinemann realized that if Douglas was going to get back into the forefront of the Navy attack bomber business, a very advanced design approach was required. The company would not stay successful building two planes here and two planes there, especially if they were nearly obsolete by the time they were built.

The Navy went for the new design and on 4 August 1944 work began on the first prototypes of the new attack bomber, which were designated BT2D (not to be confused with the aforementioned TB2D). The Navy ordered 25 prototype XBT2Ds, a quantity which as well as anything demonstrated their confidence in the design. The first of the planes, which were nicknamed Dauntless II (a good omen), flew on 18 March 1945. While twice the weight of the original Dauntless, the new bird was actually lighter than the BTD and required fewer forgings in its manufacture than either of those aircraft. Required maintenance time, a critical factor, was also greatly reduced. Fueling the BT2D took less than half the time required for the SBD or BTD. The single crewman sat high under a bubble canopy that offered visibility unprecedented in operational Navy attack bombers. There were two 20-mm wing guns, and pylons were provided to permit a variety of ordnance ranging from bombs and torpedos to rockets, drop tanks and APS-4 radar pods. The Dauntless II was designed to carry a 1-ton bomb or torpedo, but had a safe alternate overload capacity sufficient to allow it to carry three such weapons!

Exactly one month after the first flight, the Navy issued a contract for 548 BT2Ds. They were renamed Skyraider, under a

PRODUCTION CLOSE-UP

DOUGLAS ATTACK BOMBERS FOR THE US NAVY

(1937-1947)

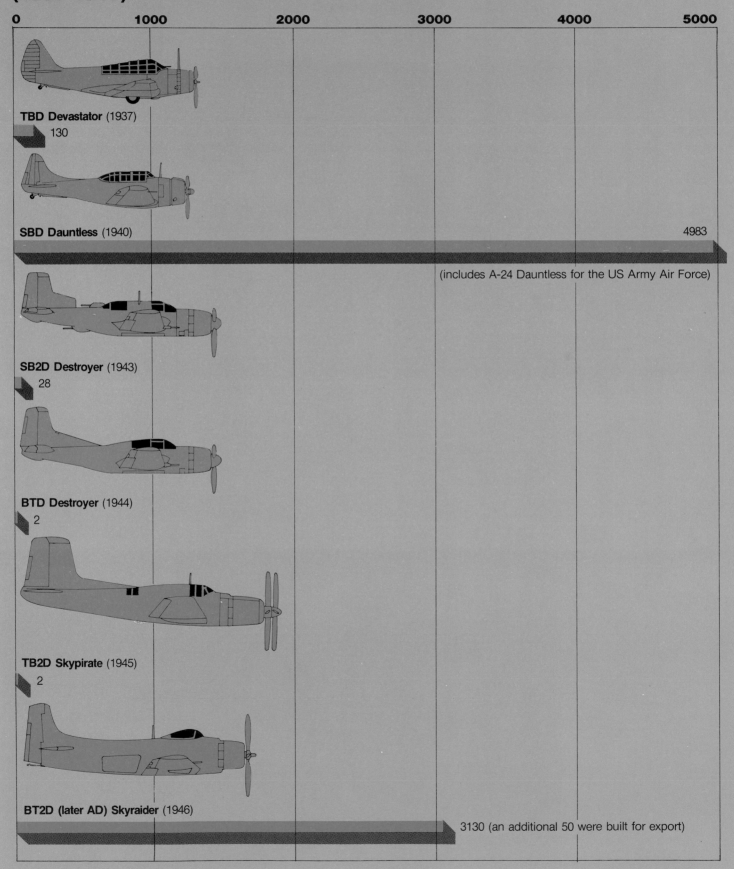

| 0 | 1000 | 2000 | 3000 | 4000 | 5000 |

TBD Devastator (1937)
130

SBD Dauntless (1940)
4983
(includes A-24 Dauntless for the US Army Air Force)

SB2D Destroyer (1943)
28

BTD Destroyer (1944)
2

TB2D Skypirate (1945)
2

BT2D (later AD) Skyraider (1946)
3130 (an additional 50 were built for export)

Above: A formation of Skyraiders from the USS *Independence* carrying drop tanks for a long-range patrol in December 1960.

scheme in which all Douglas aircraft for the Navy were to be given names beginning with 'sky.' The TB2D was known as Skypirate and the R4D transport (commercial DC-3 and USAAF C-47) had been officially called Skytrain throughout the war years. The Skyraider was certainly the appropriate plane, but the timing was wrong. Hostilities ground to a halt in August without it, and the Navy order was nearly halved. Of the original prototype order placed a year earlier, 19 planes were completed as XBT2D-1 attack bombers, two as XBT2D-1N night-attack bombers and one each as XBT2D-1P (photoreconnaissance) and XBT2D-1Q (electronic countermeasures or radar jamming systems). The last XBT2D-1 was the prototype for the next series.

On 11 March 1946, with the XBT2D-1s beginning to roll off the assembly lines and the production BT2D-1s ready to follow, the Navy merged its carrier-based torpedo bomber (VT) and dive bomber (VB) squadrons into single streamlined units known as attack squadrons (VA). With this came the elimination of the T and B prefixes in the aircraft nomenclature; thus the BT2D Dauntless II (which had become the BT2D Skyraider) became redesignated AD (Attack, Douglas) Skyraider. The prototypes were called XAD-1 and the production AD-1s began to arrive in the new VA squadrons in November 1946. Coincidentally, the letters AD are read 'Able Dog' when translated into the contemporary phonetic alphabet. The name seemed to fit the Skyraider, which was frequently referred to by its crews as Able Dog.

By 1948 the 242 AD-1s and 35 AD-1Qs were in service with eight VAs, and the first of 178 structurally enhanced AD-2s and 69 AD-3s were making their appearance. These second and third members of the Skyraider family had two additions that distinguished them from the AD-1s: APS-19 radar automatic pilot and the armor plating advocated by Admiral Hank Suerstedt of the Naval Air Systems Command (successor to the Bureau of Aeronautics).

The story of the ultimately very successful AD Skyraider is incomplete without sidestepping for a moment to the story of its ill-fated sibling, the A2D (Attack, Second, Douglas) Skyshark. The Skyshark was conceived in 1945 as the Navy's first turboprop attack bomber. Turboprop engines utilize a gas turbine to turn a propeller. Because turboprop technology was developed after the earliest jets, the early turboprops were considered to be even more advanced than jets. In any case, both were more advanced than conventional piston engines and turboprop-powered aircraft could carry more payload on less fuel than either the jets of the late 1940s or the earlier piston-engined Navy bombers. The Navy calculated that the ideal carrier plane would be a turboprop that could combine short-distance takeoffs with big payloads, and it actively solicited an A2D from Douglas. The plane that emerged from Ed Heinemann's drawing board bore a strong resemblance to the Skyraider but, to quote Heinemann, had 'a tapered nose and streamlined shape which some say resembled that feared denizen of the deep, the shark.' Hence the name 'Skyshark.'

Below: This A-1H (formerly AD-6) Skyraider of US Navy Attack Squadron 176 carries hash marks of 18 successful combat missions flown over Southeast Asia from the carrier USS *Intrepid*.

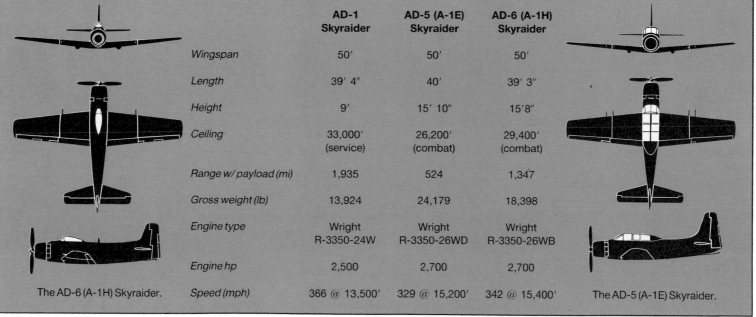

	AD-1 Skyraider	**AD-5 (A-1E)** Skyraider	**AD-6 (A-1H)** Skyraider
Wingspan	50'	50'	50'
Length	39' 4"	40'	39' 3"
Height	9'	15' 10"	15' 8"
Ceiling	33,000' (service)	26,200' (combat)	29,400' (combat)
Range w/ payload (mi)	1,935	524	1,347
Gross weight (lb)	13,924	24,179	18,398
Engine type	Wright R-3350-24W	Wright R-3350-26WD	Wright R-3350-26WB
Engine hp	2,500	2,700	2,700
Speed (mph)	366 @ 13,500'	329 @ 15,200'	342 @ 15,400'

The AD-6 (A-1H) Skyraider.

The AD-5 (A-1E) Skyraider.

The Navy ordered the first two prototypes of the new design on 25 September 1947 under the designation XA2D, but the first one did not fly until 26 May 1950. With the start of the Korean War a month later, 341 production A2D-1s were ordered.

The Skyshark was powered by an Allison XT40-A turbine engine driving two three-bladed contrarotating propellers. It had an ejection seat, four 20-mm cannons and 23 hard points for bombs, rockets and other ordnance. Despite the impressive performance specs of both the engine and airframe, and despite the Navy's big order, the first test flights during the summer of 1950 were plagued with problems. The engine was experimental and proved unreliable. The gearbox linking the engine to the props was a source of serious concern. On 14 December a power train failure resulted in the death of Douglas test pilot Hugh Wood during a flight at Edwards AFB.

Revisions to the original engine and gearbox designs led to the first flight of the production version in June 1953, but problems continued. Two nearly fatal Skyshark crashes led to the Navy's termination of the whole A2D program in September 1953 with only six production aircraft having been produced. Jet technology had matured tremendously since the Navy had first solicited the Skyshark, and the huge success of the Able Dog overshadowed the disastrous fumbling of its jinxed younger brother.

While the Skyshark was demonstrating its dubious form at the Edwards AFB test center during the summer of 1950, a hundred miles south, Douglas El Segundo was beginning to witness the production of the fourth Skyraider variant, the AD-4. The latest Able Dog was outwardly similar to the earlier Skyraiders, but its armament was doubled to four 20-mm guns and wing strengthening increased its maximum ordnance load to nearly 5 tons. The majority of the AD-4s built fell into three categories. There were 344 standard AD-4s built, 248 AD-4N night-attack versions and 194 AD-4Bs with the Low Altitude Bombing System (LABS) that permitted the Skyraider to carry tactical nuclear weapons.

The AD-5, introduced in August 1951, was a distinctly different bird. The earliest Skyraiders were single-seat aircraft, but the AD-5 had a greatly expanded cockpit area. It accommodated a two-man crew seated in a side-by-side arrangement and still had room for eight other seated personnel or four stretchers. The larger cockpit area allowed the plane to be readily used for functions other than ground attack, such as armed transport, target tug or antisubmarine warfare. The bulk of the production

A2D Skyshark	
Wingspan	50'
Length	41' 4"
Height	16' 11"
Ceiling	40,600'
Range (mi)	1,470
Max weight (lb)	22,966
Engine type	Allison XT40-A-6
Engine hp	5,035
Speed (mph)	501 @ 25,000'

Right: A Skyshark over Edwards AFB.

Below from top: A Navy hunter-killer team composed of an AD-5 (hunter) and an AD-6 (killer), an AD-5 showing the rear-of-cockpit accommodations and a flight of British Royal Navy airborne early warning (AEW) Skyraiders.

run was made up of 212 standard AD-5s and 239 AD-5Ns; these were followed by 156 AD-5W radar early-warning versions and 54 of the AD-5Ns were converted to AD-5Q electronic counter-measures/electronic warfare aircraft.

The single-place AD-6 was the Skyraider produced most, however. Like the subsequent AD-7, it was more similar to the AD-1 through AD-4 than it was to the multiseat AD-5. A total of 713 AD-6s and 72 AD-7s came off the El Segundo production line before 18 February 1957, when the line was finally shut down for the last time.

When war broke out in Korea the Skyraiders became for the Navy what the Dauntlesses had been in World War II. The North Korean invasion was barely a week old when AD-4s from VA-55 aboard the USS *Valley Forge* were sent into action. In this war there were no enemy ships to sink, but there was a wide variety of land targets for which the AD was well suited. In October 1951, a little over a year after the war began, Skyraider-equipped Marine Corps attack squadrons set up shop on the Korean Peninsula. When the war ended two years later, there were eight Marine Skyraider squadrons in Korea and two dozen AD squadrons off shore aboard the carriers of Task Force 77 of the Navy's Seventh Fleet.

The Navy's peak Skyraider strength came in 1955, by which time there were 29 squadrons in place. In the 1950s, as the Navy gradually withdrew ADs from its carrier squadrons, 93 ex-Navy Skyraiders wound up serving with the French Armée de l'Air in Algeria.

In 1962, Defense Department nomenclature changed. The very dissimilar Navy and Air Force numbering systems were merged, and a new system based on the simpler Air Force system was adopted. The Navy's manufacturer/function scheme gave way

Below: Lt Duy Chanh of the South Vietnamese air force arrives at his former US Navy A-1H Skyraider for a 23 November 1963 bombing mission.

to a function-only system and the AD series, the first attack aircraft to be numbered under the new system, became A-1. The A-1A through A-1D designations were reserved for renumbering the AD-1 through AD-4, but these had been withdrawn from active service prior to 1962 and the designations were never used. The multiseat AD-5 became A-1E and the AD-6 and 7 became A-1H and A-1J, respectively.

By this time, the United States found itself gradually slipping into the war in Southeast Asia. The US Air Force, which had been operating aging B-26s and converted T-28 trainers as counterinsurgency attack aircraft in cooperation with the South Vietnamese Air Force, felt the need for a better plane. The better plane to which they turned was the Skyraider, specifically the multiseat A-1E, which could accommodate a Vietnamese and American crewman simultaneously, and the A-1H, which saw service with both the US and South Vietnamese Air Forces throughout the war. The US Navy also used its remaining Skyraiders in Vietnam. Operating from carriers of the Seventh Fleet's Task Force 77 on Yankee Station, the A-1s were used for numerous raids against North Vietnamese coastal positions between August 1964 and February 1968.

Despite the fact that it was nearly 20 years old and an attack bomber, not a fighter, the Skyraider came out on top in two air-to-air dogfights with North Vietnamese MiGs. On 20 June 1965 Lieutenant Clint Johnson flew an A-1H from the carrier *Midway* and shot down a MiG-17. On 9 October 1966 Lieutenant (J G) W T Patton downed another one of the Russian-built jets in his A-1H. Known as 'Spads' to the Navy airmen in Southeast Asia and 'Dumptrucks' to the Air Force fliers, the A-1s proved themselves uniquely suited to the war in Southeast Asia. They combined their enormous weapons-carrying capability with a slower speed and longer duration over the target than contemporary jet-attack aircraft, which made for greater payload delivered with greater precision. The Skyraider also had a good reputation for durability; as one Navy pilot's wife told Ed Heinemann, 'when our husbands fly the Skyraider, we sleep well at night.'

The Skywarrior

The demobilization that followed World War II reduced the budgetary pie of the American defense establishment to something less than a fifth of its wartime size. Thus it followed that all the services scrambled for a larger slice of the much smaller pie. In prewar years the Navy had seen itself as the nation's first line of defense and sought to regain its primacy. During the war, however, long-range strategic airpower had proven itself a faster and more flexible alternative. In short, the Navy wanted more and bigger warships and the Air Force wanted more and bigger strategic bombers. The Air Force requested and received funding for the Consolidated B-36, the largest bomber ever built, but the Navy had its 65,000-ton supercarrier USS *United States* scrapped five days after the keel was laid.

It was not that the Navy couldn't see the future role of airpower in warfare (during the war their carrier planes had sunk more major enemy warships than their warships had); it was that they wanted a strong naval role in the future of airpower. Thus it was that in 1948 the Navy commissioned studies (including one from the Douglas-owned Rand think tank) to determine whether it was feasible to build a carrier-based strategic bomber. The major obstacle was weight. Strategic (heavy) bombers by definition carry huge loads that weigh a great deal, and there were questions about whether carrier flight decks could accommodate the loads

	A3D (A-3) Skywarrior	B-66B Destroyer	RB-66C Destroyer
Wingspan	72' 6"	72' 6"	72' 6"
Length	74' 5"	75' 2"	75' 2"
Height	22' 10"	23' 7"	23' 7"
Ceiling	40,500'	39,400'	35,500'
Range w/ payload (mi)	2,300	1,804	2,180
Gross weight (lb)	70,000	83,000	83,000
Engine type	P&W J57-P-10	Allison J71-A-13	Allison J71-A-11
Engine thrust (lb)	10,000	10,200	9,709
Speed (mph)	621 @ 1,000'	631 @ 6,000'	613 @ 8,000'

Right: A gleaming new B-66B, with bomb bay and tail guns clearly visible. The B-66B was the bomber version of the Destroyer.

Far right: A TA-4F Skyhawk snuggles up to the hose-and-drogue refueling apparatus unreeled by a KA-3B tanker.

Below right: The original prototype XA3D-1 in dark Navy blue during its first flight in 1952.

Bottom: A cutaway view of a Douglas EA-3B (A3D-2Q before 1962) Skywarrior. Most A-3/B-66 aircraft were used for electronic warfare, and the bomb bay was replaced with seating for the electronic warfare crew as shown here. Most of these in turn had the tail guns removed. The pink areas in the wing indicate the wing fuel tanks.

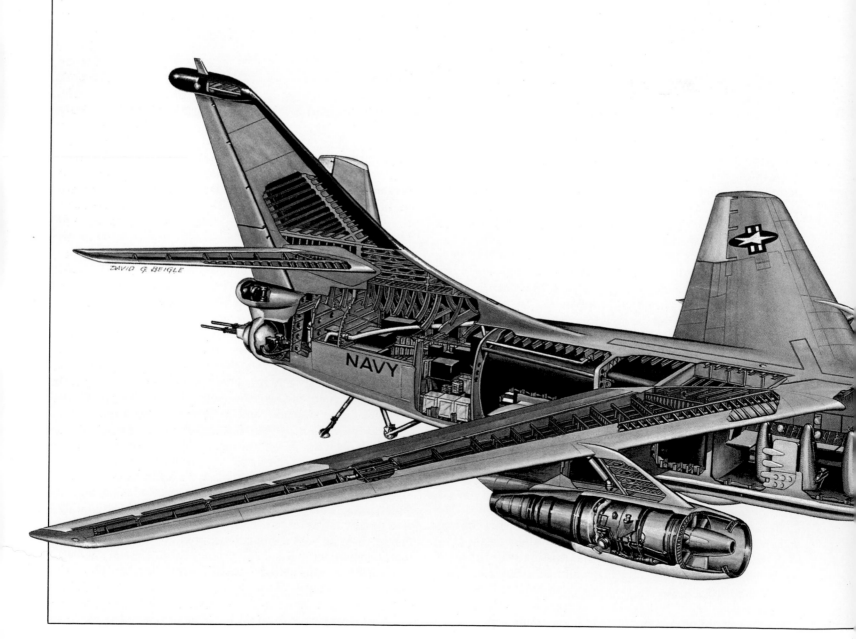

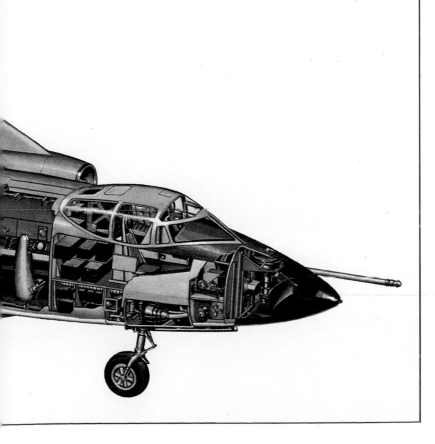

and whether strategic bombers (which traditionally required long runways) could take off from a carrier flight deck. The heaviest attack bombers operating from carriers during the war were the 8-ton Avengers built by Grumman (and later General Motors), and the Skyraiders now weighed roughly the same. North American was building its 20-ton AJ-1 (A-2 after 1962) to equip Navy heavy-attack squadrons, but these were still a far cry from the plane projected by the 1948 Rand report. The Rand study described the need for an aircraft with the capability of striking a target 2000 miles distant with a 5-ton nuclear bomb. Based on their calculations, the aircraft would probably need to have a gross weight of 50 tons, and perhaps even twice that. Douglas was one of the few companies to take up the challenge.

The challenge was met in the form of the Ed Heinemann-designed A3D Skywarrior, which first flew in October 1952. It had two Pratt & Whitney J57 (Westinghouse XJ40 on the prototype) turbojet engines mounted under high-swept wings, and it weighed only 30 tons gross. The A3D-1 (A-3A after 1962) could carry one Mk 15 nuclear bomb, and the A3D-2 (A-3B after 1962) had the capacity to carry two Mk 28 bombs plus a fuel tank in its internal bomb bay.

It is interesting to note that one of the biggest problems encountered by Ed Heinemann in the design of the Skywarrior was determining precisely what the nuclear bombs would look like and what they would weigh. Anything concerning nuclear weapons was, in those days, very top secret. It was hard to build a plane around a weapon if you didn't know what it looked like. In a conversation with General Otto Glasser of the Air Force Nuclear Weapons program, Heinemann described the problem of fitting a Hiroshima-type bomb with its 5-foot diameter into a carrier-based aircraft. 'It would seem to me,' Heinemann told Glasser, 'that the experts should have been able to come up with a smaller bomb as equally effective as what we are using today.'

As Glasser looked on, Heinemann arbitrarily picked a 32-inch diameter and showed Glasser how that size would reduce the overall size of the aircraft to acceptable limits. Glasser was dumbfounded. Heinemann had made an educated guess and had picked the exact size of the highly secret, new generation of nuclear weapons. A week later, the FBI arrived to question Heinemann about how he had guessed such a closely guarded

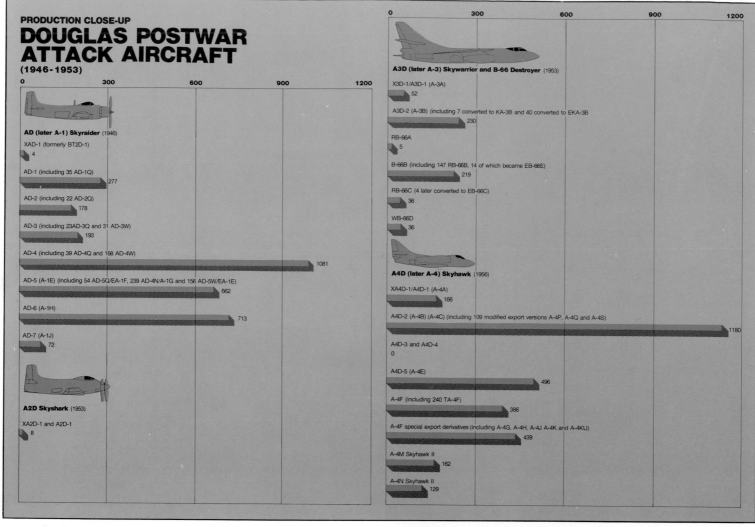

PRODUCTION CLOSE-UP

DOUGLAS POSTWAR ATTACK AIRCRAFT

(1946-1953)

AD (later A-1) Skyraider (1946)
XAD-1 (formerly BT2D-1)
4

AD-1 (including 35 AD-1Q)
277

AD-2 (including 22 AD-2Q)
178

AD-3 (including 23AD-3Q and 31 AD-3W)
193

AD-4 (including 39 AD-4Q and 168 AD-4W)
1081

AD-5 (A-1E) (including 54 AD-5Q/EA-1F, 239 AD-4N/A-1G and 156 AD-5W/EA-1E)
662

AD-6 (A-1H)
713

AD-7 (A-1J)
72

A2D Skyshark (1953)
XA2D-1 and A2D-1
8

A3D (later A-3) Skywarrior and B-66 Destroyer (1953)
X3D-1/A3D-1 (A-3A)
52

A3D-2 (A-3B) (including 7 converted to KA-3B and 40 converted to EKA-3B)
230

RB-66A
5

B-66B (including 147 RB-66B, 14 of which became EB-66E)
219

RB-66C (4 later converted to EB-66C)
36

WB-66D
36

A4D (later A-4) Skyhawk (1956)
XA4D-1/A4D-1 (A-4A)
166

A4D-2 (A-4B) (A-4C) (including 109 modified export versions A-4P, A-4Q and A-4S)
1180

A4D-3 and A4D-4
0

A4D-5 (A-4E)
496

A-4F (including 240 TA-4F)
386

A-4F special export derivatives (including A-4G, A-4H, A-4J A-4K and A-4KU)
439

A-4M Skyhawk II
162

A-4N Skyhawk II
129

secret. Douglas El Segundo was apparently cleared of any question of its being a spy nest, because the company later was given a contract to build TX5 and TX7 nuclear weapons on an interim basis, pending construction of the Sandia Corporation facility at Albuquerque.

The Skywarrior first entered service with the Navy's Heavy Attack Squadron One in March 1956. A decade later, the fast-moving world of aviation and weapons technology had rendered the A-3 obsolete in its original role. Still a reliable and serviceable aircraft, the Skywarrior got a new lease on life. There was a need for a large aircraft that could be used as a carrier-based, air-refueling tanker; 50 A-3As became KA-3As and 39 A-3Bs became EKA-3Bs with an electronic countermeasures capability added to the refuelling capability. During the war in Southeast Asia there was no call for carrier-based nuclear strikes, but carrier-based KA-3 tankers saved countless Navy planes and pilots who might otherwise have been lost at sea or over enemy territory.

The Skywarrior as originally conceived was a means for the Navy to get into the strategic-bombing business dominated by the Air Force, so it is ironic that the Air Force should have decided to buy Skywarriors of its own. This decision was made in 1952 before the Navy had even entered its first A3Ds into service. Designated B-66 and called Destroyer, the Air Force version began service in 1956, nearly a year after the Navy A3D. The basic bomber version of the Destroyer was the B-66B, but by the time war came in Southeast Asia, the Destroyer, like the Skywarrior, was no longer serving as a bomber. Most of the Destroyer production run, built at Douglas Long Beach and Douglas Tulsa, were WB-66D weather reconnaissance and

Above: An A3D bound for service in the US Navy rolls out of the Douglas plant at El Segundo. Note the folding of the tail as well as of the wings.

Below: A multipurpose EKA-3B Skywarrior of the US Navy's Tactical Electronic Warfare Squadron 33 with a TA-4J Skyhawk over the Pacific north of Hawaii.

EB-66/RB-66 reconnaissance/electronic countermeasures versions, and this was the job to which they were assigned in Southeast Asia. When USAF fighter bombers such as F-105s and later F-4s went into North Vietnam during the Rolling Thunder bombing offensive, Destroyers went along not as bombers but as radar-jamming platforms to confuse enemy radar and to help prevent enemy surface-to-air missiles from finding their mark among the fighter bombers. In addition to electronic countermeasures capability, the EB-66s also had their tail guns removed to facilitate the installation of chaff dispensers to further clutter enemy radar scopes. The ECM Destroyers served with the Air Force through most of the war years in Southeast Asia as well as in Europe, where they operated with the 39th TEW Squadron out of Bitburg/Spangdahlem until the mid-1970s.

In the end the Skywarrior/Destroyer was an aircraft of ironies. Developed as a Navy bomber to spite Air Force bombers, it was ordered by the Air Force as well. Ultimately it proved very useful to both services but to neither as a bomber.

The Skyhawk

The diminutive A4D Skyhawk (A-4 after 1962) must be recognized as one of the two or three most successful combat aircraft in the history of the Douglas Company. In production between 1954 and 1979, the Skyhawk has served three nations in three wars and has earned the praise of pilots and maintenance crews alike.

In the midst of the Korean War, while Douglas was upgrading the Skyraider, grappling with the Skyshark and developing the Skywarrior, the need for a jet-powered light attack bomber was making itself evident. Bothered by the nagging problem of bigger, heavier and more complex carrier aircraft, Ed Heinemann proposed the development of an aircraft that would contradict all these trends. 'In order to increase reliability,' Heinemann observed, 'secondary systems were being added. In the final analysis, though, reliability of basic systems was reduced by the

Left and below: Douglas A-4 Skyhawks of the US Navy's Blue Angels aerobatic team photographed by the author during the 1983 Fleet Week exercises over San Francisco Bay.

Right: A Douglas EKA-3B Skywarrior photographed by Harry Gann during a mission over Mount Shasta in Northern California.

secondary systems, or because of it. In many cases, for the same total amount of engineering effort expended, the primary system could have been developed to a much greater degree of safety and efficiency. If [an] aircraft's gross weight is increased by 10 percent due to additions in the form of equipment, and performance is to remain constant, then the wing area, power plant, fuel and structure must be increased by as much as 100 percent.'

The El Segundo team went to work on the smaller, lighter attack bomber that was to embody the theories of its designer and was to be known as 'Heinemann's Hot Rod.' The first Hot Rod, the A4D-1, which first flew on 22 June 1954, weighed just over 4 tons empty as against the Skyraider's 5 tons and Dauntless's 3 tons. Its combat weight was 6 tons compared to an 8-ton gross weight for the Skyraider and 5-ton gross weight for the much more primitive Dauntless. The first Skyhawk had a presentable top speed of 677 mph at sea level and could carry nearly 3 tons of ordnance, including Mk 7 and Mk 8 nuclear weapons.

The A4D-2 (A-4B after 1962) that first appeared in March 1956 had provisions for inflight refueling and had wing racks to accommodate a pair of Bullpup antiradar missiles. In August 1958 the A4D-2N (A-4C after 1962) was introduced. It was based

on the early Skyhawks but had the added ability to operate in difficult weather conditions. The A4D-3 and A4D-4 were designations reserved for developmental experiments that never came to fruition. About this time the entire US military was turning to the new 1962 nomenclature scheme, and with it, the A4D become the A-4. The designation A-4D would logically have been the new designation of the A4D-3 or A4D-4 had they been built. It was purposely never assigned to any aircraft, however, to avoid confusion between the old A4D series and a single variant of the new series.

The next Skyhawk, first designated A4D-5 but then called A-4E, was first delivered to squadron service in May 1962. The A-4F, first flown in August 1966, featured a number of new innovations, the most visible of which was a hump-like avionics/ECM pod molded into the fuselage behind the cockpit that earned the A-4F the nickname Camel. The 'hump' was also retrofitted on some A-4Es and became standard equipment on all subsequent A-4 models.

In addition to 146 A-4Fs supplied to the US Navy, the A-4F also served as the basis for a number of foreign orders. Though they were basically A-4Fs, there were subtle detail variations, and

each foreign delivery was assigned a new model letter. Eight A-4Gs went to the Royal Australian Navy (and remained in service until retirement of the carrier HMAS *Melbourne* in 1985), 90 A-4Hs to the Israeli Air Force, 10 A-4Ks to the Royal New Zealand Air Force, and 30 A-4KUs to the Kuwaiti Air Force. A lesser number of two-seat trainer versions of these aircraft have also been produced, including 240 TA-4Fs, two TA-4Gs, 10 TA-4Hs, 279 TA-4Js (also to Israel), four TA-4Ks and six TA-4KUs.

The Skyhawk II, still basically an A-4F, made its first flight on 10 April 1970. Upgraded systems included a better engine, a drogue parachute (which had been used on the Israeli A-4H), a head-up avionics display, larger canopy and more ammunition for its two 20-mm cannons. The first 162 Skyhawk IIs were ordered by the US Marine Corps under the designation A-4M. This order was followed by 117 A-4Ns delivered to Israel and a canceled order for A-4Ts from the French Navy.

Rebuilt older Skyhawks have also been assigned new designation letters. A hundred A-4Cs rebuilt for the US Naval Reserve became A-4Ls, ex-US Navy A-4Bs went to the Argentine Air Force and Navy as 50 A-4Ps and 16 A-4Qs, respectively. A total of 51 former US Navy A-4Bs were rebuilt for the Air Force of Singapore as A-4S (including 11 TA-4S). It has been announced that Malaysia will also receive 65 rebuilt A-4Cs and A-4Ls. At the end of 1983 it was reported that Australia's A-4Gs and TA-4Gs would be sold to Brazil (reportedly offered to New Zealand but rejected) for operation from its aircraft carrier *Minas Gerais* (ex-Royal Navy *Colossus* class), which would give Brazil the second naval air arm in South America to operate Skyhawks.

The combat career of the Skyhawk began with the first American carrier-launched raids on North Vietnam on 5 August 1964. Flying from the carriers *Ticonderoga* and *Constellation*, respectively, 16 A-4Cs and 15 A-4Es constituted nearly half of the strike force that day and a respectable percentage of the total US Navy effort through the rest of the war. At the same time that American pilots were flying Skyhawk missions over North Vietnam, the Israel Air Force was receiving the first of its A-4Hs. The first 48 of these appeared in October 1967, four months after the Six Day War, and these made up the first direct American combat-aircraft sale to Israel. The first Middle East combat missions flown by Skyhawks came during the series of skirmishes known as the War of Attrition, which began in 1969. In June 1972 the A-4N Skyhawk II made its first appearance with the Israeli Air Force. When Egypt and Syria launched their full-scale invasion of

Above left: The Douglas XA4D-1 Skyhawk prototype during early flight tests in Southern California in 1954.

Above: A TA-4J two-place training Skyhawk touches down on a US Navy aircraft carrier during exercises in the Gulf of Mexico.

Above: Three A-4F Skyhawks from the USS *Bon Homme Richard* over the Gulf of Tonkin in June 1969 during the Vietnam War.

Below: Douglas A-4Ps, being readied for delivery to the Argentine Navy. In 1982 these planes would see action against the British in the South Atlantic.

Israeli-occupied territory on 6 October 1973, the Skyhawks were an integral part of the counterstrike against Arab airfields and troop concentrations.

The Skyhawk was absent from combat for nearly nine years after the end of the Yom Kippur War on 24 October 1973. Then came the Argentine invasion of the British-held Falkland Islands (Las Islas Malvinas) in the South Atlantic in April 1982. As a British task force sailed south to confront the invaders, the Argentine military mobilized for war. Among their assets were the A-4Qs of the Comando de Aviación Naval Argentina (CANA) as well as some A-4Bs and Cs (A-4P) in the Fuerza Aerea Argentina (FAA).

Skyhawks joined the mobilization and were deployed to forward bases on the Argentine mainland, the FAA base at Rio Gallegos and the CANA base at Rio Grande. (The largest runway in the Falklands, at Port Stanley, was too short to accommodate combat jets.) The Skyhawks first taste of combat came on 1 May when the British task force first came within range of the mainland bases. Exactly half of the sorties flown in the first air attack were flown by 28 Skyhawks of the FAA.

The next major action by Argentine Skyhawks came three weeks later in the wake of the British landings at San Carlos Bay, resulting in the fierce air battles of 21 through 25 May. The bravery of the Argentine pilots, attacking at deck level amid a fire storm of antiaircraft fire, won praise even from British Minister of Defence John Nott. By this time the land-based FAA and CANA Skyhawks were being augmented by CANA A-4Qs operating from the aircraft carrier *25 de Mayo* (ironically a

Above: A pair of 'camel-humped' A-4M Skyhawk IIs in service with US Marine Corps Attack Squadron 223. The 'hump' was an integral avionics/ECM pod.

Left: An A-4N Skyhawk II in Douglas company markings, but painted in the camouflage scheme of the Israeli Air Force, to whom it would be delivered.

Below: A cutaway view of an A-4E (A4D-5 before 1962) without the camel's-hump electronics pod, showing the compact inner structure of the Skyhawk's fuselage. The pink areas are the wing fuel tanks. Note the 20-mm cannon in the forward wing root.

Lower right: A Skyhawk of US Navy Attack Squadron 144 ('Roadrunners') aboard the USS *Bon Homme Richard*, returning from a June 1969 bombing mission.

	A4D-1 (A-4A) Skyhawk	A-4F Skyhawk	A-4M Skyhawk
Wingspan	27′ 6″	27′ 6″	27′ 6″
Length	39′ 4″	41′ 4″	41′ 4″
Height	15′ 2″	15′	15′
Ceiling	46,600′	38,600′	40,600′
Range (mi)	1,489	460	1,048
Gross weight (lb)	15,093	19,356	19,833
Engine type	Wright J65-W-4	P&W J52-P8A	P&W J52-P408
Engine thrust (lb)	7,700	9,300	11,187
Speed (mph)	609 @ 35,000′	647 @ 3,500′	687 @ 5,000′

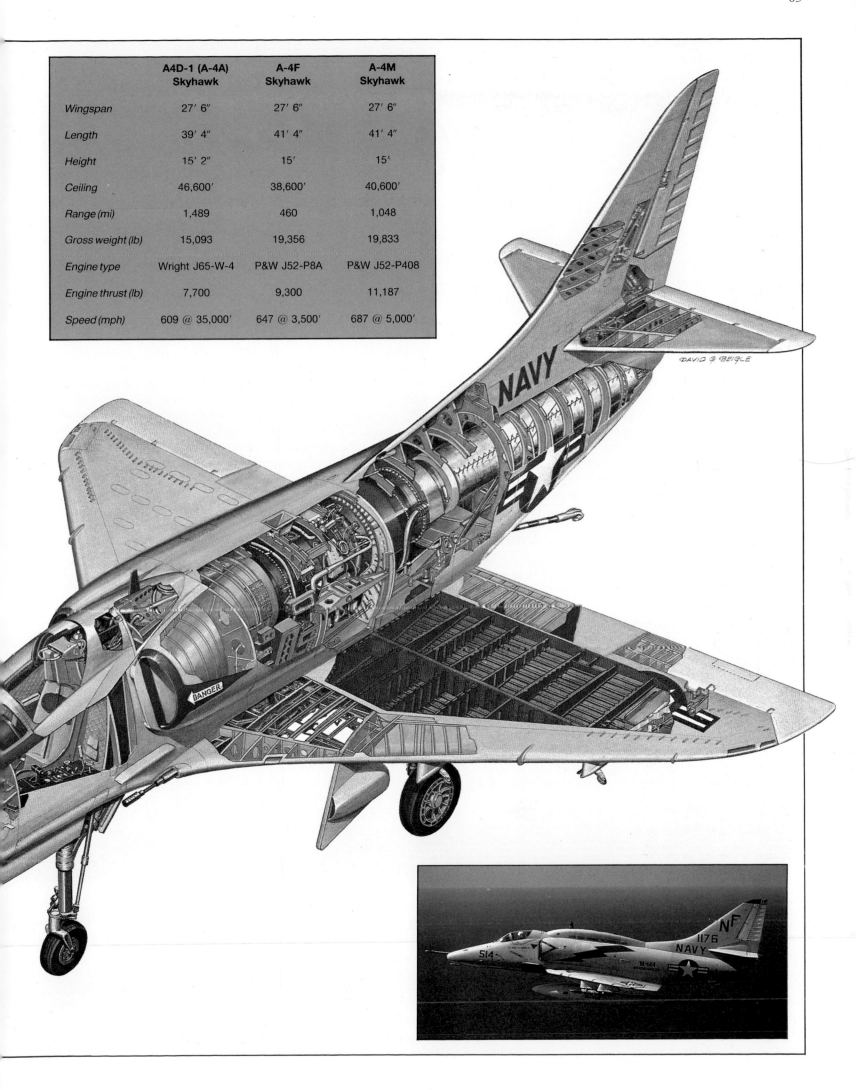

DAVID G. BEIGLE

Above: The A-4 Skyhawk assembly line at Palmdale in the California desert north of Los Angeles.

former British *Colossus*-class carrier) that never ventured far enough from shore to provide any advantage in range to its aircraft. Had the Argentine carrier been able to operate closer to the war zone, it might have improved the chances for Argentina's success in the conflict. As it was, the Argentine planes were operating at the limit of their range, while the British Harrier fighters were operating from nearby carriers.

The attrition rate was severe during the battle for the San Carlos beachhead. The CANA *3a Escuadrilla de Caza y Ataque* lost six A-4Qs in two days, while the FAA *IV Brigada Aerea* lost eight Skyhawks and wrote off two more to battle damage. On the other hand, the air strikes succeeded in sinking the British frigates *Ardent* and *Antelope* and the destroyer *Coventry*, and they also caused severe damage to the British landing force. During the 44-day conflict, the FAA Southern Command had reportedly flown between 445 and 505 missions, 255 of them by Skyhawks. The FAA admitted to the loss of 34 jet combat aircraft including 20 A-4s, while CANA lost more than half of the dozen A-4s that it was reported to have had in service at the beginning of the war.

For Douglas El Segundo and later Douglas Palmdale, the Skyhawk became something of an institution. With 2960 of them produced over a quarter of a century, it was possible for a Douglas employee to have spent virtually his entire career with the Skyhawk. For the aircrews, the plane called Heinemann's Hot Rod or Bantam Bomber was a durable, reliable and effective weapons system.

A Hand at Jet Fighters

The contribution made by the Douglas Aircraft Company to the field of combat aircraft falls almost entirely into the category of light attack bombers. From the DTs in the beginning, through the Devastator, Dauntless, Havoc and Invader of World War II, to the Skyraiders and Skyhawks of the postwar years, almost everything belongs in the same category. There was, however, a narrow thread of naval fighters drawn through this lineage. The first of these was the little-known XFD-1, a single biplane produced and delivered to the Navy in June 1933. It was a two-place radial-engined aircraft with an enclosed cockpit developed to answer the BuAer Specification 113. The Design 113 contract was later won by the Vought XF3U-1 and the Douglas bird was stricken from the record. So insignificant

was the plane in Navy eyes that they reused the FD designation again at the end of World War II.

During World War II, with the proliferation of small aircraft companies supplying airplanes to the Navy, it was impossible for each company to have an identification letter assigned solely to it. Thus, many of the letters were assigned to more than one company, usually to a single major supplier and several that might supply only one or two aircraft types. Douglas had been assigned D since 1922, but during the war three other companies were also assigned that letter: Radioplane, Frankfort and a small upstart company from St Louis called McDonnell. The tiny company that two decades later was to grow large enough to swallow Douglas received its own letter, H, in 1946 following the demise of Hall, Howard and Snead, who had each held it during the war. Before the change, however, the revived FD designation was assigned to McDonnell (for its Phantom I jet fighter), and the F2D designation (for the Banshee fighter project) as well.

Both the McDonnell FD and F2D became FH and F2H before actually going into production, so the FD and F2D designations were never applied to service aircraft for either McDonnell or Douglas.

The first Douglas fighter ever to go into service was also the first jet fighter ordered by the Navy strictly for use as a night fighter. Originally conceived during the Second World War (like the McDonnell Phantom I and Banshee), the Douglas fighter was given the designation F3D when it was ordered in April 1946. The new plane first flew on 23 March 1948 and was named Skyknight, occasionally spelled Skynight in reference to its fly-by-night design. It was no small airplane. To fly and fight by night in those days required a large volume of vacuum-tube radar and avionics. There was a half ton of electronics in the nose of the Skyknight that took up an area sufficiently wide for the two-man crew to sit side-by-side comfortably behind it and the unorthodox large flat windshield. The first of 28 F3D-1s appeared in February 1950 and the first of the principal version, 237 F3D-2s, appeared one year later. The F3D-1 had a 3100-lb-thrust Westinghouse J34-WE-24 turbojet engine and the F3D-2 was designed around the 4600-lb-thrust J46-WE-3. The latter engine was unavailable, so the F3D-2s had to be built with a 3400-lb-thrust J34-WF-36.

Though designed for carrier operations, the Skyknight found itself serving operationally with land-based Marine units in Korea. On the night of 2 November 1952 Marine Major William Stratton and Master Sergeant Hans Hoglind shot down a Yak-15 in the first jet-to-jet aerial victory scored at night. One Marine night-fighter squadron went on to rack up the best night-fighter record of the Korean War, but this has been attributed more to

Top: A Douglas F3D-2Q Skyknight in US Marine Corps markings. The Skyknight served with both Navy and Marine Corps squadrons.

Above: An F3D Skyknight, its large flat windshield clearly visible, in dark colors for nighttime operations. Because of its night-fighter mission, the F3D was often called Skynight rather than Skyknight.

Below: The Douglas XFD-1 was the first Douglas fighter. It was so forgettable that its designation was reassigned.

the 20-mile range of the APQ-35 radar than the Skyknight's dogfighting ability. The Skyknight developed a good reputation with the US Air Force as well, with Marine F3Ds having provided fighter cover for USAF B-29 raids over North Korea. The Air Force actually looked seriously at the Skyknight as a possible answer to its night-fighter requirement, but went ahead with the Northrop F-89 Scorpion instead.

After Korea the F3D remained in service as an electronic reconnaissance/electronic countermeasures aircraft with the Navy and Marines for nearly two decades. The Skyknight was redesignated F-10 in 1962 under the big Defense Department nomenclature change. Later in 1962, the Skyknight was credited with having detected the first radar emissions from Cuba, which led to the discovery of the Russian missiles that precipitated the Cuban missile crisis. Some F-10s went on to serve in Southeast Asia until the last one was retired in 1970.

The design of the orthodox, straight-winged F3D was ordinary and almost boring by comparison to the F4D which followed, even though the two got their start at roughly the same time. In a sense, the design of the Skyknight was an exercise in the adaptation of accepted and proven elements of design to the aircraft under development. The F4D Skyray was designed with the benefit of the most advanced theories available at the time. It is no secret that German aircraft design was well ahead of the rest of the world throughout the early 1940s. The Germans had several types of jet aircraft in operational units when jets were still experimental in Great Britain and the United States. When Germany was defeated in the spring of 1945, scientists and engineers were sent to study the captured German files. The swept-wing designs of the Messerschmitt company influenced the development of Boeing's B-47 and North American's F-86. Meanwhile the delta-winged, tail-less aircraft like the Me 163 designed by Dr Alexander Lippisch were observed by emissaries from Consolidated (later Convair) and translated into a lineage of delta-wing fighters for the Air Force that still are in service. Gene Root and Amos Smith from Douglas were also intrigued by the Lippisch deltas. Ironically, Jack Northrop and Ed Heinemann had tinkered with the idea of a delta-winged aircraft (Northrop Model 25) before the war but had dropped it. Employing Lippisch data, the Douglas team, including Heinemann, tackled the

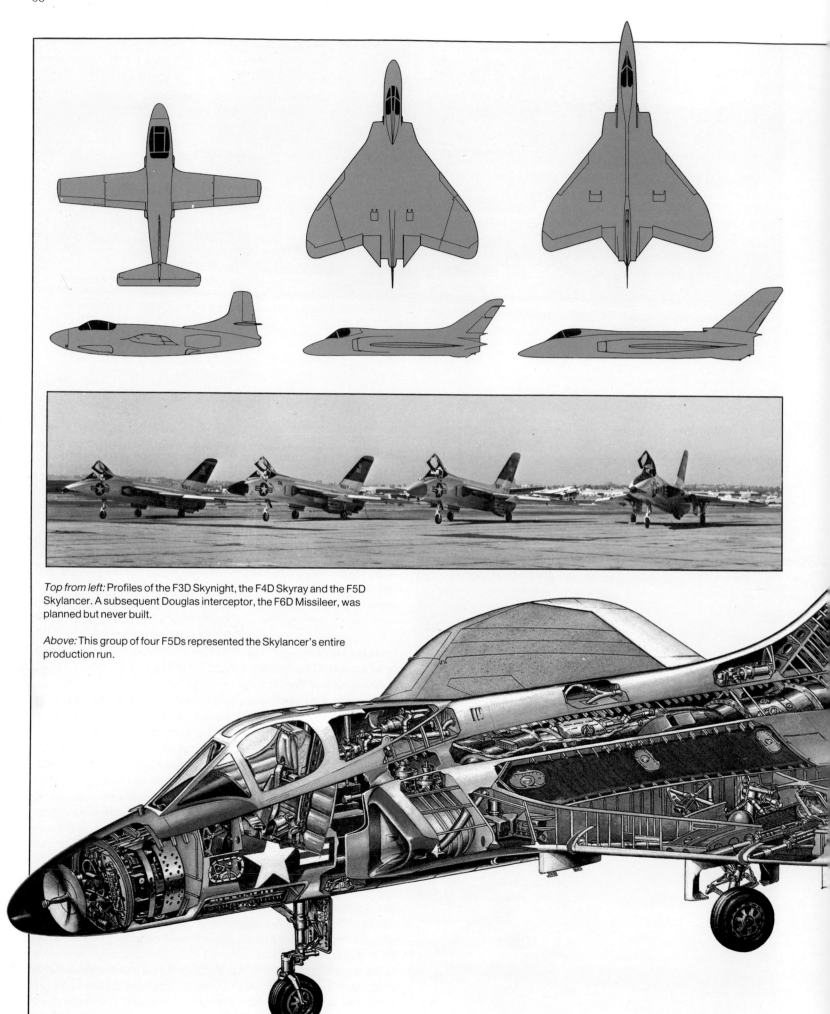

Top from left: Profiles of the F3D Skynight, the F4D Skyray and the F5D Skylancer. A subsequent Douglas interceptor, the F6D Missileer, was planned but never built.

Above: This group of four F5Ds represented the Skylancer's entire production run.

	F3D Skyknight	F4D Skyray	F5D Skylancer
Wingspan	50′	33′ 6″	33′ 6″
Length	45′ 5″	45′ 8″	53′ 10″
Height	16′ 1″	13′	14′ 10″
Ceiling	34,000	55,000	—
Range (mi)	1,068	593	1,226
Gross weight (lb)	24,485	26,000	29,122
Engine type	Westinghouse J34-WE	P&W J57-P-8	P&W J57-P-8
Engine thrust (lb)	3,250	16,000	16,000
Speed (mph)	478 @ 33,000′	723 @ 50,000′	791 @ 35,000′

Right: The XF4D-1 Skyray prototype streaks into a steep climb.

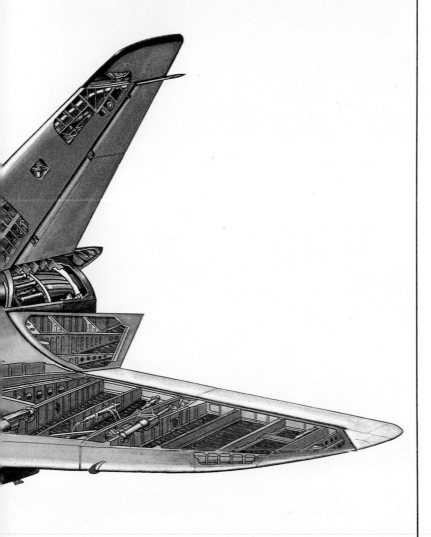

Above: A cutaway view of the F4D-1 Skyray, a sleek fighter jet that was on the leading edge of aircraft design when it was first introduced.

problem of building a practical delta-winged fighter for the Navy in response to the latter's request for a plane that could climb to 40,000 feet in five minutes.

In the era of the Skyraiders, when jets were still not fully trusted, the Douglas Model 571 was an odd bird. Nevertheless, a contract was signed in December 1948 under the designation F4D-1 and the plane, called Skyray because of its similarity to a Manta Ray, was first flown on 23 January 1951. The first prototype XF4D-1 was fitted with a 5000-lb-thrust Allison J35 turbojet, but the second was retrofitted with a 11,600-lb-thrust Allison J40. This engine gave the extra push to set a 753-mph world speed record in October 1953. Meanwhile it was decided to fit the production versions with a similarly rated Pratt & Whitney J57 turbojet. The plane that the Navy requested was supposed to climb to 40,000 feet in five minutes; the Skyray could do it in two. In 1957 and again in 1958, a Skyray-equipped interceptor squadron was named the top interceptor squadron in the North American Air Defense Command (NORAD), even through it was the only Navy unit assigned to the Air Force-dominated Command.

There were 422 Skyrays built, including the two prototypes, and they continued to roll off the El Segundo production line until December 1958. The F4D-1 (F-6A after 1962) equipped both Marine squadrons and Navy carrier squadrons until the last one retired in February 1964, six months short of the first salvos of the US Navy participation in the war in Southeast Asia.

PRODUCTION CLOSE-UP
DOUGLAS POSTWAR FIGHTERS
(1950-1956)

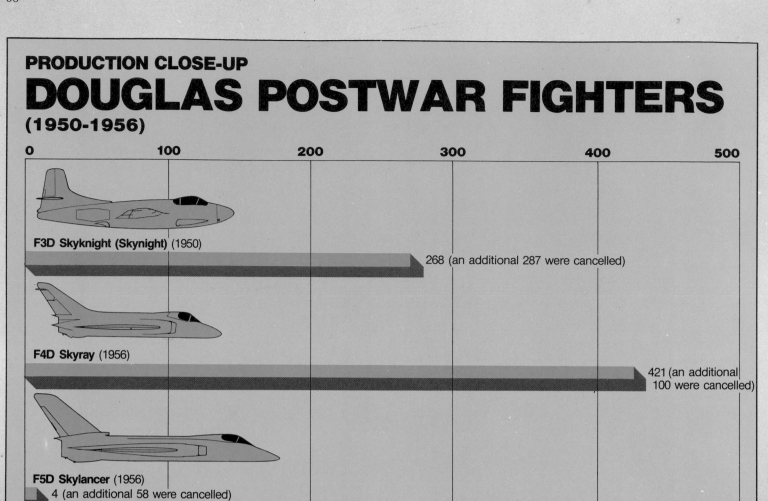

0   100   200   300   400   500

F3D Skyknight (Skynight) (1950)

268 (an additional 287 were cancelled)

F4D Skyray (1956)

421 (an additional 100 were cancelled)

F5D Skylancer (1956)

4 (an additional 58 were cancelled)

The first F4D-2 began life as one of the F4D-1s, but modifications to this 'Super-Skyray' were so extensive that the program was redesignated F5D and the plane became the Skylancer. Ed Heinemann had designed the Skyray and he won the 1954 Collier Trophy for his design. However, he gave credit for much of the Skylancer to three other Douglas engineers—John Barter, Nate Carhart and Jonnie Jorgenson (the project engineer)—who saw it through. The J57-powered F5D had a wing layout very similar to that of the Skyray, and their wingspans were identical. The Skylancer, though, was 10 feet longer and much sleeker in appearance. Inside it was an all-new aircraft, with greatly improved avionics systems and a wider range of weapons systems available. The first of four prototypes made its maiden flight on 21 April 1956, and the Navy placed an order for 58 production aircraft. Despite the improvements and the promise, the performance did not match the requirements and the production order was canceled. The four prototypes were turned over to NASA for experimental purposes, where they were used in the early development of the X-20 Dyna-Soar space-shuttle program. The test pilot for this phase of the program was Neil Armstrong, who later became the first human being to walk on the moon.

The Skylancer, fourth and last of Douglas' fighters (the proposed F6D Missileer was never built), faded from the scene before its more successful predecessor, the Skyray, but both were extinct when Donald Douglas crossed paths with the man from St Louis who was to become the premier builder of fighters.

Above: An F4D-1 Skyray of VF-13 lines up for a landing aboard the carrier USS *Essex* (CV-9) on 8 January 1960.

Below: In the land of Skyrays. A lineup of F4Ds of Navy Fighter Squadron 74 with a few A4Ds, A3Ds and Vought F8Us in the background.

McDONNELL OF ST LOUIS

A Giant Comes to Life

The McDonnell Aircraft Company of St Louis was just three months old and had a staff of 15 when the war clouds exploded over Europe. The entire American aircraft industry was quickly swept up in the Roosevelt Administration's attempt to increase by tenfold the size of the US Army Air Corps. In the space of two years the small St Louis company grew from fledgling newcomer to a firm of 400 employees with two and a half million dollars' worth of orders on its books. But McDonnell was not alone. All across the country small firms grew large and large ones grew larger while still smaller firms started up and proliferated. For every one of the majors such as Boeing, Consolidated, Grumman and, of course, Douglas, there were a dozen smaller companies whose products would never become household words, but whose role in the war effort was essential nonetheless. For most of the smaller companies the role was as subcontractor, supplying parts for products designed by the majors. For McDonnell it was supplying tails and engine cowlings for Boeing's bombers and Douglas's C-47s. The company that would one day swallow Douglas began as one of a myriad of its supplicants. Douglas netted well over a billion dollars during the war and it designed and built nearly 30,000 aircraft. McDonnell netted about five percent as much by building subassemblies and produced just two McDonnell-designed aircraft, though it built a few Fairchild AT-21 trainers.

On 29 July 1941 the US Army Air Force contracted with McDonnell to design and build a twin-engined interceptor designated P-67 and alternatively called Bomber Destroyer because of its mission and Bat because of its unusual design. The contour of the P-67's wings was molded into that of the fuselage and engine nacelles like the membrane of a bat's wing stretching between its body and forearms. The design was ahead of its time insofar as it permitted the fuselage to provide some of the lift normally provided only by the wings. The Bat was larger than Lockheed's P-38 Lightning, the best known of America's twin-engined fighters, but much smaller than Northrop's P-61 Black Widow, the largest operational USAAF fighter. Its designated armament, consisting of six 37-mm cannons, was among the heaviest carried by any fighter.

The first prototype XP-67 rolled out of the company's factory at Lambert Field in late 1943, but its first flight did not take place until 6 January 1944. In the initial trials, the Bat left a great deal

to be desired. Its formidable armament portended a serious threat to enemy bombers, but the bomber destroyer's performance was not exceptional. Fear of enemy bombers had waned, as would interest in the P-67. It is well documented that the USAAF bought a wide variety of prototypes during the war years, but that the bulk of its money was bet on proven winners. The second prototype XP-67 was canceled and the first was destroyed by fire on 6 September 1944. It was perhaps a climactic end to the only propeller-driven fighter program ever undertaken by McDonnell.

Left: James Smith McDonnell punching the McDonnell plant time clock at an unaccustomed 8:34 am. Mac had owned the shop for three years when this picture was taken in 1942.

Below: The McDonnell Company moved into its general offices at Lambert Field near St Louis in 1939.

Even as a fiery inferno consumed the Bat, another program was taking shape on the McDonnell drafting tables. The contract for this program came to McDonnell at least to some extent because it was such a small firm. The major manufacturers were all up to their elbows with their major programs. Because these programs were seen to be so important, experimental or marginal programs were often assigned to competent but smaller firms. Among the most important experimental programs of that or any other era was the development of operational jet aircraft. Bell had gotten the ultrasecret contract to build the first USAAF jet fighter in 1941 and on New Year's eve of 1942 the telephone rang in James Smith McDonnell's office. It was the Navy calling about jet aircraft. McDonnell was summoned from St Louis to Washington DC the following day to discuss his building the Navy's first jet fighter. The contract was signed at the end of the week, on 7 January 1943, and two years and two weeks later, on 26 January 1945, the Navy's first jet and the second plane designed by McDonnell Aircraft Company took to the air on its first flight. The prototype had been designed and built under the designation XFD-1. The D ironically shared by the huge Douglas Company was later dropped, and the letter H was assigned to the up and coming McDonnell.

The FH-1 carried the given name of Phantom. 'Mr Mac,' as the founder of the company was known, had a keen interest in animism and the spirit world that dated back to his days as a student at Princeton, and this was the reason for the succession

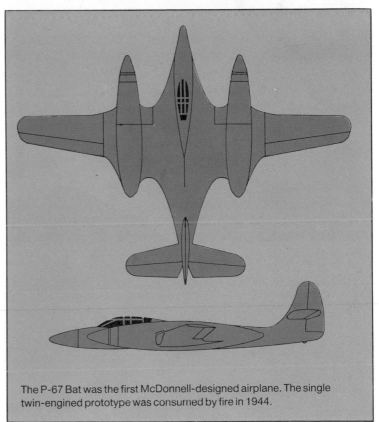

The P-67 Bat was the first McDonnell-designed airplane. The single twin-engined prototype was consumed by fire in 1944.

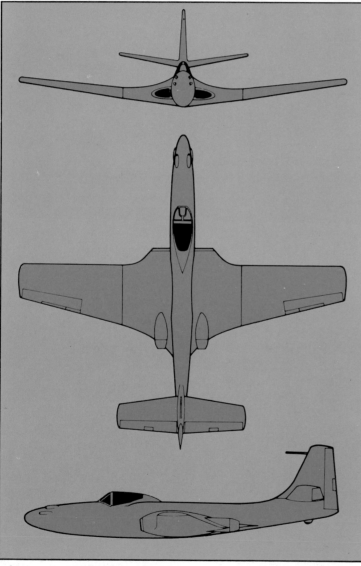

Left and upper left: The McDonnell FH-1 (originally FD-1) Banshee was McDonnell's second plane and the US Navy's first jet.

Above: A pair of McDonnell F2H Banshees from the carrier USS *Midway* (CVA-41) on patrol over Greece in March 1952.

Top right: A pair of McDonnell F3H Demons from the carrier USS *Constellation* (CVA-64) on patrol during March 1962.

production contract. The first prototype was, however, the only Phantom built before the war ended and it never got near combat. On 21 July 1946, an FH-1 took off from the USS *Franklin D Roosevelt* and the aircraft carrier reached the jet age.

The first of the 60 production aircraft remaining in the Phantom contract after postwar demobilization began to role off the McDonnell line in January 1947; by July, the first all-jet Navy fighter squadron, VF-17 aboard the USS *Saipan*, was becoming operational with FH-1s. Even as the Phantom was barely entering squadron service, McDonnell engineers were at work on a successor.

The Banshee

The McDonnell Banshee, given the Navy designation F2H, (originally F2D), was first ordered in March 1945, shortly after the first flight of the Phantom. The first flight of the XF2H-1 came on 11 January 1947. Outwardly, the new bird was very similar to its predecessor. The two planes were within a foot of being the same size on every dimension. Inside, however, the Banshee snarled with the power of a pair of J34-WE-22 turbojets, delivering nearly twice the thrust available to the Phantom.

Armament on the F2H, like the FH, consisted of four 20-mm cannons, but a bomb-carrying capacity was also added. The operational F2H-1 Banshees first joined the fleet in August 1948, with the first F2H-2s appearing in November 1949. There had been 56 F2H-1 fighters and there were to be 334 F2H-2s in the fighter configuration. There were also 14 F2H-2N night fighters and 88 F2H-2P photoreconnaissance aircraft, with the latter carrying six cameras in their noses instead of the standard 20-mm cannons of the fighter versions. Twenty-five F2H-2s were later modified to carry either Mk 7 or Mk 8 nuclear weapons. The F2H-3 and F2H-4 Banshees that continued in production until October 1953 were designed as all-weather fighters with APQ-41 and APG-37 radar, respectively.

The Banshee first went into combat in August 1951 and served as one of the principal fighters aboard the carriers of the US

of McDonnell aircraft being assigned names like Phantom, Banshee, Goblin and Voodoo. In a postwar interview, he is recorded as having observed that 'inanimate objects possess a conscious life or vitality' and that 'it is good and nourishing to treat all things as alive.'

The life breathed into the Phantom made it the fastest US Navy combat aircraft of World War II. Powered by a pair of 1600-lb-thrust Westinghouse WE-19-XB-2B turbojets, the FH-1 reached top speeds of 500 mph and earned the company a 100-unit

Seventh Fleet's Task Force 77 for the duration of the Korean War. After the war, the F2H continued in service with the Navy until September 1959. In November 1955 the Canadian Navy acquired 39 former US Navy F2H-3s, which remained in service until September 1962.

The Demon

The Banshee was flying its first missions over Korea when its successor first rolled off the line at St Louis. Given the designation F3H by the Navy and the evocative name Demon by its creator, the new plane was the first swept-wing fighter McDonnell built for the Navy, and the only single-engined McDonnell fighter that ever went into production. The idea behind the Demon was for an efficient single-engined, carrier-based, all-weather fighter. It had some roots in common with the F-88 fighter that McDonnell was then building for the Air Force. The two planes were roughly the same size, and while both had swept wings, the F-88 was powered by a pair of Westinghouse J34s like the Banshee, but the Demon had a single 10,900-lb-thrust Westinghouse J40. The company had hoped that the

	FH-1 Phantom I	F2H Banshee	F3H Demon
Wingspan	40' 9"	41' 6"	35' 4"
Length	38' 9"	39'	59'
Height	14' 2"	14' 5"	14' 7"
Ceiling	41,100'	48,500'	44,000'
Range (mi)	695	1,278	1,130
Gross weight (lb)	10,035	14,234	29,998
Engine type	Westinghouse J30-WE-20	Westinghouse J34-WE-22	Westinghouse J40-WE-22
Engine thrust (lb)	1,600	3,000	6,500
Speed (mph)	479 @ sea level	587 @ sea level	616 @ sea level

Below: The McDonnell factory floor as it appeared in 1940. The company got its start building parts here for other manufacturers.

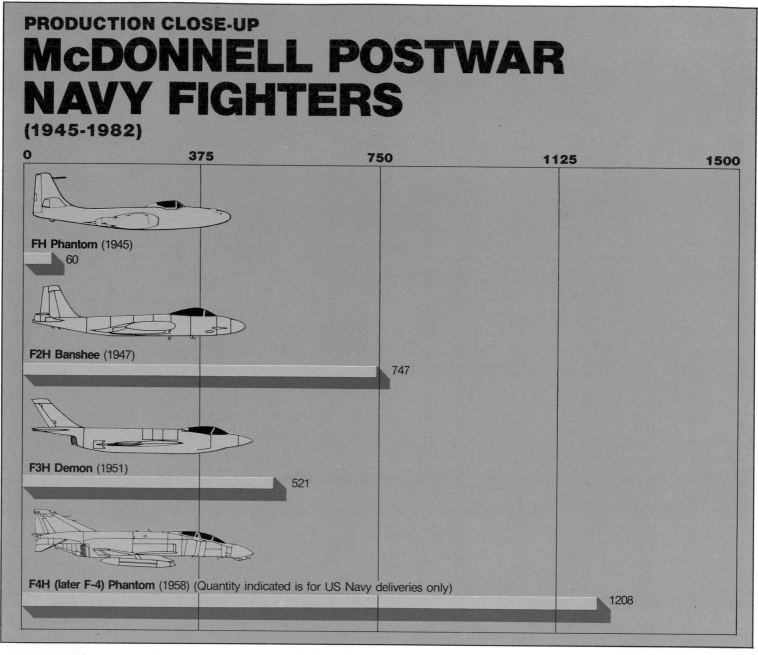

PRODUCTION CLOSE-UP
McDONNELL POSTWAR NAVY FIGHTERS
(1945-1982)

| 0 | 375 | 750 | 1125 | 1500 |

FH Phantom (1945) — 60

F2H Banshee (1947) — 747

F3H Demon (1951) — 521

F4H (later F-4) Phantom (1958) (Quantity indicated is for US Navy deliveries only) — 1208

Allison J71 would be available, but it did not appear until the F3H-2.

The XF3H-1 prototype first flew on 7 August 1951, and the first of the 56 production F3H-1Ns (N for the all-weather capability) flew on 24 January 1954. Serious difficulties immediately reared their heads—not a single J40 was able to satisfactorily handle a 15-ton airplane, which was 50 percent heavier than the twin-engined Banshee. Difficulty turned to disaster with the loss of six of the aircraft and four pilots. The Navy had fumbled $200 million with the J-40 by the time the Allison J-71 finally became available in December 1954.

The F3H-2 did not find its way into service until March 1956, just over a year after the F3H-1s were grounded as unsafe. Production of the second Demon model, first based with the VF-14 aboard the USS *Forrestal*, was divided between F3H-2N and F3H-2M. These aircraft were generously armed with four Sparrow (or two Sidewinder) radar-guided air-intercept missiles and four 20-mm cannons. Designated F-3 after 1962, the Demon remained in production until November 1959 and in squadron service until September 1964, when the last ones were retired. The Demon, a single-engined fleet interceptor, was a singularly unimpressive fighter but it was significant in the history of military aviation. It provided the stepping-stone between the early straight-winged McDonnells and the F4H, which became the F-4 and the greatest American fighter since the Sabre Jet.

The Goblin

McDonnell's first venture into the realm of Air Force combat aircraft after World War II and the ill-fated P-67 Bat was probably the most unusual prototype the Air Force ever saw built. At the same time that the very conventional Phantom and the Banshee programs were underway for the Navy, the Army Air Force ordered the strange little bird which it designated P-85 (F-85 after 1948). The idea behind the P-85 grew out of the World War II requirement for fighters to escort long-range bombers. To counteract enemy interceptors over hostile territory, bombers needed fighters to protect them. As technology allowed the development of longer and longer range bombers, their newfound extended range outstripped the ability of the smaller fighters to escort them, even with external fuel tanks.

As the war ended, the huge Convair B-36, with its 5000-mile combat radius, was designed to be the cornerstone of the postwar Air Force. Its range was so great that it seemed to be technologically impossible to build a light maneuverable fighter that

Above: An F3H Demon being readied for launch from the catapult of the USS *Coral Sea* (CVA-43).

Below: The sleek and futuristic XF3H-1 Demon prototype at Lambert Field after its 1951 rollout.

Above left: The XF-85 is lowered from a B-29 for its first test flight. It was unable to reattach itself to the trapeze after this flight and had to land using its landing skid.

Above: The second Goblin, still designated XP-85, has its fuel tanks topped off before a test flight.

Below: A study in scale: the first XF-85 Goblin with its B-29 'mother ship.'

could accompany it to the target. In another decade aerial refueling would be a practical solution, but in 1946 it was not a viable option.

The immediate solution was as unorthodox as it was obvious. If the fighters could not match the range of the big bombers they were designed to protect and if bases closer to the target were not available, why not carry the fighters the way it carried other defensive armament? The fighter could ride the bomber to enemy territory, preserving its fuel and range, and take off when needed.

The idea for an aerial aircraft carrier was not new. The US Navy had operated fighters experimentally from its dirigibles in 1931. A trapeze and hangar apparatus allowed the airships USS *Akron*, USS *Macon* and USS *Los Angeles* to carry, release and recover as many as five aircraft at a time. The aircraft (Curtiss F-9Cs) were used not only to defend the airship, but to extend its reconnaissance range as well by allowing it to look in six directions at once. Technically the system worked, but the Navy ultimately scrapped the idea. This was partly because of doubts about whether the fighters could adequately protect a blimp and partly because of the demise of the general idea of maintaining a fleet of airships. Bombers were far less vulnerable

than airships. Escort fighters were a proven and valuable defensive measure when the USAAF commissioned McDonnell to design a parasite fighter that would live off the mother ship for most of the mission and operate on its own for only brief periods.

By October 1945 the Second World War was over, Convair's huge B-36 bomber was taking shape as the centerpiece of the postwar Air Force, and McDonnell was given a contract to build the parasite fighter, P-85. The parasite was required to be small enough to fit in a B-36 bomb bay but to have the performance to contend with the jet fighters that might be sent to attack it. The McDonnell engineers tackled their unusual task and by June 1946 a mock-up of the fighter, called Goblin in the McDonnell tradition, was ready for inspection. The Goblin was a strange looking

Below: A gleaming swept-wing delight, the prototype XF-88 Voodoo was photographed at McDonnell's big Lambert Field hangar on 11 August 1948. Even though it wasn't quite right for them, the Air Force liked it and urged its further development, which resulted in the F-101.

little aircraft, and was described alternatively as a 'fat little bug' or an 'amusement park airplane.' Nevertheless, it met the design specifications. It was less than 15 feet long, with a wingspan of 21 feet 1 inch that folded to 5 feet 5 inches when it was tucked into the B-36 bay. McDonnell also designed and built the trapeze to hold the Goblin in place within the B-36, then lower and release it at the start of a mission. The Air Force liked what it saw in St Louis that June day in 1946, and the company got the nod for a pair of prototypes.

On 23 August 1948 the first XF-85 went up for its initial flight. The B-36 was not available for the flight test, so the trapeze was carried aloft by a modified B-29. The flight itself was a success, but when the pilot eased the tiny craft back to its rendezvous with the mother ship, it collided with the trapeze and had to make a forced landing on its Me 163-type landing skid. After the initial snafu, the flight test series continued and the XF-85 prototypes performed well despite their small size and unusual basing mode. The little parasite had a perfectly acceptable top speed of 648 mph at sea level, and its mission endurance of 20 minutes at full power was considered adequate because it would be carried to and from the mission by another airplane.

During the seven test flights the XF-85 demonstrated a maximum endurance of 109 minutes, but doubts were starting to creep in from official circles. Theoretically the system was valid and it had passed a series of practical tests; however, retrieving the fighter was a complicated process that would be no small feat in in the heat of battle. Furthermore, what would happen to a fighter with an hour's endurance if the bomber were shot down after the launch? It certainly would not be able to reach friendly territory. If the bomber was in fact shot down, either before or after the launch, it would automatically mean the loss of the Goblin because, by definition, a parasite depends on the host organism to sustain it. Bearing all this in mind, the Air Force canceled the F-85 program after the construction of two Goblins,

seven flight tests and the expenditure of $3.1 million for research, development, tests and evaluation. It was not the last USAF experiment with aerial aircraft carriers, but it marked the end to McDonnell's first postwar Air Force contract and the smallest fighter ever built for the postwar USAF.

The Voodoo

Even with the F-85 program in the works, McDonnell was still keen for a more conventional fighter contract with the Air Force. The Phantom and Banshee programs were working out well for the Navy and the company felt this expertise could be put to some use. In June 1946 the company was able to interest the Air Force in the idea of a jet-powered, long-range penetration fighter intended to escort Strategic Air Command bombers. It was the conventional approach to the same question but addressed another way by the F-85. The USAAF ordered two prototypes for a plane similar to the Navy's Banshee under the designation F-88. Nicknamed Voodoo, the plane first flew on 20 October 1948, six months late due to a midstream change of specifications that called for a 35-degree swept wing rather than a straight wing like that of McDonnell's two Navy fighters. The performance of the first XF-88 prototype pointed up the need for a redesigned intake. This took nearly two years to complete and in August 1950, shortly after the flight of the XF-88A second prototype, the program was scrapped. Most of the USAF budget had been directed toward bombers and strategic forces, and the Voodoo had failed to perform its intended task well enough. The Air Force by this time had in service both the Republic F-84 Thunderjet and the North American F-86 Sabre Jet, which between them could do everything the F-88 could do or was intended to do. Most important, they had already been tested and were in production, while the F-88 was still not ready for mass production.

A Canadian Armed Forces CF-101B Voodoo interceptor of No 425 Squadron photographed by Terry Panopalis at Canadian Forces Base Trenton on 10 September 1983. The CF-101B Voodoo was the mainstay of the Canadian contribution to the North American Air Defense Command (NORAD) until it was replaced by another McDonnell Douglas product, the CF-18 Hornet.

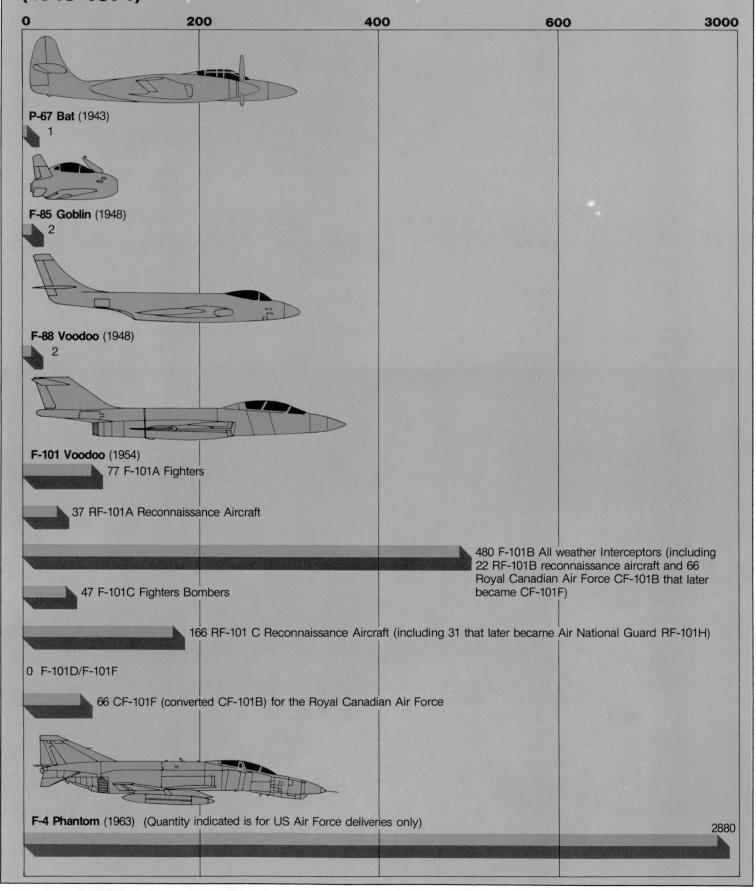

PRODUCTION CLOSE-UP
McDONNELL US AIR FORCE FIGHTERS
(1943-1974)

| 0 | 200 | 400 | 600 | 3000 |

P-67 Bat (1943)
1

F-85 Goblin (1948)
2

F-88 Voodoo (1948)
2

F-101 Voodoo (1954)
77 F-101A Fighters

37 RF-101A Reconnaissance Aircraft

480 F-101B All weather Interceptors (including 22 RF-101B reconnaissance aircraft and 66 Royal Canadian Air Force CF-101B that later became CF-101F)

47 F-101C Fighters Bombers

166 RF-101 C Reconnaissance Aircraft (including 31 that later became Air National Guard RF-101H)

0 F-101D/F-101F

66 CF-101F (converted CF-101B) for the Royal Canadian Air Force

F-4 Phantom (1963) (Quantity indicated is for US Air Force deliveries only)
2880

The Voodoo was far from dead, however. The F-88 had been well liked and attributed with many desirable qualities. In January 1951 the Air Force again went shopping for a long-range fighter after seeing the results coming back from the Korean War. In October 1951 funds earmarked for the F-84F and F-86F were diverted to McDonnell for production of the Voodoo, which still bore the designation F-88. The basic airframe was to serve immediately as an interim long-range fighter, and as an 'ultimate' long-range fighter later. As technology progressed the systems of later aircraft in the series were upgraded, and the earlier airframes were retrofitted.

On 15 January 1952 the USAF offered a contract for the new Voodoo under the designation F-101A; the contract was signed on 11 June, with the Air Force accepting the terms inserted by McDonnell. However, the Air Force later recorded that 'cost increases, judged excessive by the Air Force, led to renegotiation of the contract.' The contract was finally concluded in November 1956 as a modified, fixed-price incentive, in which the cost ran about five percent more than the target cost. McDonnell made neither the 10 percent maximum profit nor the 8 percent target profit permitted in the original F-101 contract. The contractor's profit reached 6.85 percent of the total cost, or about as much as a cost-plus-fixed-fee contract would have allowed. Other F-101s followed almost the same buying pattern. As with the original model, the manufacturer began production under a temporary letter contract that was later replaced by a more formal, negotiated agreement. The Air Force endorsed the letter contract procedure to make sure that McDonnell's work would not be consumed by lengthy negotiations.

The last of 77 F-101As were delivered in October 1957, with the unit cost of the aircraft listed at $2,906,373. Of this total price, $2,364,143 went to McDonnell for the airframe and most of $429,016 to Pratt & Whitney for the pair of J57-P-13 engines. The balance went for electronics, ordnance and armament.

The first F-101A was delivered as scheduled in August 1954 and test flown at the Edwards AFB flight test center on 29 September. Flight testing continued for two years, during which a tendency of the Voodoo to pitch up during flight was diagnosed. This problem still unsolved, production went forward, reaching a rate of eight aircraft per month by the end of 1956 when production was temporarily halted. A three-month review of the entire F-101 resulted in the green light for further production on 26 November 1956. The 41st F-101A to come off the St Louis assembly line became the first operational Voodoo on 2 May 1957 with the 27th Fighter-Bomber Wing at Bergstrom AFB. The unit was transferred from SAC to TAC two months later. The F-101A, a fighter conceived a decade earlier for the Strategic Air Command, served for just 59 days before becoming part of TAC, where it served for more than 12 years. Only 50 of the 77 F-101As ever went into squadron service, however, the rest being classed as 'preproduction.' Transfer of F-101As to the Air National Guard began in 1966 and by 1970 they had been phased out of USAF inventory entirely.

Meanwhile, the first reconnaissance version of the Voodoo, the RF-101A, had made its first flight in June 1956. Outwardly the RF-101A was very similar to the heavier F-101A and had the same capability to carry nuclear bombs. The major difference, however, was in the long flat nose housing the long focal Fairchild KA-1 framing camera, one vertical and two side oblique Fairchild KA-2 framing cameras and a CA1 KA-18 strip camera. First operational service for the RF-101A came in May 1957 with the 363d Tactical Reconnaissance Wing at Shaw AFB as a replacement for much slower subsonic RF-84s. The RF-101A went into service even before all the above-mentioned equipment was

Above: A single-place F-101A fighter (*top*), with an RF-101 reconnaissance aircraft. Compare these with the two-place F-101Bs on the next page.

	XF-88 Voodoo	F-101A Voodoo	F-101B Voodoo
Wingspan	39' 8"	39' 8"	39' 8"
Length	54' 2"	67' 5"	71' 1"
Height	17' 3"	18'	18'
Ceiling	36,000'	38,900'	52,100'
Range (mi)	1,737	677 (combat)	829 (combat)
Weight (lb)	18,500	48,001	45,461
Engine type	Westinghouse J340-WE-22	P&W J57-P-13	P&W J57-P-55
Engine thrust (lb)	3,000	15,000	16,900
Speed (mph)	641 @ sea level	1,005 @ 35,000'	1,094 @ 35,000'

available and continued in service until 1970. Beginning in 1966, 18 of the 35 original RF-101As were extensively modified to accommodate photographic and electronic components far superior to those with which they had originally been equipped. These modified aircraft were redesignated RF-101G because of the modifications and remained in service until 1979. The flyaway cost of the original RF-101As was $1,604,963, or about 55 percent of the cost of the F-101A. The flyaway cost of each RF-101G was $2,979,745 in current dollars. Considering inflation, it was still somewhat less than the cost of the original F-101A, which carried the burden of all the original development costs except for $6.6 million that was written off to the F-88 phase of the Voodoo program.

The second major Voodoo subprogram was the F-101C, which was designated later but developed earlier than the F-101B interceptor variant. The F-101C program closely paralleled the F-101C program, and the two aircraft were similar in most respects. In fact, the initial contract for the F-101C, initiated in March 1956, called for an additional number of F-101As. The designation did not become F-101C until September of that year. The first of 47 structurally strengthened F-101Cs were delivered to the 523d Tactical Fighter Squadron a year later in September 1957, with the last being delivered in May 1958.

When it was first deployed, the F-101C was the fastest tactical fighter in service and captured a world speed record of 1207 mph on 12 December 1957. In addition to speed, another striking feature of the F-101C was its 1000-mile unrefueled range. Given its capability of being refueled, this Voodoo offered a great deal of flexibility in terms of the distances to which it could be deployed. On 28 June 1958 four F-101Cs flew nonstop from Andrews AFB in Maryland to Liege, Belgium, at an average speed of 640 mph. Two months later seven Voodoos completed a 6100-mile nonstop deployment from Bergstrom AFB, Texas to RAF Bentwaters in England.

The reconnaissance version of the F-101C, designated RF-101C of course, was ordered and delivered at the same time as the fighter version, and entered operational service in September 1957 with the 432d Tactical Reconnaissance Wing. The first overseas deployment of the RF-101C came at the end of 1958, with Voodoos based at Nouasseur AB, Morocco; Laon AB and Phalsbourg AB in France; Misawa AB in Japan and Kadena AB on Okinawa. By 1960 Voodoos of all model types deployed overseas, especially in the Pacific, were showing signs of a serious corrosion problem. Many had to return to the United States for reskinning of the wings and fuselage at a cost of 8400 man-hours per aircraft. In 1963 the Air Force decided to build a corrosion-control facility at Kadena AB.

In 1962 all the reconnaissance Voodoos, both RF-101A and RF-101C, were retrofitted with new high-resolution cameras and flash cartridge pods to give them a limited night capability. Another modification permitted 'buddy-refueling,' or the refueling of one RF-101 by another. No sooner had these modifications taken place than the RF-101C found itself operational in its first potentially explosive crisis situation. When Soviet nuclear-armed missiles were discovered in Cuba, Air Force RF-101Cs were directed to make regular low-level reconnaissance flights over the island, to monitor first the Soviet buildup and later the dismantling of the Soviet arsenal. The efforts of the recon Voodoos helped the United States keep tabs on the situation and thereby eliminate the threat of nuclear blackmail and/or a third world war. These operations also served as a laboratory in which the Air Force could study both the hardware and tactics of reconnaissance.

Despite the modifications made in early 1962, shortcomings were evident and an across-the-board USAF recon updating called Modification 1181 was put into effect. Modification 1181 had first been proposed by TAC in 1960 but had been deferred because of cost. With the lessons learned in the Cuban missile crisis fresh in mind and a new crisis brewing in Southeast Asia, it was time to make changes. These changes revolved around the Hycon KS-72A framing camera that was being developed for McDonnell's RF-4C and other equipment. Costs were indeed high; they ran $180,000 per RF-101 on top of the $3 million in basic costs. Initial testing in 1963–64 showed a number of bugs in the system, and all of the aircraft were not fully modernized until 1967. However, when completed, Modification 1181 and the KS-72A camera gave the RF-101C (and the RF-4C as well) an improved low-altitude photographic capability that could take full advantage of the aircraft's speed and performance. Other advantages offered included a high-altitude true vertical photographic capability and an increase in sensor reliability

Left and above: A flight of Canadian CF-101B interceptors and a single USAF F-101B at Tyndall AFB, Florida in September 1958.

through the use of automatic exposure control and an improved camera-control system.

The RF-101 was the only Voodoo to serve in Southeast Asia during the war. The first deployments were made to Thailand in 1961, with reconaissance operations initially flown over Laos and later South Vietnam and North Vietnam. When American fighter bombers first went into North Vietnam in February 1965 at the start of the Rolling Thunder air offensive, the RF-101s provided before and after reconnaissance support. By 1967 all but one of TAC's RF-101C Squadrons were in the Southeast Asia war zone, but by 1969 the RF-101Cs began to be replaced by RF-4Cs in first-line units and turned over to Air National Guard units. By 1971 the last RF-101C was turned over to the Air Guard. The transition to the Guard complete, the RF-101A and F-101C were rebuilt and redesignated RF-101G and F-101H, respectively. The aircraft served with the Air Guard for eight years before the final phaseout in 1979.

The idea for the F-101B interceptor came about very early in the development of the F-101A program, and the F-101B designation dated back to August 1955. Behind the F-101B was the need for an interceptor to succeed the Northrop F-89 Scorpion and serve until deployment of the Convair F-106 'ultimate interceptor.' The Air Defense Command (ADC) liked the idea of the Voodoo because its long range gave it the capability of guarding the perimeters of the United States where ground radar was less than adequate.

The first F-101B flew from Lambert Airport (across the taxiway from the McDonnell factory) on 27 March 1957. It had been four years since ADC first gave its blessing to the idea of a Voodoo interceptor, two years after the contract was signed and a year after the first flight was originally supposed to have taken place. The F-101B was built five feet longer than the F-101A to accommodate a second crewman and was powered by a 16,900-lb-thrust Pratt & Whitney J57-P-55 as opposed to the J57-P-13 that delivered

a maximum of 15,000 lb of thrust for the F-101A. The $1,754,066 unit cost of F-101B was less than the F-101A but half a million more than the F-101C, despite the fact that 480 F-101Bs were built, more than all the other F-101 variants combined.

Following the first flight of the F-101B in 1957, nearly two years of testing ensued. Many potential problems had been corrected in advance because of experience with the F-101A, but several problems unique to the interceptor version also arose. There was, of course, the problem of the badly designed radar observer's cockpit, but the major problem inherent in the F-101B was attributable to Hughes Aircraft, not McDonnell. Hughes had the contract to develop the fire-control system. The system they developed, designated MG-13, was (according to the official Air Force record) 'merely a refinement of the E-6 fire control system of the F-89D and could not control the weapons of an interceptor as fast as the F-101B. Headquarters USAF denied replacement of the MG-13 with the MA-1 system of the F-106 because of the cost involved. This left only one course of action: to improve the Central Air Data Computer that was the heart of the MG-13 system.'

When the first F-101B was delivered to the Air Defense Command on 5 January 1959, it was a thoroughly tested aircraft and fully capable of the advanced performance for which it was designed. A year later most of the F-101Bs to be built were in service, with 70 percent of them combat ready. The last of them was delivered in March 1961, the same year that 66 were transferred to the Royal Canadian Air Force under the designation CF-101B. The CF-101Bs were actually late production Voodoos that were modified with upgraded systems and hence superior in some respects to the F-101B in use by the USAF. Those American F-101Bs built with comparable systems were given the designation F-101F. In 1961, with the McDonnell Douglas merger only six years away, the McDonnell F-101B and F-101F aircraft were coincidentally modified to carry the Douglas-developed MB-1 (later AIR-2) Genie nuclear-armed air-intercept rocket.

The phaseout of the F-101B and F began in 1968 with the retirement of the first seven ADC Voodoo squadrons. Some of the surplus interceptors were turned over to Canada, some to the Air National Guard and the rest put into storage. By the spring of 1971, there were no F-101B or F aircraft in the USAF, but they continued in service with the Air National Guard until 1982 and with the Canadian Armed Forces well into the 1980s until replaced by McDonnell Douglas CF-18s.

Originally conceived as a long-range escort fighter, the Voodoo ultimately achieved its only combat success as a reconnaissance aircraft. The interceptor version, first considered as an 'interim' interceptor, wound up serving in that role for 20 years.

THE DOUGLAS TRANSPORTS

The First Family of American Commercial Aviation

The greatest line of commercial transports the world has ever seen was born and then died as a result of two of the most spectacular (at the time) air crashes ever to curse the midwestern United States, and indeed the country as a whole. The first crash involved a TWA Fokker F-10A trimotor, with the legendary Notre Dame football coach Knute Rockne on the passenger roster. When the Fokker went down in a thunderstorm near Bazaar, Kansas, on 31 March 1931, killing everyone on board, it prompted TWA to solicit a safer airliner. This led to the Douglas DC-1, which in turn led to 10 DC designations that spanned the greatest years of world aviation history.

The second crash took place at Chicago's O'Hare International Airport on 25 May 1979. It involved a DC-10, the last of the DC liners, and 273 people, all of whom died in what was the largest aviation disaster in American history. Though the DC-10 was ultimately cleared of blame in the Chicago crash, the public hysteria and the government's reaction to both the crash and the emotion led to a loss of public confidence in the DC-10 that was never fully restored. Orders for the DC-10 dropped off. The DC-11 project, which was never a high priority for James Smith McDonnell anyway, was scrapped and the DC-9-80 (DC-9 Super 80) program was redesignated MD-80. All future McDonnell Douglas commercial transports carried the MD for McDonnell Douglas prefix rather than DC for Douglas, Commercial.

Many of the planes in the 10-plane DC dynasty marked milestones in aviation history. Within the DC series there were representatives of all the steps in the advance of commercial aviation technology. There were the earliest and the best twin-engined monoplanes as well as earliest and latest four-engined propliners. The DC-3 had been the greatest airliner of its era and, as some would argue, of all time. The DC-4 helped pioneer successful four-engined air transportation, and the DC-7 was perhaps the best four-motored propeller-driven airliner ever built. The DC-8 was a member of the first generation of jetliners, and the DC-10 was one of the first three American wide-body jetliners.

When one considers the great families of American commercial aircraft, only the Boeing 700 jetliner series comes to mind as a possible rival to the DC series, and the DC series had a 20-year head start. Though Boeing has been America's premier builder of jetliners since the 1960s, the DC jets continue to thrive. The heritage of McDonnell Douglas commercial transports will

endure. Fifty years after they were first introduced, DC-3s still fly the world's skyways. The DC-8 will probably survive in service as long or longer than Boeing's 707. The DC-9, which began as a 70-passenger short-haul jetliner, was stretched, or enlarged, several times, evolving into the DC-9 Super 80 and then into the MD-80, the first McDonnell Douglas jetliner. The DC-10 is still in widespread use by the world's major international airlines. By the turn of the century the DC-series assembly lines will be only a distant memory, but the DC jets—the DC-9 and DC-10—will probably still be flying and the new lineage of MD series liners will be going strong.

The DC-1 Program

On the morning of 31 March 1931 the TWA (Transcontinental & Western Air, later Trans World Airlines) airliner enroute from Kansas City to Wichita, Kansas was flying at about 500 feet to avoid a thunderstorm when it suddenly went into a 55-degree dive and smashed into a field between Bazaar and Cottonwood Falls, Kansas. Because Notre Dame coach Knute Rockne was aboard the Fokker F-10A trimotor monoplane, the crash attracted a great deal of media attention. Some speculation centered on sabotage. A copyrighted story in the *South Bend News-Times* reported that Rockne had been the

Opposite and above: The Douglas DC-1 on its first flight and later parked at the Grand Central Air Terminal in Glendale, California.

Below: The letter from TWA's Jack Frye to Don Douglas that started it all.

victim of a hit man who had placed a bomb aboard the plane in an effort to kill Reverend John Reynolds of Notre Dame, who had been a witness to a gangland slaying in Chicago and whose place Rockne had taken at the last minute.

Structural failure of the Fokker's wing was listed as the probable cause of the crash, and coupled with the media attention generated by Rockne's death, the publicity was anything but positive for the airline industry. Suddenly there was a need for a new generation of safer airliners. In Seattle, Boeing was developing its Model 247 monoplane, a plane that was generally accepted as representative of a significant advance in technology over the Fokkers, Fords and others that made up the bulk of the nation's air-transport fleet. For TWA, however, there was a catch. The Boeing 247 was being developed for Boeing's own airline, United Air Lines, and would not be available elsewhere on the market. TWA was eager not to be left behind. Civil air transport was on the verge of realizing its potential as a major form of long-distance transportation within the United States, and the airlines with the best equipment stood to reap huge profits.

Jack Frye, vice-president for operations at TWA, anticipated what was coming and actively started soliciting the type of design that his airline needed to get out from under the cloud of the Rockne crash and compete with the Boeing 247. His letters of inquiry went to the major American airplane manufacturers, including Consolidated, Curtiss-Wright, General Aviation (later North American) and Glenn Martin. One of his letters, dated 2 August 1932, also crossed the transom of the office of Donald Wills Douglas at Clover Field, Santa Monica.

Douglas had little experience in the civil market. The first Douglas design, the Cloudster, had spawned a whole series of military progeny, but only 59 nonmilitary M-2 mailplanes were built in the likeness of the Cloudster. Eleven of the Douglas Dolphin amphibians had been sold on the civilian market, but aside from these, Douglas built only military aircraft. Donald

TRANSCONTINENTAL & WESTERN AIR INC.
10 RICHARDS ROAD
MUNICIPAL AIRPORT
KANSAS, CITY, MISSOURI

August 2nd,
19 32

Douglas Aircraft Corporation,
Clover Field,
Santa Monica, California.

Attention: Mr. Donald Douglas

Dear Mr. Douglas:

Transcontinental & Western Air is interested in purchasing ten or more trimotored transport planes. I am attaching our general performance specifications, covering this equipment and would appreciate your advising whether your Company is interested in this manufacturing job.

If so, approximately how long would it take to turn out the first plane for service tests?

Very truly yours,

Jack Frye

Jack Frye
Vice President
JF/GS   In Charge of Operations
Encl.

N.B. Please consider this information confidential and return specifications if you are not interested.

SAVE TIME — USE THE AIR MAIL

Above and opposite: A DC-2 over central Holland and landing at Amsterdam's Schiphol Airport in 1984. For the DC-2's 50th anniversary KLM had acquired an original DC-2 and painted it in the colors of the since-departed *Uiver.*

Below: The DC-1 at Malaga, Spain after her final flight in December 1940.

Douglas was persuaded to submit a design, and he assigned Harry Wetzel and Dutch Kindelberger to head the design team as general manager and chief engineer, respectively. The specifications were not easy. TWA needed a fast plane and a safe plane. It also needed a plane that could maintain sufficient altitude to cross the high mountains of the Continental Divide. Time was also important, as TWA was in a hurry. The Douglas team met the challenge and submitted a design that was accepted by TWA on 20 September 1932. Douglas stock rose in value from $7.12 per share to $16. The contract called for a payment of $125,000 in gold for development of the first prototype and $58,000 each for the production aircraft, exclusive of engines.

Work began on the prototype at once and continued through March 1933, when the Boeing 247 made its maiden flight, and into the spring and summer. The resulting airplane, designated DC-1 (Douglas, Commercial, First) rolled out of the hangar at Clover Field in June 1933, less than a year after Jack Frye had contacted Donald Douglas. She was $182,000 over budget but she was a beautiful airplane—sleek and silvery, larger and more powerful than the 247. At noon on Saturday, July 1st, she took off for the first time with chief company test pilot Carl Cover at the controls. Carburetor problems in the two Wright Cyclone engines made the first flight very nearly the last flight, but thanks to Cover's skill and the aerodynamic integrity of the DC-1 itself, the maiden voyage ended safely. The engines were pulled and put on blocks. They ran perfectly on the ground, with none of the sudden mysterious cutoffs that had plagued Cover in the air. Finally the problem was diagnosed. The fuel-line floats were installed in a way that could simply be called backward. Whenever the aircraft climbed, the fuel line automatically shut down. The floats were reversed and the problem was solved.

When the DC-1 was finally delivered to TWA in December 1933, not only was it thoroughly flight tested, it had one of the plushest interiors in the air. Passenger comfort was a high priority and the difficult problem of noise control had been met. The bulkheads and fuselage wall were soundproofed with kapok and thick carpets covered the floors. The seats were made of sound-absorbing material and were mounted on rubber supports. Even the engines were mounted on rubber insulators. A small galley was included to provide passengers with hot coffee and warm soup. The sound-deadening insulation also permitted the cabin temperature to be maintained at a toasty 70 degrees F even if the plane was a mile over the Rockies and it was well below zero outside. The lavatory in the rear of the DC-1 was larger than those on the later DC-9. TWA was delighted with its DC-1, and promptly gave Douglas a $1,625,000 contract for 25 production versions, which were designated DC-2 (Douglas, Commercial,

Second). The price of the production aircraft was allowed to increase by 12 percent over the $58,000 specified in the September 1932 contract, because the United States had since been taken off the gold standard and the value of silver certificates was seen to be less than that of gold.

Even as the DC-2s were delivered into the TWA fleet, the DC-1 (TWA aircraft number 300) was at work alongside them. On 18 February 1934, two hours before the nation's airmail system was federalized, Jack Frye and Eddie Rickenbacker flew the last sacks of civilian-transported airmail from Burbank to Newark. Despite encountering a hellish blizzard over Ohio, they managed to set a transcontinental-transport aircraft speed record of 13 hours and 4 minutes in the DC-1. On 30 April 1935 'Old 300' set a new transcontinental record, covering the distance from Los Angeles to New York in 5 minutes over 11 hours.

In January 1936 the DC-1 was secretly sold to the notorious millionaire, playboy, aviator and major TWA shareholder Howard Hughes. He intended to use Old 300 in an attempt to break the round-the-world speed record. Hughes had the plane retrofitted with 875-hp Wright Cyclone engines and installed extra fuel tanks, which boosted the plane's range to 6000 miles. At the last minute, Hughes switched to a Lockheed Lodestar and the DC-1 was parked at the airport in Burbank. It remained there until May 1938, when the eccentric future billionaire sold it to Viscount Forbes, Earl of Granard, for a transatlantic flight that the Viscount intended to make, but which quickly fell through. Forbes had the DC-1 shipped to England, where he used it for a couple of jaunts to the Continent before he sold it to the Société Française des Transports Aeriens (SFTA) in August. Some mystery seems to surround this transaction and the fact that it turned up a month later in Spanish Republican registry in the service of Lineas Aeros Postales Españoles (LAPE). Her silvery

skin painted camouflage drab, the DC-1 flew between Paris and Barcelona via Toulouse until Barcelona fell to the Nationalists under Francisco Franco in March 1939. Members of the Republican Government escaped to Toulouse in the DC-1, which was turned over to the Nationalist Government when the war ended in April. Repainted in the colors of Iberia Airlines, the plane served on a domestic passenger run between Seville and Tetuan via Malaga until December 1940, when she crashed on takeoff at Malaga. The engines had cut out just like they had for Carl Cover in Santa Monica so many years before. Fortunately the plane was only a few inches off the ground when the engines died and no one was killed or even seriously injured. The plane, however was a total loss. It was as though Old 300 had decided that her time was over.

The final disposition of the wreck is not known but evidence supports the legend that portions of her structural assemblies were salvaged and used to build an *andas*, or ceremonial throne, used by the Confraternity of Our Lady of Hope in Malaga to transport a statue of the Madonna during Holy Week festivities. It is interesting to note, as pointed out by Spanish aviation historian Felipe Ezquerro (and quoted by Mauno Salo in the *Journal of the American Aviation Historical Society*), that in Spain, the Madonna is known as the 'queen of the skies.'

The DC-2 Program

At first glance, the plane that rolled out onto Clover Field on 11 May 1934 looked like she could be the DC-1's twin. In reality the DC-2 was different in several important ways. She was two feet longer to accommodate an additional passenger on each side of the aisle, and she was capable of faster speeds and longer range.

Left: A 1934 DC-2 freight-loading demonstration using crates from TWA's own supply closet. The distinctive headlights distinguished the DC-2 from the later DC-3.

Top: A TWA DC-2 *Sky Chief* over downtown Kansas City in August 1934.

Above: KLM's DC-2, *Uiver*, arriving at Waalhaven Airport, Rotterdam after the 1934 MacPherson Trophy race to Melbourne in which it took first place in the transport division.

Transcontinental and Western Air took possession of its first DC-2 on 13 May 1934, just two days after her first flight and assigned her its number 301. Just five days after that, TWA had her in service on the Newark to Chicago run, on which the new plane broke the speed record for that route four times in the next eight days! By the first of August TWA began advertising its Sky Chief service (an oblique reference to the Santa Fe Railroad's Super Chief), which was a Newark-to-Los Angeles run featuring DC-2s that left the East at 4:00 pm and arrived in Los Angeles at 7:00 am. If the business traveler slept during the flight, he could be ready to go to work without having lost a day of travel time. This concept, which hardly seems revolutionary today, was an astounding innovation in 1934. The traveling public was just starting to accept flying as a serious means of transportation and not just as a somewhat risky novelty.

Not only did the airlines and the public take to the idea of the DC-2, but professional airplane designers liked her as well. Anthony Fokker, the *Vliegende Hollander* (Flying Dutchman), who was among the greatest designers in the world at the time, took one look at the DC-2 and bought a license to sell the new aircraft in Europe. Tony Fokker's first customer was KLM. Five months after the DC-2's first flight, Super Chief DC-2s were flying coast to coast in the United States and KLM had its DC-2 flying regular runs between Amsterdam's Schiphol

Left: The interior appointments of a Douglas DC-2 executive transport.

Below: A pair of DC-2s are loaded at Los Angeles for shipment to the KLM subsidiary in the Netherlands East Indies.

Above: President Franklin Roosevelt awarded Don Douglas the 1936 Collier Trophy for his development of the DC-2. The Douglas DC-2, for all of its ingenious originality, was only just the prelude to the plane that was to revolutionize American air travel.

Airport and Batavia (now Djakarta) on Java in the Netherlands East Indies.

In October 1934, one of the KLM DC-2s took part in the first major international air race for a DC aircraft. The route ran more than 11,000 miles, from London to Melbourne, with the Mac-Pherson Robinson Trophy and $75,000 at stake for the winner. Flying against a number of racing planes from six countries, including a brand-new Boeing 247, the DC-2 (nicknamed *Uiver*) carried paying passengers and flew the regular KLM route rather than the shorter distance of the race. Ninety hours later the DC-2 finished second to a de Havilland Comet; many of the others did not finish at all. The DC-2's reputation was assured. Orders came in from around the country and around the world. Eastern, Western, Braniff and Northwest airlines all became committed to the plane. Pan Am/Grace bought the plane for its Latin American service and Pan Am's Chinese subsidiary, China National. In Europe, Ceskoslovenska Letecka Spolecnost of Czechoslovakia followed KLM's lead and bought six of the durable Douglases. Ultimately there were 156 DC-2s produced at Santa Monica and the plane earned Donald Douglas the 1936 Collier Trophy. But it was only a hint of what was to come.

The DC-3 Program

Transcontinental & Western Air had defined the need that was met by the Douglas DC-2, and in doing so it helped launch a product that earned it new customers. Among the airlines lining up for the plane was the small, newly emerging American Airways, soon to become American Airlines and later one of the largest airline companies in the country. American's chairman, Cyrus Rowlett ('CR') Smith, was pleased with the 15 DC-2s that he bought for his Flagship Fleet, but he wasn't content. He wanted still more than was offered by the acclaimed best liner flying in the United States. He wanted a longer DC-2 and one with Pullman-type sleeping compartments such as those offered by the railroads. CR Smith went to Donald Douglas to propose the idea, but the planemaker was more than a little reluctant to retool his plant to build another plane when the newly introduced DC-2 was selling so well. Smith was persistant and he finally convinced the Scotsman with a guaranteed order for 20 of the yet undesigned aircraft.

The design work on the new plane, which was to be called the Douglas Skysleeper Transport (DST), began in the fall of 1934. The aircraft that took shape was similar in appearance to the DC-1 and DC-2, but it represented the ultimate refinement of the earlier designs. It carried the Douglas model number DC-3 and it was one of the greatest airliners ever built in the United States. Some would argue that it was the greatest airliner ever produced anywhere.

	DC-1	DC-2	DC-3
First flight	1 July 1933	11 May 1934	17 December 1935
First delivery	13 September 1933 (TWA)	13 May 1934 (TWA)	8 August 1936 (American Airlines)
Wingspan	85'	85'	94' 6"
Length	60'	62'	64' 6"
Height	16'	16' 4"	16' 11"
Engines	Wright SRG1820F3	Wright SRG1820FS2	Wright R1820
Engine hp	710	835	1,200
Gross weight (lb)	17,500	18,560	30,900
Max payload (lb)	3,500	4,070	8,018
Passengers	12	14-18	14-28
Cargo space (cu ft)	220	188	293
Operating altitude	10,000'	10,000'	10,000'
Cruising speed (mph)	190	200	192
Range (mi)	998	1,058	1,495

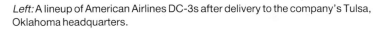

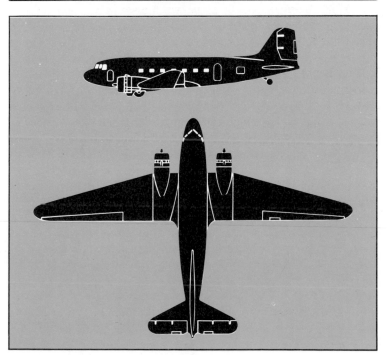

Left: A lineup of American Airlines DC-3s after delivery to the company's Tulsa, Oklahoma headquarters.

Right from top: The first Douglas transports, the DC-1, DC-2 and the DC-3. Each plane had a payload slightly larger than its predecessor.

Below: A sideview of a Continental Airlines DC-3 showing the aft cargo hold and the steps inside the fold-down door.

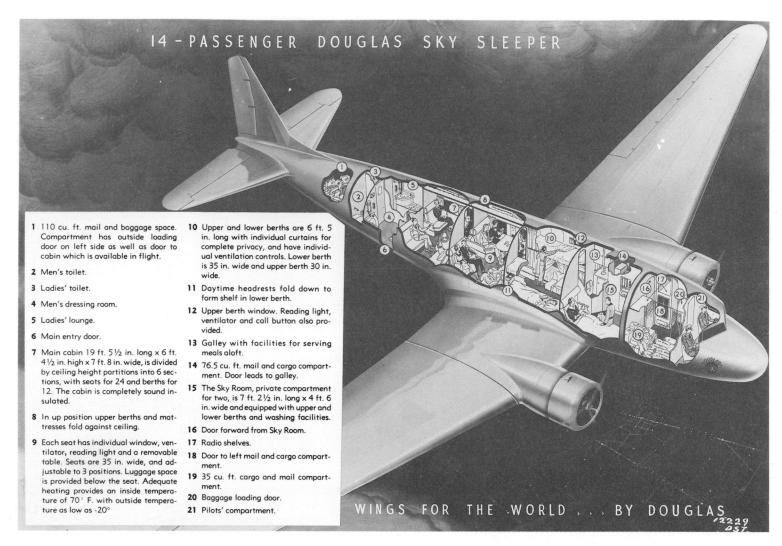

14 - PASSENGER DOUGLAS SKY SLEEPER

1 110 cu. ft. mail and baggage space. Compartment has outside loading door on left side as well as door to cabin which is available in flight.

2 Men's toilet.

3 Ladies' toilet.

4 Men's dressing room.

5 Ladies' lounge.

6 Main entry door.

7 Main cabin 19 ft. 5½ in. long x 6 ft. 4½ in. high x 7 ft. 8 in. wide, is divided by ceiling height partitions into 6 sections, with seats for 24 and berths for 12. The cabin is completely sound insulated.

8 In up position upper berths and mattresses fold against ceiling.

9 Each seat has individual window, ventilator, reading light and a removable table. Seats are 35 in. wide, and adjustable to 3 positions. Luggage space is provided below the seat. Adequate heating provides an inside temperature of 70° F. with outside temperature as low as -20°

10 Upper and lower berths are 6 ft. 5 in. long with individual curtains for complete privacy, and have individual ventilation controls. Lower berth is 35 in. wide and upper berth 30 in. wide.

11 Daytime headrests fold down to form shelf in lower berth.

12 Upper berth window. Reading light, ventilator and call button also provided.

13 Galley with facilities for serving meals aloft.

14 76.5 cu. ft. mail and cargo compartment. Door leads to galley.

15 The Sky Room, private compartment for two, is 7 ft. 2½ in. long x 4 ft. 6 in. wide and equipped with upper and lower berths and washing facilities.

16 Door forward from Sky Room.

17 Radio shelves.

18 Door to left mail and cargo compartment.

19 35 cu. ft. cargo and mail compartment.

20 Baggage loading door.

21 Pilots' compartment.

WINGS FOR THE WORLD . . . BY DOUGLAS

Above: This cutaway rendering was filed in 1937 but was actually drawn in 1935. While the tail is incorrectly drawn, the interior is an accurate representation of that of a DST.

Right: A Braniff DC-3 in postwar colors photographed about 1955.

The first of the DC-3 DST version, which first flew on 17 December 1935 (the 32nd anniversary of the Wright brothers' first flight) was the picture of luxury. Twelve plush seats, three feet wide, were provided in six compartments. Each pair of seats could be folded together to form a bed, while a second berth folded down from the roof in each compartment. In the front of the plane, just aft of the cockpit, was the Sky Room. Generally known by the nickname 'honeymoon suite,' this area was a totally separate compartment with two beds and a private bath. Thus the DST could accommodate 14 overnight passengers in berths, or twice that number for shorter daytime runs.

The first DST was delivered to American Airlines on 7 June 1936, followed by the first standard (nonsleeper) DC-3 to American on 18 August. United Air Lines, which had been a subsidiary of the Boeing Company until 1934, saw the future in the new Douglas and became the second customer for the DC-3 on 25 November. The DC-2 had proven the better of the Boeing 247 and the DC-3 assumed the lead that Douglas was to hold over the Seattle planemaker for the next quarter of a century. United's DC-3s were powered by the 1200-hp Pratt & Whitney R1830 Hornet as opposed to the R1820 Wright Cyclone of the American DC-3. They were also equipped with a Sky Lounge offering air travelers the kind of amenities that could be expected in a railroad club car. The orders from American and United were soon followed by orders from other airlines. TWA bought

Above: A Transcontinental & Western Air DC-3 over California's rugged Tehachapi Mountains. TWA was known as the Lindbergh Line because of Charles Lindbergh's participation in the company.

over 30 in the next two years and Eastern's Great Silver Fleet took over two dozen. These airlines were followed by Braniff, Western and World. Pan American was again a customer, as was KLM. Pan Am had pioneered air service into South America in 1927 and, with the advent of the DC-2 and DC-3, it was able to establish a network of routes that connected all of the continent's major cities. Its major competition was the German airlines such as Deutsche Luft Hansa and Condor, which connected Latin America to Europe and also maintained their own extensive route network on the continent. Pan Am went head to head against the Germans with a fleet of 33 Douglas aircraft, and by early 1941 it had triple the business of its European competition. When war came the influence of the German airlines disappeared. The efforts of Pan Am with its fleet of reliable DC-3s proved a valuable extension of American foreign policy and helped keep South America united behind the allied cause.

It has been estimated that 93 percent of the world's airline passengers were traveling in the sleek DC-3 even as early as 1939. The plane was not only comfortable; it was durable, reliable and especially economical. It was the single major factor in airline profitability in the late 1930s.

The outbreak of World War II in Europe in September 1939 promised big changes in the airline industry, first in Europe and soon worldwide. Commercial airports became combat airfields and profitable air routes became hostile airspace. Airliners became military transports.

Above: This DC-2 became the US Army Air Corps' first C-32 and the first military version of a DC airliner.

Left: When this China National Airways (a Pan Am subsidiary) DC-3 lost her right wing in a 1941 Japanese strafing attack, it was successfully replaced with the wing of a DC-2.

The military career of the Douglas DC birds had actually begun in 1936 when the US Army Air Corps purchased a pair of DC-2 passenger transports under the designation C-32. This order was followed by 18 DC-2s in freighter configuration under the designation C-33 and two under the designation C-34 which served until 1942 as general staff VIP transports based at Bolling Field in the District of Columbia. In 1937 one of the C-33s was retrofitted with a DC-3 tail under the official designation C-38 and the unofficial designation 'DC-2½.' The single C-38 served as the prototype for 35 DC-2½s delivered to the US Army Air Corps until 1938 under the designation C-39. The C-39s comprised the backbone of the first serious effort by the USAAC to establish an air-transport capability. Their mission was to transport supplies between the growing network of Air Corps supply centers across the country. A couple of C-39s were also converted to VIP transports on the order of the C-34 and redesignated C-41 and C-42. (Because of the number of DC-3 components in the C-39 and C-42, Douglas historian Harry Gann considers them to be DC-3s rather than DC-2s.) Aside from a number of commercial DC-2s impressed after Pearl Harbor under the old C-32 designation, C-39s and their derivatives were, in 1938, the last aircraft that were even partly of DC-2 construction to be purchased by the Army. Like the commercial carriers, the military had its eyes on the DC-3.

The US Army Air Corps became the US Army Air Force in June 1941 at a time when the Second World War in Europe was

Above: The five DC-2s acquired by the US Navy and Marine Corps in 1934 were designated R2D-1, but were virtually identical to the US Army Air Corps C-32 pictured on the facing page.

Right: The Army's C-33s, shown during prewar maneuvers and during engine maintenance, were really C-32s with reinforced floors for carrying heavy cargo.

running in favor of the Axis. An urgent need to develop a strong national defense was the order of the day in the United States. It was well recognized that transport aircraft would play a role as important in the future of the USAAF as that played by combat aircraft. With the overwhelming success of the DC-3 on the civil air routes, it was no wonder that the same airframe became the standard USAAF transport. The first DC-3s were ordered by the USAAF in 1941 under the designation C-47, but there was no way to predict that the simple designation would become a legend, that over 10,000 would be built and that the plane would be listed by General Dwight Eisenhower as one of the four pieces of equipment 'most vital to our success in Africa and Europe.'

Only 122 Douglas transports were delivered in 1941, but following the attack on Pearl Harbor the order for C-47s was bumped up to 965, all of which were delivered from the new Douglas plant in Long Beach in 1942. The C-47 was followed by by 2954 C-47As from the Long Beach plant and another 2300 C-47As from the Douglas plant in Oklahoma City, which also delivered 3064 C-47Bs before the end of 1944. The C-47 differed from the DC-3 principally in its lack of carpeting, soundproofing and interior detail as well as in the size of its door. The door size was more than doubled to accommodate oversize cargo, and structural strengthening was also required to provide for a door so large. Unlike the C-47, the electrical system of the C-47A was upgraded to 24 volts to facilitate the addition of an electric

Below: A Transcontinental & Western Air DC-3 in service after the start of World War II. During the war the slogan 'the Lindbergh Line' (*see picture on page 95*) gave way to slogans having to do with winning the war, like the one shown here.

Right: The USAAF C-47B, like the earlier C-47 and C-47A, was similar to the civilian DC-3 from which it was derived. The subtle differences included the larger single cargo door on the left side, a deleted small cargo door on the right side, engine superchargers, a navigator's dome above the cockpit, different radio masts, deicer boots and of course the gun ports in the passenger windows, which would have been of little use to civilian passengers.

Above: The US Navy and Marine Corps received 20 C-53 paratroop transports from the USAAF, which were redesignated R4D-3. The C-53 was simply the paratroop version of the C-47.

Below: C-47s bound for service with the USAAF, Britain's Royal Air Force (as Dakotas), the Soviet air force and Chiang Kai-shek's Nationalist Chinese air force. The Soviets later built their own C-47s as Lisunov Li-2s.

Above: The widened door and strengthened floor that distinguished the C-47 from the DC-3 permitted the aircraft to carry a wide variety of oversize cargo, including entire jeeps.

conveyor-belt motor. The C-47B retained the 1200-hp R-1830 engines of the earlier planes but added high-altitude superchargers and provision for additional fuel tanks.

There were countless modifications to the C-47 fleet, some taking place at the factory and some in the field. There were VIP transports, designated VC-47A and VC-47B, and there were SC-47s used as search and rescue aircraft. A couple of C-47s were fitted with pontoons and redesignated C-47C. There were trainer versions designated TC-47 and reconnaissance versions designated RC-47. Some of the C-47 fleet were transferred from the USAAF to the US Navy under the designation R4D (Transport, Douglas, Fourth). The Navy equivalent of the C-47 was the R4D-1, while C-47As were designated R4D-5 and C-47Bs were redesignated R4D-6 and R4D-7. The R4D-2 designation was applied to a pair of Eastern Air Lines DC-3s drafted into the Navy, and R4D-4 was assigned to 10 DC-3s ordered by Pan American but delivered directly to the Navy.

The USAAF also drafted its share of commercial DC-3s. For various accounting reasons, no DC-3-type aircraft were designated C-47 if they had been either part of a commercial order or had served with a commercial carrier. The first groups of these were 36 DSTs and standard DC-3s drafted just after Pearl Harbor, which were designated C-48. These included 16 United Air Lines DSTs and one Northwest DC-3 that became air ambulances. Another assortment of 138 Santa Monica-built DC-3s was drafted under the designation C-49. These were mostly aircraft originally ordered by TWA or Eastern, but also included

Above: The single XC-47C was actually an early C-47 fitted with two Edo Model 87 amphibious floats. Kits were later shipped to the Pacific Theater, where an unknown number of field modifications of C-47s to C-47C standard took place.

Right: A C-47B over the Southern California coast.

some that had been ordered by American, Braniff, Delta, Chicago & Southern and the Netherlands East Indies. While there was really no consistent difference between the DC-3s that received the C-48 and C-49 designations, those 14 DC-3s that received the subsequent C-50 designation had a gross weight of 29,000 to 29,300 lb as opposed to a weight of 25,000 lb for a standard DC-3 or DST. The C-51 designation went to a single DC-3 that had been ordered by Canadian Colonial but which was put into USAAF service before delivery, while a half dozen DC-3s on order from United, Eastern and Swift Flite received the designation C-52. Two other later model DC-3s were drafted later in the war as C-68s, and four TWA DC-3s temporarily taken over the USAAF were designated C-84. In retrospect these eight designations really applied to the same type of airplane, one that was almost indistinguishable from the C-47. Had it not been for the urgency of war, time might have been taken to consolidate the designations.

Many of these DC-3s that were commandeered from the airlines just after Pearl Harbor and well into 1942 were seized along with their crews. The USAAF contracted with the airlines for whom the planes had originally been built to provide the air and ground crews to keep them flying. These drafted DC-3s gave the USAAF Air Transport Command a large immediate airlift capability without having to wait for the enormous tide of C-47s that would would not come in until mid-1942. They went on to provide an indispensible link in the airlift network within the continental US and Alaska, and on the North and South Atlantic routes as well.

Even as the C-47s were streaming off to war, a second DC-3-based aircraft had been designed and was being built specifically for military service. Designated C-53 by the USAAF and R4D-3 by the US Navy, the plane was really just a troop transport version of the C-47. Designed to carry paratroopers, the C-53 had a conventional passenger door rather than a cargo door and hence was a bit more like the basic DC-3 than the C-47 was. In fact two of the original batch of 219 C-53s were ordered by Pan Am and should logically have been designated within the C-48 through C-52 series. Only one C-53A, equipped with full-span slotted flaps and hot-air wing deicing, was built. The C-53B designation went to eight C-53s specially modified for cold weather and long range. The C-53C was a series of 17 DC-3s that had become C-53Cs except that, like the C-47A, they had a 24-volt electrical system. Like the DC-3s, the C-48 and C-52, all the C-53s were built at Santa Monica, while the C-47s were built at either Long Beach or Oklahoma City.

Of the US Navy's R4D series, all but 66 purchased directly

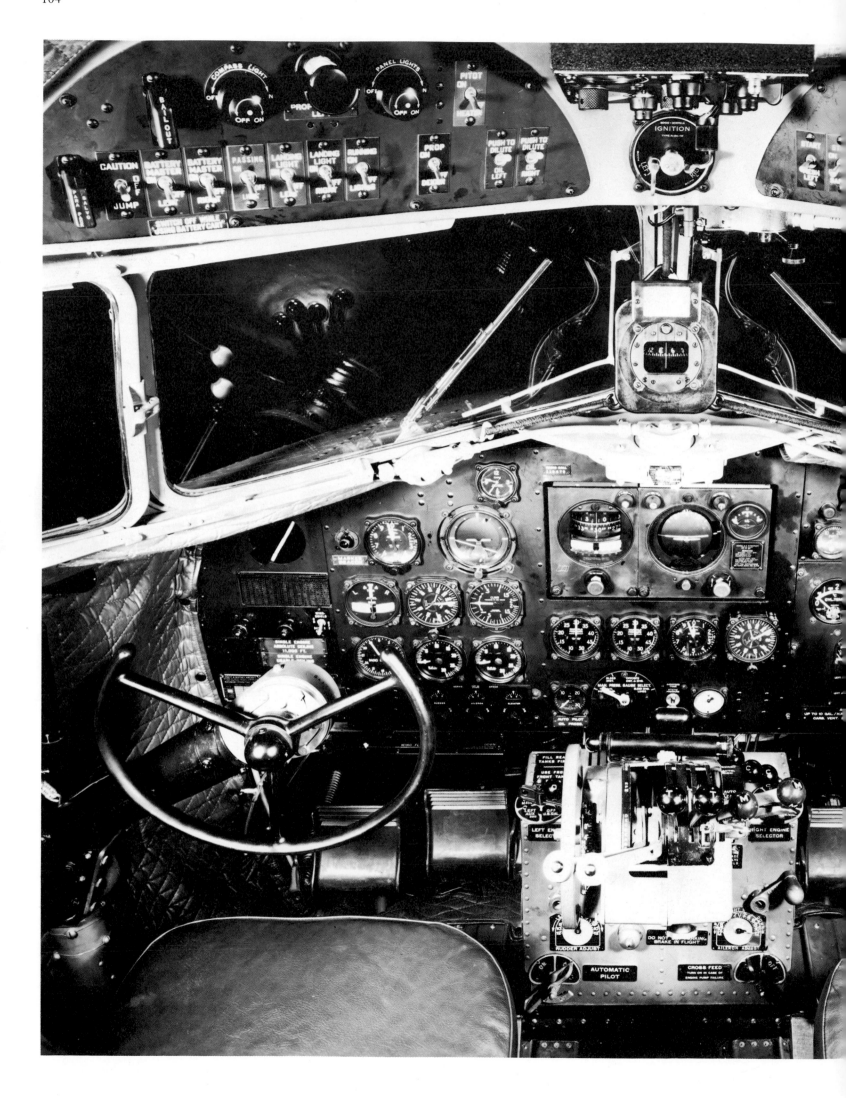

Above: A C-47B, lights blazing and engines roaring, prepares for takeoff from Santa Monica in September 1943.

Left: The interior detail of a C-47's cockpit as photographed at the factory on 7 November 1942.

from Douglas and 19 commandeered from Eastern Air Lines and Pan Am were hand-me-downs from the C-47 and C-53 stocks originally delivered to the USAAF. The latter transferred over 600 of its DC-3-derived transports to the Navy, which helped form the basis of the Naval Air Transport Service (NATS)—a far-flung net of air routes connecting naval installations around the world. Like the USAAF's Air Transport Command, forerunner to the postwar Military Air Transport Service (MATS), NATS was virtually nonexistent before 1942, but within a matter of 18 months it grew to become one of the world's largest 'airlines.'

The US Navy was not the only client to receive C-47s from the USAAF. Britain's Royal Air Force also received a large number of them under the designation Dakota I, III and IV. The Dakota II designation was reserved for six civilian DC-3s that had been commandeered by the RAF. The British air arm also operated five C-49s, one C-53, one C-68 and two DC-2s that it purchased in the United States directly from civilian sources, without those planes having served in the USAAF.

The British were not the only Allied nation to receive substantial numbers of DC-3-derived transports. The Soviet Union, America's other partner in the 'Grand Alliance,' received a few C-47s under Lend-Lease just as the British had. They then obtained from Douglas a license (that was never paid for) to manufacture the DC-3. Somewhere on the order of 2000 were built by the Russians under the designation Li-2. The designation attributed the DC-3 to the Lisunov Design Bureau, thus disguising the plane's American origins. After the war, the basic DC-3/Li-2 design formed the basis for the Ilyushin Design Bureau's Il-12 and Il-14, many of which survived as late as the 1980s.

Like the DC-3 in civilian service and the C-47 (*et al*) in US military service, the Dakota became something of a living legend in the RAF. It was so much so that some aviation writers in Britain have come to use the name Dakota when referring to all DC-3 derivatives in military service. (The name Dakota correctly applies only to aircraft in RAF service and those transferred to other air services such as those turned over to nations of the British Commonwealth after the war by the British.) In USAAF/USAF/US Navy nomenclature the correct given name of the C-47/R4D was Skytrain, while that of the C-53 was Skytrooper. This system was adopted in line with the Douglas policy of assigning official names beginning with the prefix 'sky.'

Named Skytrain, Skytrooper or Dakota, the durable Douglases became a familiar sight on the world's skyways during World War II. They were equally at home in the icy gales between Greenland and Iceland or in the hot desert sands of Libya and Tunisia. They were a reliable workhorse on the vast distances between the Pacific islands or in the backwater jungles of southern Asia.

Despite her more than adequate supply of official names, this plane came to be known both to those who flew her and those who knew her simply as the Gooney Bird. No other unofficial name that developed during the war came to be universally well known. Indeed there probably was no single airplane in the war that was held in such high regard by the people who knew her as the Gooney Bird.

The C-47 was an integral part of the trans-Himalaya airlift that kept forces in China supplied from India when the land supply lines were cut. Flying over the 'Hump,' as it was called, caused pilots to encounter some of the worst weather in the world—violent storms, severe cold and bone-wrenching updrafts—not to mention Japanese interceptors. The tortuous flights over the Hump put the C-47 airframes to a severe test, but the challenge was met. Indeed the challenge had been met even before the war when China National (CNAC), the Pan Am subsidiary, had flown its DC-2s and DC-3s over the same rugged air routes.

During World War II, C-47s dropped not only paratroops and supplies but, in a couple of documented cases, they dropped bombs and napalm as well. They delivered everything from mail and spare parts to entire jeeps. They sprayed South Pacific jungles with insecticide and rescued interned American airmen from neutral Sweden. They carried loads far in excess of what they were designed to carry. While the DC-3 was designed for a maximum of 28 passengers, there is at least one recorded instance of 68 passengers being evacuated out of the path of the Japanese Army. One of them was General Jimmy Doolittle, who had ended up in China after leading the first American raid on Tokyo, and who hitchhiked out of China aboard a CNAC DC-3.

Below: A group of local residents inspect a C-47 during a 1942 stopover in New Guinea. Both they and the crew were intrigued.

Two wonders of the world, recorded at Giza near Cairo in Egypt on 23 October 1943. The Gooney Birds flew into nearly every nook and cranny in the known world during and shortly after World War II.

Above: This C-47A of the 92nd Troop Carrier Squadron flew a number of missions during the war, including two trips over Normandy on 6-7 June 1944.

Below: The XCG-17 glider prototype (a C-47 sans engines) and a US Coast Guard R4D-1 in postwar markings.

Half a world away more than a thousand C-47s, C-53s and Dakotas took part in the largest military operation in history, Operation Overlord, the Allied invasion of Europe. Between the night of 5/6 June and the night of 7/8 June 1944, the transports carried 20,000 paratroopers and tons of parachute-dropped equipment to the Normandy beachheads. During Overlord and again during Operation Market Garden in the Netherlands three months later the C-47s carried troops and towed gliders loaded with troops. The gliders, generally Waco CG-4s, greatly extended the troop-carrying capacity of the Skytrains. The process was economical because the Skytrain/glider combination could carry more men for the amount of fuel and engine wear expended than could transports by themselves. A number of transport glider experiments were carried out on both sides during World War II, but in the United States, of the 20 glider types to be given the CG (Cargo Glider) designation, only the Waco CG-4 was produced in any quantity (over 16,000 were ordered between 1942 and 1945). Among the others was the Douglas XCG-17, a C-47 converted to a glider by removing its engines and fuel tanks. The Skytrain glider experiment was successful with the XCG-17 gliding better and gliding at higher speeds than the CG-4. The glide ratio of the XCG-17 was 14 to 1 compared to 12 to 1 for the CG-4, and it could be towed at 290 mph, almost 100 mph faster than the CG-4. Nevertheless the program was dropped after the preparation of the single prototype. The C-47 airframes were in too much demand as powered transports.

The ubiquitous C-47 was a popular demand. She had the reputation of a go-anywhere, do-anything workhorse, and it was a reputation well deserved. Even after the end of World War II and the onset of postwar demobilization, the Skytrains continued to be present in large numbers in the arsenal of the US Army Air Forces. Of the 4522 C-47/C-53 aircraft on hand in September 1945, 2125 remained at the beginning of 1947. This was a larger number than any other single type of aircraft, combat or non-combat. Many of these Skytrains were on hand in 1948 when the Russians blockaded the western sectors of Berlin, cutting all the overland road and rail routes into the city. The Western Powers, particularly the United States, responded with one of the biggest airlifts in history, keeping the besieged city supplied and fed through the bitter winter of 1948–49. By the time of the Berlin Airlift, MATS had taken delivery of a sizeable number of the larger Douglas C-54 Skymasters (civilian designation DC-4), but the old C-47s were also present in large numbers hauling food, medicine, spare parts and even coal. There was one case of a C-47 being assigned to carry a load of aluminum planking into Berlin. On the flight into the blockaded city, the pilot found his plane particularly sluggish and hard to fly, but he made it and delivered his cargo. On closer examination he discovered the reason for Skytrain's poor performance: the planking had been mislabeled. It was steel, not aluminum, and its weight was double the maximum weight that could be carried in a C-47. Again the old Gooney Birds were distinguishing themselves with service above and beyond the call of duty.

By the time war broke out in Korea, the MATS fleet contained a variety of larger four-engined transports, and these were immediately put to work ferrying supplies from the continental United States to dispersal points in Japan and Korea. Once the supplies were on the ground at rear echelon bases, however, it was the Skytrain's turn to carry the ball. Once again, the Gooney Birds were trucking oversize loads into primitive forward air-fields, as they had so many times during World War II. In the

Above from top: One of several DC-3s that were re-engined in the postwar years with turboprops, and one of many surplus C-47s that would experience an easy transition from USAAF to small-airline service, frequently with the same pilot.

Below: A US Navy R4D-5L races a dog sled down a frozen Alaska runway. The R4D-5L was the specially winterized version.

Above: An ex-military, now civilian-registered, DC-3 photographed by the author at Beale AFB in June 1983. The large cargo doors that distinguish the ex-C-47s from the original DC-3s are clearly visible in this photo.

Left: A civilian nonairline DC-3 (ex-USAAF C-47) photographed by Phil Brooks at Indianapolis International Airport in November 1978.

Above: The US Air Force C-47 *Delta Queen II*, photographed at Tan Son Nhut AB in South Vietnam circa 1970. Although it is named after the steamboat *Delta Queen*, the delta referred to here is that of the Mekong, not the Mississippi.

Below: An American-registered DC-3 sporting the colors of Air BVI (British Virgin Islands).

Above: A DC-3 in the final colors it would wear in service with United.

Below: Swivel recliners (now considered unsafe aboard airliners) in the deluxe interior of an early United Airlines DC-3 Mainliner.

Bottom: The fifth DC-3 to be built was later sold to Ozark by American Airlines. It is now reportedly the oldest surviving DC-3.

wake of the Chinese offensive of December 1950, C-47s were sent to the aid of the 1st Marine Division trapped in the Chosen Reservoir area deep in North Korea. Flying onto a hastily prepared 2000-foot runway, the Skytrains managed to evacuate over 4600 casualties in six days.

Throughout its career, the Gooney Bird was called upon to fly a great variety of missions, but during the 1950s, the Skytrains were used in two operations that were poles apart and yet quite similar. In 1952 US Air Force C-47s landing on a 2500-foot strip laid out on pack ice, helped establish Ice Station Bravo at the North Pole. Four years later during Operation Deepfreeze, a Navy R4D nicknamed *Que Sera Sera* spearheaded the establishment of the first permanent settlement at the South Pole.

A generation after its exploits in World War II and Korea, the C-47, still part of USAF inventory, found itself at war again, this time in Southeast Asia. In 1961, when American operations first began in Vietnam, they were on a low profile and designed to support and train the air force of South Vietnam. The old Skytrains were less sophisticated than the newer airlifters, but they had proven their ability to operate in these same jungles in the 1940s and their age was ideal for the low-profile operations that were planned.

They began as transports, serving both with the US Air Force and later more so with South Vietnam's air force. By late 1964, however, the Gooney Birds had become warbirds. As the war and the American involvement in it grew, there came a need for an aircraft that could deliver a concentrated and protracted barrage of gunfire on a specific target. The period of time to which even the slowest aircraft could deliver firepower to a stationary target was limited to just a few seconds. What was needed therefore, was an aerial gun platform that could concentrate gunfire for several, or even many, minutes on such targets as enemy troop concentrations and strong points, especially in the dead of night.

It was determined that this could be achieved by mounting the guns so that they fired at a 90-degree angle to the side of the aircraft rather than straight ahead or straight behind. The plane would then circle with the guns pointing to the center of the circle. The circle would then become the base of an inverted cone, with the line of fire forming the cone itself and at the point of the cone where all the lines of fire converged would be the target. A transport aircraft would be the ideal platform because it would be relatively slow and because it would, by definition, have a large open fuselage in which to mount guns and ammunition. The gunships came to be the most heavily armed aircraft in Southeast Asia. Most carried a sizeable number of fixed-mounted guns, including several 20-mm, 40-mm and, in some cases, 75-mm cannons.

The first gunships were 20 C-47 Skytrains redesignated AC-47 and organized at the end of 1965 into the 4th Air Commando Squadron. They were initially nicknamed Spooky (all USAF gunships had nicknames beginning with 's'), but came to be known as Puff the Magic Dragon or Dragon Ship because of the fire and smoke they breathed. Puff was an immediate success. No enemy hideout could withstand the firestorm that it created.

By the time that American involvement in the war ended in 1973, the last C-47s were being phased out of American military service after over 30 years. More than a decade later, however, hand-me-down C-47s and British Dakotas were still in service with a number of smaller air forces around the world, just as over 400 conventional DC-3s were still in service with two dozen airlines around the world.

Above and below: AC-47 Spooky Dragon Ships in South Vietnam in 1965 and 1966. The ten .30-caliber machine guns (*below*), later replaced by 20-mm Gatling guns, turned the AC-47's large cargo door into a roaring furnace of fiery death.

This Millardair Super DC-3 was photographed in Toronto in January 1984. It carries the legend 'Douglas C-117,' but the US Air Force designation for the Super DC-3 was actually C-129. The C-117 designation was assigned to late-model C-47Bs that were modified as VIP staff transports after World War II. In the blizzard of designations that befell the DC-3 family, however, it is not impossible that this Super DC-3 might have once carried a C-117 designation either in USAF or Canadian Armed Forces service.

The Super DC-3

In the demobilization that followed World War II, the C-47 may have been the single plane retained in the largest numbers, but there still were over 2000 of them sold on the surplus market. This was more than double the number of commercial DC-3s that had been delivered to the airlines before the war. Surplus Skytrains were being snapped up by small airlines and individuals (many of them ex-USAAF C-47 pilots) at a price far lower than that which Douglas would have to charge to build them new. In a few short years, during the late 1930s, the DC-3 had single-handedly revolutionized commercial air travel and made itself the most valuable airliner in the world. Just five years later, the market for factory-new DC-3s had been virtually destroyed by the glut of surplus C-47s and the advent of larger, faster, four-engined transports.

The more modern four-engined liners, like Lockheed's Constellation, Boeing's Stratocruiser, and Douglas's own DC-4 and DC-6, were taking on the transcontinental routes pioneered by the DC-2 and DC-3, but there was still a market for a fast and efficient short-range airliner to service shorter feeder air routes. Using the advanced technology developed during the war, both Martin and Convair were moving to fill the gap. Douglas engineers also studied the situation, and concluded that the best plane for the job would be an upgraded DC-3, a Super DC-3. A new program was born.

The process of developing the Super DC-3 was actually a modification process. Rather than building the new bird from the ground up, the Douglas Santa Monica team started with a pair of conventional DC-3 airframes. The first of the new planes rolled out in the spring of 1949. She was 3 feet, 3 inches longer, which translated into 10 more seats. The tail, similar to the tail that was being used on the DC-6, was a foot higher. She was powered by a pair of Wright R-1820s delivering 1475 hp, 275 hp better than the standard DC-3 a decade earlier, and the rated range of the sleek new plane was nearly 50 percent greater than its predecessor.

The aviation press sang the virtues of the new plane and everyone who flew the Super DC-3 had nothing but praise for it. Donald Douglas and his son Donald Jr personally undertook a 10,000-mile sales and promotion trip in the first prototype (civil registration number N30000). Nobody had a bad word to say about the plane and from the words that *were* said it sounded like there would be airline orders in excess of 60 planes. However, when the dust settled from the promotional tour and the ink had dried on the sales contracts, Douglas had sold exactly three Super DC-3s, and all of them to Capital Airlines.

Despite her flawless performance, the airlines wanted more seating and tricycle landing gear, among other things. The bottom line was that they were in the market for a new airplane, not a rebuilt old one.

Capital received the first of its Super DC-3s on 30 July 1950 and in 1951 the original prototype, N30000, was sold to the US Air Force under the designation YC-129 (tail number 51-3817). Eventually the YC-129 was transferred to the US Navy under the designation XRAD-8. Nearly 30 years earlier the Navy had helped to justify the Cloudster by being the first to order a series of Cloudster derivatives. The Navy helped do the same for the Super DC-3. A contract was issued under which 100 R4D-5s and R4D-6s were brought up to Super DC-3 standard under the designation R4D-8.

Were it not for the Navy order, the Super DC-3 program would have been a failure. It was simply a matter of economy. The Super DC-3 cost nearly 20 times as much as a surplus C-47 and

Above: A Douglas Super DC-3 in its original company colors during the 1949 sales tour. The tour that showed great promise but garnered four sales.

Below: The Super DC-3 prototype shown at the left was sold to the US Air Force in 1951 and redesignated C-129. It later became another Navy R4D-8.

Above: The US Navy saved the Super DC-3 project by contracting with Douglas to convert 100 R4D-5s and R4D-6s to R4D-8 (Super DC-3) standard.

it wasn't 20 times better. The original was too good to start with. It was hard for an airliner's accounting department to justify $200,000 for a rebuilt version of a plane that was selling for around $8000.

It is now over 30 years since the Super DC-3s were delivered to Capital, and over 400 examples of the original DC-3 and a few Super DC-3s as well are still in operation, nearing the end of their first half century of service and looking like they could go another half century.

The DC-4 Program

The DC-3 story, the Super DC-3 chapter aside, has to be taken as one of the greatest aircraft success stories in history. Nevertheless the first serious talk of a DC-4 came up before the first prototype DC-3 was delivered. Four-engined transports were on the minds of airline executives just as four-engined bombers were on the minds of Air Corps officers, but in 1936 four-engined aircraft of any sort were still a bit unusual. Boeing was working on its Stratoliner and Clipper, but it was to Donald Douglas that United Air Lines came with $300,000 and a desire to buy a four-engined transport. W A ('Pat') Patterson, like airline executives all over the country, liked the DC-2 and had a lot of confidence in the firm that built it. So, like TWA with the DC-1/DC-2 and American with the DC-3/DST, United was coming to Douglas with a necessity that would mother a Douglas invention.

Donald Douglas knew that Patterson's $300,000 would not cover the cost of developing the new plane, but he also knew that the future contained four-engined transports and that if this

Above and below: The DC-4E as first flown and, later, at New York's Floyd Bennett Field as a United Air Lines Super Mainliner.

program (provisionally designated DC-4) was to be a success, it would more than make up for any losses incurred on the prototype. After four other airlines also expressed interest, Douglas went for it. A development contract was signed and Douglas engineers went to work on the new plane, designated DC-4E for DC-4 Experimental.

The plane that resulted was three times the size of the DC-3, had four engines, and triple tail surfaces. The development costs ran to $1,634,612, more than five times the seed money. The DC-4E could accommodate 30 overnight passengers in berths and 42 on day flights. The galley was actually a complete kitchen and the interior appointments equalled or surpassed those of the

DC-3/DST. When test pilot Carl Cover took her up for the first time on 7 June 1938 he is reported to have remarked, 'She flies herself, I just went along for the ride.'

The airlines were anxious for this wonderful new plane that could fly nonstop between Chicago and San Francisco, but it was May 1939 before the only DC-4E to be built was painted in the colors of a United Air Lines Super Mainliner. By this time, war was imminent in Europe and the development of civil airliners was beginning to take a back seat to the production of warplanes. Before the war began, however, Douglas redesigned the DC-4 and set to work building a block of 24 DC-4A production aircraft. The DC-4A was smaller than the prototype, with a

wingspan of 117 feet 6 inches compared to 138 feet 3 inches for the DC-4E, and a length of 93 feet 5 inches compared to 97 feet 7 inches for the earlier aircraft.

As the Santa Monica assembly line was being set up to build the smaller, single-tailed DC-4A for United and American in September 1939, the DC-4E was sold to Japan purportedly to serve as an airliner. The Douglas transport, however, was a practical pattern for Nakajima to refer to in the development of its four-engined G5N Shinzan bomber, which would have been very similar in appearance to the Douglas transport. The Shinzan program ended in failure, and the DC-4E herself reportedly met her end in a crash that took her to the bottom of Tokyo Bay.

Above: A Douglas Model DC-4A as a US Army Air Forces C-54 (*top*) during World War II and a commercial DC-4 in the postwar colors of Pan American's clipper *Racer*.

The war started for the United States before the conventional DC-4s were finished, and the first 24 were commandeered on the assembly line under the USAAF designation C-54 and the code-name Skymaster. Just as the USAAF needed the versatility of the durable C-47, it needed the range and cargo capability offered by the four-engined DC-4, so it ordered 252 more under the designation C-54A. Of these, 155 were built at Santa Monica and the rest at a Douglas plant in Chicago. Of the total, 57 were transferred to NATS under the designation R5D-1.

The C-54A was followed by 220 C-54Bs, 120 of which were built in Chicago. The major innovations offered in the C-54B were integral wing tanks and the provision for use as an air ambulance. Delivered between 1942 and 1944, the stretcher-carrying C-54Bs evacuated thousands of American casualties to the United States from the world's battlefronts. Thirty of the C-54Bs were transferred to NATS as R5D-2 and one to the RAF for use as a personal executive transport for Prime Minister Winston Churchill.

The one C-54C was actually a C-54A specially modified as the personal executive transport of President Franklin D Roosevelt. It was equipped with sleeping compartments for six and a special elevator to accommodate the wheelchair-bound chief executive.

Left: Vernon Tree's outstanding rendering of the commercial DC-4's interior powder rooms, dining areas and sleeping quarters, which were more like those of a deluxe streamliner than those of today's commercial airliners.

Above and below: Stateroom detail and the special elevator that equipped the C-54C used by President Franklin D Roosevelt.

This Skymaster carried Roosevelt to his overseas conferences with other Allied leaders and went on to serve his successor, Harry Truman. Nicknamed *Sacred Cow*, this single C-54C was later redesignated VC-54C and it remained in service until 1961.

All of the 380 C-54Ds were built in Chicago, and all of the 125 C-54Es and 162 C-54Gs were built in Santa Monica. The C-54F was a projected troop-transport version. The C-54Gs, registered in 1945, were the last Skymasters to be built, but several existing aircraft were modified and given designations through C-54L. The C-54M was a series of 38 earlier C-54s modified to haul coal during the Berlin Airlift of 1948–49. While they never received

any DC-4 derivatives directly from Douglas, the Navy received 30 C-54Bs from the Air Force that were redesignated R5D-2, 95 C-54Ds redesignated R5D-3 and 20 C-54Es redesignated R5D-4. The R5D-5 designation fell to earlier R5Ds re-engined with 1450-hp R2000 engines similar to those of the Air Force C-54G. The R5D-6 designation was reserved for a transfer of C-54Js that never took place. Ultimately 11 R5Ds from US Navy and US Coast Guard inventories were transferred back to the US Air Force under designations ranging from VC-54N to RC-54V.

A further series of C-54 modifications took place after the war, resulting in aircraft designated XC-112, XC-114, XC-115 and

Above: A Navy DC-4, designated R5D-1, over the pineapple fields of the Hawaiian island of Molokai in about 1945.

Below: The North Star was a Rolls-Royce Merlin-powered version of the DC-4 (C-54GM) built under license by Canadair in Canada during the mid-1950s.

YC-116. The XC-112 was a single C-54B retrofitted with four 2100-hp R-2800 engines. First flown in February 1946, it was destined to become the prototype for Douglas's DC-6 series. The XC-114 was a single C-54G retrofitted with four 1620-hp V-1710-131 engines, and the YC-116 was a single similarly engined aircraft with a thermal deicing system. The XC-115 was a C-114 variant with four 1650-hp V-1650-209 engines that was never built.

When World War II ended, so too did the C-54 production line. Douglas had hoped to come back to the keen interest the airlines had expressed in the DC-4 before the war. His hopes were to be dashed by the same phenomenon that had killed further factory-new sales of DC-3s. This phenomenon was the used-plane market. The US military had thousands of surplus C-47s and C-54s. The DC-4E prototype had cost more than a million dollars. The factory-new production DC-4s cost much less but it was hard to compete with used C-54s that sold for $10,000. Nevertheless the company *was* able to take 79 commercial DC-4 orders in the postwar market. This more than made up for the original 24 commercial DC-4s ordered on the eve of the war that had been drafted as USAAF C-54s before they were delivered to the airlines. Canadair also bought the rights to build a DC-4 derivative in Canada with 1760-hp Rolls-Royce Merlin engines. Canadair eventually built 71 of these CL-2 North Stars for such customers as Trans-Canada Airlines, British Overseas (BOAC) and the Royal Canadian Air Force. Of all the Douglas-built DC-4 variants, the Canadair North Star was most like the experimental XC-114.

Commercial postwar sales of DC-4s suffered like those of the DC-3, but the plane's record was solid. In the years immediately after World War II, new and used DC-4s carried more passengers than any other four-engined transport. Though she was soon upstaged by the DC-6, the DC-4 continued in service and more than two dozen were still in service four decades after she was first introduced.

The DC-5 Program

The fifth aircraft type to receive the Douglas Commercial designation was also the most enigmatic. It came and went in a short space of time, completely overshadowed by the DC-3 and DC-4. With only 12 examples built, there were fewer DC-5s than any other of the DC series except the DC-1. While the DC-1 was clearly part of the same family as the DC-2 and DC-3, and the DC-6 and DC-7 were clearly developments of the DC-4, the DC-5 was related to no other model.

Within the Douglas family tree her closest relative was the DB-7 bomber that eventually became the A-20 Boston/Havoc, and it was the DB-7 that sparked the idea for the DC-5. The DC-3 program was in full swing at Douglas Santa Monica in 1938 when an idea evolved at Douglas El Segundo that the DB-7 they were developing might have possibilities as an airliner. Work started on a prototype in September 1938 and the new plane was finished four months later. The plane that first flew on 12 February 1939 at El Segundo had a fuselage similar to that of the DC-3, but it was camouflaged beneath wing and tail surfaces like the fuselage of the DB-7. It was roughly the same size as the DC-3 and carried on average the same number of passengers. Her differences were more pronounced than her similarities to her older cousin. She had been designed by Ed Heinemann and the El Segundo team with tricycle landing gear and the ability to land and take off in relatively short distances.

The four previous DC airliners had been built in response to airline requests, but the DC-5 was built simply because it seemed

Below: A KLM DC-5 with canted horizontal tail surfaces, ready for delivery in 1940. Compare it with the DC-3 in the background.

like a good idea and other airline orders were not immediately forthcoming. Ironically the first prototype was eventually sold as a personal executive aircraft to William Edward Boeing, founder and former owner of the Boeing Airplane Company, historically Douglas's biggest competitor.

Late in 1939 the US Navy became the DC-5's first customer, ordering three aircraft for itself under the designation R3D-1 and four for the US Marine Corps under the designation R3D-2. The deliveries did not take place until after a tragic accident in July 1940 that resulted in the death of Douglas test pilot Bill Benson and the loss of one of the undelivered R3D-1s. The aileron cables had been accidentally rigged backwards and the plane crashed near the Standard Oil refinery at El Segundo. The remaining

Above: Designer Ed Heinemann and test pilot Carl Cover with one of the original DC-5s at Douglas El Segundo in 1939.

Above: The Douglas DC-5 as originally configured with straight horizontal tail surfaces as compared to those in the photograph below.

R3D-1s and R3D-2s were delivered in September and October. With the exception of the loss of one R3D-2 in December 1941, all the planes survived the war. After the war started in February 1942 the Navy commandeered Bill Boeing's executive transport under the designation R3D-3 and retained it in service until June 1946. The Navy retired the rest of its DC-5 derivatives in late 1945, but the Marines held on to theirs until October 1946.

The first and only airline order came on the heels of the Navy order, but deliveries of the commercial DC-5s were actually made before the first Navy deliveries. KLM, the national airline of the Netherlands, was pleased with the DC-2s and DC-3s it had purchased from Douglas and was interested in the short takeoff and landing characteristics of the DC-5. Indeed, it was a Dutch test pilot named Vandermaas (he was also head of the aeronautical engineering department at the University of Delft) who helped Douglas work out some of the early bugs in the DC-5 design. Because of the war in Europe, all four of the DC-5s purchased by KLM were shipped to the Netherlands East Indies for use by KNILM, KLM's subsidiary in that part of the world. The first and second aircraft were delivered on 30 April and 30 May 1940. With the Netherlands having been defeated by Germany on 15 May, the Dutch Government went into exile and the business of delivering the remaining pair of DC-5s went ahead. On 24 July 1940 the final two DC-5s, nicknamed *Eend* (Duck) and *Boschduif* (Wood pigeon) were loaded aboard the SS *Silverwood* at San Pedro, California, for delivery to the East Indies. On their arrival in Surabaya, two of the DC-5s were seen marked with orange triangles, indicating that they had been transferred to the Netherlands East Indies Air Force.

The Japanese captured the Dutch colony a year and a half later, along with at least one of the DC-5s. By March 1945 one of the DC-5s had shown up in Australia, where it was commandeered by the USAAF, with two of the missing DC-5s transferred to USAAF rosters in absentia. The use of the DC-5 by the USAAF at this stage was ironic because General Henry ('Hap') Arnold, commander of the USAAF, had decided five years earlier not to buy the type when it was first offered for sale by Douglas. Designated C-110, this sole survivor was sold to Australian National Airlines in December 1946. A couple of years later, it found its way to the Israeli Air Force where it served until 1955 under the nickname *Bagel Lancer*.

The failure of the only DC liner to come out of El Segundo was probably due to its being overshadowed by the DC-3, which put a damper on commercial sales before the war. When the war came, its lack of experience caused the military services to turn to more proven transports (again the DC-3), and this in turn caused Douglas to replace it on the El Segundo production line with urgently needed A-20s and SBDs. When all is said and done, however, this ugly duckling of the DC family tree did give rise to some interesting tales.

Below: A good three-quarter view of the DC-5 in company markings photographed on the apron at Douglas El Segundo in January 1940.

Right: This US Navy R3D-1, one of seven Navy DC-5s, served as a VIP transport at NAS Anacostia near Washington in the District of Columbia.

DC-5

First flight	12 Feb 1939	*Max gross weight (lb)*	21,000
First delivery	30 Apr 1940 (KLM)	*Max payload (lb)*	4,026
Wingspan	78′	*Passengers*	26
Length	62′ 2″	*Cargo space (cu ft)*	278
Height	19′ 10″	*Operating altitude*	10,000′
Engines	Wright GR18720-G102A	*Cruising speed (mph)*	184
Engine hp	1,100	*Max range (mi)*	1,024

Above: The C-118A Liftmasters of the USAF Military Air Transport Service were the Air Force equivalent of the commercial DC-6.

Above: The Scandinavian Airlines DC-6 nicknamed *Leif Viking* shortly after it was delivered for service.

Below: Most of the DC-6s still in service in the 1980s, such as this Challenge Air Transport freighter, operate with small nonscheduled airlines.

The DC-6 Program

Both the DC-3 and DC-4 were promising airliners whose civilian careers had been interrupted by military service. The military careers of both planes secured their place in aviation history, but the proliferation of used DC-3s and DC-4s on the market after the war cut deeply into the number of potential postwar airline orders for Douglas. The company had received far more orders for the DC-3 before the war than for both planes combined in the years after the war. The DC-6, on the other hand, was a product of the war which would nearly equal the phenomenal success enjoyed by the DC-3 in the late 1930s. Douglas received over 500 orders from 44 airlines, nearly six times the number of airline orders received for the DC-4. On top of this there were 101 orders from the US Air Force and 65 from the US Navy.

The DC-6 was very similar to the DC-4 in its overall appearance, with the same wing span and wing structure. The bridge between the two was the USAAF YC-112 long-range transport, which was a greatly modified C-54 (Douglas Model DC-4) with four Pratt & Whitney R-2800-22W engines generating 2100 hp, 45 percent more than those of the DC-4/C-54 series. The YC-112 first flew on 15 February 1946 and served as a prototype first for the commercial DC-6 series, and the later USAF version that was designated C-118. With the war over, the Air Force lost interest in the long-range transport it had ordered, while Douglas, the company that built it for them, took up where it left off. The company immediately began soliciting commercial orders, and on 28 March 1947 both American Airlines and United Air Lines took delivery of gleaming new DC-6s. There was seating for 52 passengers, 20 percent more than in the DC-4 and 85 percent more than the DC-3.

Just as the DC-6 was getting off to a running start, though, disaster struck. A DC-6 went down in Bryce Canyon, Utah, killing everyone aboard. Shortly thereafter another DC-6 burst into flames over New Mexico. This time, an emergency landing

Above from left: Profiles of the full family of Douglas four-engined propeller airliners, the DC-4, DC-6 and DC-7.

Below: Pan Am's DC *Clipper Mignight Sun* was of several to enter the Pan American fleet after World War II.

Right: The DC-7C Seven Seas, such as this one for Sabena of Belgium, was the ultimate Douglas prop-driven transport.

	DC-4	DC-6	DC-7
First flight	14 Feb 1942	15 Feb 1946	18 May 1953
First delivery	18 Jan 1946 Western Air Lines	28 Mar 1947 American Airlines United Airlines	4 Nov 1953 American Airlines
Wingspan	117' 6"	117' 6"	117' 6"
Length	93' 5"	100' 7"	108' 11"
Height	27' 7"	28' 5"	28' 7"
Engines	P&W R2000	P&W R2800CB16	Wright R3350
Engine hp	1,450	2,400	3,250
Max gross weight (lb)	82,500	107,000	144,000
Max payload (lb)	26,000	23,490	40,000
Passengers	80	102	110
Cargo space (cu ft)	3,575	4,939	5,436
Operating altitude	10,000'	28,000'	25,000'
Cruising speed (mph)	207	308	334
Max range (mi)	4,255	2,990	5,635

saved the plane, but the nation's entire fleet of DC-6s was grounded. As in the wake of the DC-10 disaster 32 years later, an entire type of Douglas transports was grounded. The company moved swiftly to diagnose the problem (which turned out to be fuel overflow sucked into a cabin heater duct) and to correct it. On 21 March 1948, four months after the grounding and a year after the first DC-6 deliveries, the plane was back in the air.

Even as the company was racing to get the basic DC-6 back in the air, plans were being laid for newer, larger DC-6s. There was a larger all-cargo version designated DC-6A and a passenger version with seating for up to 102 designated DC-6B. The DC-6A first flew on 29 September 1949 and the first commercial delivery was made to Slick on 16 April 1951. The DC-6B did not make its first flight until 10 February 1951, but the first delivery was made to United Air Lines on 11 April of the same year.

In the meantime the Korean War broke out and the US Air Force and Navy took renewed interest in the long-range capabilities of the DC-6. The Air Force ordered 101 of the new DC-6As under the designation C-118A and named them Liftmaster. Those C-118As used for Korean War aeromedical evacuation were designated MC-118A. The Navy ordered 65 under the designation R6D-1. Of the latter Liftmasters, 40 were lent to the USAF MATS during the Korean War and most of these were returned. Those R6D-1s acquired permanently were redesignated C-118B. In 1966 two used commercial DC-6Bs were procured by the USAF under the designation C-118A (though they should logically have been designated C-118C) for transfer to the air force of Chile.

By the time the Korean War ended, the role of the DC-6 as a first-line civil airliner had virtually ended as well. This time it was not so much a matter of surplus C-118s on the market as with the DC-3 and DC-4, because fewer military versions had been built than civilian versions. The real reason for the end of the DC-6s (and this had contributed in part to the earlier downfall of the DC-3 and DC-4) was obsolescence in the face of advancing technology. The most recent version of Lockheed's Constellation was outflying the DC-6 and Douglas itself was building a plane, the DC-7, to outfly them both. The airlines wanted only the newest aircraft to serve as their flagships in the sky.

The DC-6 had been the first plane to fly a regularly scheduled around-the-world route and she ultimately outlived the planes

that tried to replace her. The DC-6 continued to serve smaller airlines in third-world countries until well into the 1980s, long after the DC-7 had passed from the scene.

The DC-7 Program

The man that lit the spark that launched the DC-7 was C R Smith of American Airlines, the same man who had been responsible for Douglas building the DC-3. In 1934 Smith had wanted a larger, longer range DC-2. Now, nearly two decades later, he wanted a larger, longer range DC-6. It was another guaranteed order for Douglas and Douglas accepted it. The plane that first flew on 18 May 1953 represented the kind of improvement in performance and capacity over the DC-6 that the DC-6 had over the DC-4 and that the DC-3 had over the DC-2. She was powered by 3250-hp Wright R-3350 radial engines, the most efficient engine of its type that had yet been designed.

The DC-7 began service with American Airlines on 4 November 1953, allowing the company to offer coast-to-coast, nonstop service. A DC-7B version first flew on 21 April 1955 and went into service with Eastern Air Lines a month and four days later. The ultimate DC-7, however, and also the ultimate Douglas piston-engined airliner, was the DC-7C. Given the nickname Seven Seas, which was as much a commentary on her range as it was a

Above: In 1946, the Douglas Aircraft Company public relations department decided to have some interior photos taken to aid the marketing of the then brand-new DC-6. Among the models selected for the sessions were young ladies who had come to Southern California more interested in the motion picture industry than the aircraft industry. The girl seated on the right, Norma Jean Baker, became successful in this endeavor as Marilyn Monroe.

Below: The Navy equivalent of the DC-6 was originally designated R6D-1, but this was changed to C-118B after 1962.

A Transcontinental DC-6 photographed against the cumulus of gathering dusk by Phil Brooks at the Salt Lake City airport in March 1982.

The American Airlines DC-7 flagship *Missouri* was among those DC-7 flagships that helped flesh out this airline's long-distance transcontinental routes during the early 1950s.

Above: The first DC-7C Seven Seas, shown here on the apron at Santa Monica, was painted in the same company colors as the small aircraft in the background.

Below: Northwest bought Douglas DC-7C Seven Seas transports at a time when it was expanding its service over one of those seven seas, the Pacific Ocean.

Above: This Aviateca DC-6, nicknamed *Esquipulas*, was photographed by E William Helmer at Caoba, Guatemala, in February 1977. Like many small third-world airlines, Aviateca still flies DC-4s and DC-6s on many of its short but high-density intracountry routes, like the one from Guatemala City to Tikal. When the passenger load is small, a small Convair 340 flies the route, but on peak days, the airline switches to one of its larger DC-6s. Because the runway at Tikal is too short for the DC-6, it has to land on this dirt strip in the jungle at Caoba. Here the passengers wait under a make-shift shelter for a Convair to shuttle them the last 23 miles to Tikal.

play on words, the DC-7C first flew five days before Christmas in 1955. She had the range to fly anywhere in the world and carried nearly four times the passenger load of a DC-3, and 30 percent more than the DC-4.

The DC-7C was first put into service by Pan American Airways on 18 April 1956, servicing its vast route network in the Pacific. She was a splendid plane, luxurious and yet powerful. Like the Super DC-3, however, the Seven Seas was a plane that came too late. She went into service with Pan Am just two years before the Boeing 707, America's first jet-powered airliner. When Douglas began work on the DC-7, turbojet engines were not yet economical enough for commercial airliners. With the DC-7, Douglas had decided to rely on stable, proven technology, and for the moment not to gamble on a jet airliner. Boeing, on the other hand, despite its enormous success with multiengined bombers, had never enjoyed anything approaching that degree of success with any commercial airliner. Douglas was the leader and Boeing was out to gamble on a challenge to that leadership by being the first American planemaker to leap into the unknown of jet airliners.

The DC-8 Program

The first commercial jet transport, Britain's de Havilland Comet, had first flown in July 1949 and had gone into airline service three years later. A series of disastrous crashes, however, resulted in the plane being grounded in 1954, the same year that the prototype of America's first jetliner made its maiden flight. Douglas had been studying the idea of a jet transport, but, noting the Comet fiasco, it was moving much more cautiously than Boeing. Douglas was more seriously preoccupied with a possible DC-7D and an even larger turboprop airliner. It was not until 7 June 1955, a year after the first flight of the Boeing 707 prototype (Boeing Model 367-80), that Douglas announced that it was undertaking the development of a commercial jet transport under the company designation DC-8. The designation had actually been used a few years earlier to describe a possible airliner version of the B-42 Mixmaster bomber. The prototype was never built and Douglas reassigned the DC-8 designation to its new jet-transport project.

The plane first flew three years later on 30 May 1958. It was similar in outward appearance to the 707, whose first production versions were about to go into service with Pan Am. It had the same swept wings as the 707, and the same engine placement. It was nearly 40 feet longer than the DC-7C, but carried roughly the same number of passengers. The first DC-8's range was better than that of the original DC-7, but 16 percent less than that of the DC-7C. Speed was another story. The four Pratt & Whitney 13,500-lb-thrust JT3C-6 turbojets of the DC-8 gave a cruising speed 75 percent faster than that of the DC-7C. The DC-8 became airline certified on 31 August 1959 and entered airline service simultaneously with United Air Lines and Delta on 18 September,

Far left: The prototype DC-8 as it appeared during its first flight on 30 May 1958.

Left: A Canadian Pacific airliner with an F-104 Starfighter chase plane, during a test flight in which this DC-8 became the first and only American-built jetliner to achieve supersonic speeds.

Below: Two United DC-8s (with the DC-8 prototype in the background) on the flight line at Long Beach.

nearly a year after the first Boeing 707s. Boeing had seized the lead and the DC-8 would never catch up.

The initial DC-8 Series 10 aircraft with 13,500-lb-thrust Pratt & Whitney JT3C-6s were followed by the first flight of the DC-8-20 aircraft on 29 November 1958. The Series 20 aircraft were powered by 16,800-lb-thrust Pratt & Whitney JT4A-9s and first went into service with Eastern Air Lines on 3 January 1960. The Series 30 and 40 aircraft were designed for intercontinental service and were powered by Pratt & Whitney JT4A-11 and Rolls-Royce Conway turbojets, respectively, both of which delivered 17,500 lb of thrust. The DC-8-30 and DC-8-40 had made their first flights early in 1959 and both entered service on 7 February 1960, a month after the DC-8-20.

The DC-8 Series 50, which first flew on 20 December 1960, was a notable milestone in DC-8 development. First entering service with KLM on 3 April 1961, it was the first DC-8 to be powered by turbofan engines instead of turbojets. The Pratt & Whitney JT3D-3 turbofans delivered 18,000 lb of thrust and gave the Series 50 a 12 percent longer range than the Series 40, and 58 percent longer range than the original Series 10. The Series 50 was also the first to be offered to customers in all-freight (DC-8-50AF), convertible-freight or passenger (DC-8-50CF) versions. Of the 88 DC-8-50s delivered, 15 were the windowless all-freight versions and 39 were convertibles.

	DC-8-10	DC-8-40	DC-8-63
First flight	30 May 1958	23 Jul 1959	10 Apr 1967
First delivery	3 Jun 1959 (UAL)	7 Feb 1960 (ACA)	15 Jul 1967 (KLM)
Wingspan	142' 5"	142' 5"	148' 5"
Length	150' 6"	150' 6"	187' 5"
Height	42' 4"	42' 4"	42' 4"
Engines	P&W JT3C-6	RR Conway R0012	P&W JT3D-7
Max gross weight (lb)	355,000	355,000	355,000
Max payload (lb)	117,744	117,744	117,744
Passengers	259	259	259
Cargo space (cu ft)	12,580	12,580	12,580
Operating altitude	35,000'	35,000'	35,000'
Cruising speed (mph)	570	589	584
Max range (mi)	4,773	6,757	7,015

Above: A cutaway interior view of a typical DC-8 in passenger configuration, with cutaway details of wing structure and engine nacelles as well. The smaller cutaway at the right shows the interior of a D-8-62F Jet Trader loaded with cargo pallets and cargo containers.

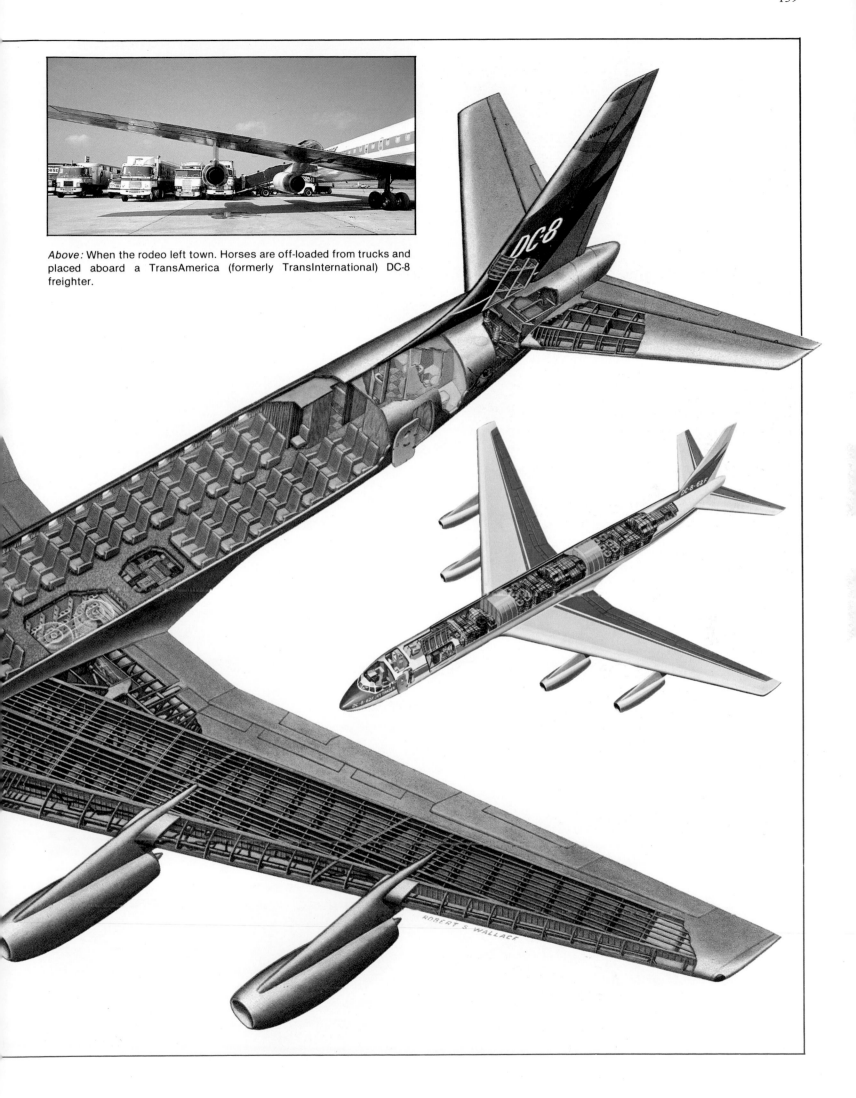

Above: When the rodeo left town. Horses are off-loaded from trucks and placed aboard a TransAmerica (formerly TransInternational) DC-8 freighter.

Above: A Capitol Airlines DC-8-61F Jet Trader. A long-time DC customer, Capitol once flew DC-3s, was the only commercial carrier to buy Super DC-3s and now flies DC-10s.

Left: An early freight loading demonstration with a DC-8-50F freighter.

While there had been a considerable number of changes made in the DC-8-10 through DC-8-50 lineage, the basic airframe of the 294 aircraft built under these designations remained relatively constant. The series that followed, known as the Super Sixty series, had the same nose, wing and tail as the earlier DC-8s, but the fuselage was 'stretched,' making the series 36 feet, 11 inches longer than its predecessors. The stretching was accomplished by inserting a 'plug,' or fuselage section, both in front of and behind the wing. This more than doubled the passenger capacity. The increase in passenger capacity from model to model, going back to the DC-4, had been relatively modest, and the Super Sixty series DC-8 submodel had made possible the biggest percentage increase of capacity since the transition from twin-engined DC-3 to four-engined DC-4.

The first flight of the DC-8-61 took place on 14 March 1966, followed by the DC-8-62 on 29 August 1966 and the DC-8-63 on 10 April 1967. First deliveries of the DC-8-61 were made to United Air Lines on 26 January 1967, of the DC-8-62 to the Scandanavian Airlines System (SAS) on 3 May 1967 and of the DC-8-63 to KLM on 15 July 1967. A DC-8-63CF convertible-freighter version first flew on 18 March 1968, first entering service on 21 June of the same year with Seaboard World.

Of the three subseries within the Super Sixty series, the DC-8-62 was smaller than the other two, with a standard passenger capacity of 189 compared to a standard capacity of 220, and a maximum capacity of 259 in the DC-8-61 and DC-8-63. Both the DC-8-62 and DC-8-63 were originally equipped with 19,000-lb-thrust Pratt & Whitney JT3D-7 turbofans, delivering more power and more range than the DC-8-61. The smaller DC-8-62 had a longer range than any other Douglas Commercial transport before or since, including the larger DC-10.

By 1983 a new generation of DC-8s was appearing on the world's airways. The new birds, referred to as the Super Seventy series, are actually DC-8-60s re-engined with General Electric-SNECMA CFM56-2-1C turbofan engines. The retrofitting, involving about a hundred DC-8-60s, was undertaken at the McDonnell Douglas Tulsa facility. The operation involved both passenger- and freight-configured aircraft, with the DC-8-61 and 60F becoming DC-8-71 and 71F and so on through DC-8-72, 72F, 73 and 73F. There was no increase in the passenger capacity of 259 for the DC-8-61 and 63 in the transition to DC-8-71 and 73, but the range was increased from 7150 to 8790 miles and 7700 to 9080 miles, respectively. The new engines also helped boost the range of the DC-8-62, already the longest-range DC jet, from 8500 to 9940 miles in the DC-8-72 incarnation. In addition to the increased range provided to the DC-8, the CFM56s are both more cost effective and quieter.

While the DC-8 re-engining process was underway, McDonnell Douglas was in the midst of a parallel effort to convert a large proportion of the world's DC-8 passenger fleet to an all-freight configuration. The Sixty and Seventy series freighters provided a cargo capacity of between 89,100 and 109,217 lb, depending on model and configuration.

Below: A Venezuelan VIASA DC-8-61 photographed in February 1983.

Right: An early test flight featuring a SNECMA turbofan-powered DC-8 Series 70 for United Air Lines.

The DC-9 Program

With the exception of the enigmatic DC-5, the trend with each model of Douglas Commercial transports since the beginning was to be larger than its predecessor. The plane that the company announced in 1962 broke with that trend. The proposed DC-9 was smaller than either the DC-8 or the DC-7, and the basic version carried fewer passengers than some versions of the DC-6 and DC-4. The idea was to develop a jet transport for the short-range markets of the world. Boeing had seized the long- and medium-range markets with its 707 and 720, and the new 727 would be another medium-range jetliner. Boeing had come to dominate the commercial market more completely than any company since Douglas stunned the market with the DC-3. The Seattle planemaker, however, still had shown no intentions of getting into the short-range jetliner market (it would, eventually, with its 737) and Douglas felt it could easily compete with the smaller companies who were already there.

The DC-9 Series 10 first flew on 25 February 1965 and made its first in-service airline flight for Delta Airlines on 8 December 1965. It was 104 feet 4 inches long, 83 feet shorter than a DC-8 Super Sixty, 46 feet shorter than a standard DC-8 and very different in appearance. The forward fuselage was similar but the rest of the design was decidedly dissimilar. The DC-9 had two engines instead of four, and they were located in the aft fuselage rather than on the wing. The horizontal tail surfaces were located at the top of the vertical tail plane like the Boeing 727 and the BAC 111, which also had their engines located aft.

Noting its experience with the DC-8, Douglas designed the DC-9 with fuselage stretching in mind, and three distinctive stretched series developed in the first decade after the introduction of the DC-9-10. The DC-9-20, which was developed for SAS, had a DC-9-10 fuselage but it had the longer wing developed for the stretched DC-9-30. The Series 30 first flew on 1 August 1966 and went into service with Eastern Air Lines in February 1967.

Above: The first Douglas DC-9 Series 30 rolls out at Long Beach in July 1966.

Right: DC-9s on the Douglas Long Beach assembly line. Since the DC-9 is the most successful DC airliner, this assembly line may run for a quarter century.

Below: Commercial transport then and now: a DC-9 Series 40 dropped thousands of flowers in the path of the liner *Queen Mary* as she steamed into the port of Long Beach on her last voyage in December 1967.

The DC-9-30 was 15 feet longer than the Series 10 and 20. The DC-9-40, first flown on 28 November 1967, was 6 feet longer than the Series 30.

Seven years after the first flight of the DC-9-40, Douglas, by then part of McDonnell Douglas, introduced the DC-9-50. Making its first flight on 17 December 1974—the 39th anniversary of the first flight of the DC-3—the DC-9-50 was 133 feet 6 inches long with a wing span of 93 feet 4 inches. The wing span (and the wing) was the same as for all the previous DC-9s except the DC-9-10. The DC-9-50 was, however, 29 feet 2 inches longer than the Series 10 and 8 feet longer than the Series 40. The Series 50 accommodated a regular passenger load of 122 (or 139 in a high-density arrangement) compared to 70 to 90 in the original DC-9.

An American International Airlines DC-9 photographed by Bryant Petitt during the uphill climb of the morning sun at Atlanta's Hartsfield International Airport in August 1983. Hartsfield at this time was the second busiest airport in the United States (after Chicago's O'Hare) and as such was visited by hundreds of DC-9s every day.

Above: These Hughes Airwest DC-9 'Flying Bananas' photographed by Phil Brooks at San Francisco International in 1979 became part of the Republic Airlines fleet when the two airlines merged shortly thereafter.

Below: A US Air DC-9 photographed by Marion Pyles at Cincinnati Airport in April 1982.

Above: The DC-9 flying hospitals: the US Navy's C-9B Skytrain II (*top*), the USAF's C-9A Nightingale and the medevac-configured interior common to both.

The DC-9-50 was powered by a pair of Pratt & Whitney JT8D-17 turbofans delivering 16,000 lb of thrust. This compared to the 12,250-lb-thrust JT8D-5s of the DC-9-10. The intervening DC-9s were each available with a variety of Pratt & Whitney turbofan powerplants ranging from the 14,000-lb-thrust JT8D-1 to the 15,500-lb-thrust JT8D-15.

The DC-9 was also the first of the DC series to see military service since the DC-6 had become the C-118 back in the early 1950s. In 1962 the military nomenclature was changed and the numbering system restarted at 1, so subsequent numbers were much lower than they had been in the 1950s. As a result, the military transport version of the DC-9 could also conveniently be given the number 9, thus being designated C-9. First ordered in August 1967 and first delivered a year later, the military C-9s are all DC-9-30 airframes and are used almost exclusively as aeromedical transports or hospital planes. Twenty of them are in use by the US Air Force under the designation C-9A with the name Nightingale. Fourteen were delivered to the US Navy under the designation C-9B and named Skytrain II out of deference to the given name of the C-47/R4D of World War II fame. There are three VC-9Cs in use by the Air Force as executive transports and two DC-9-30s were procured by the Navy under the designation C-9K for transfer to the air force of Kuwait.

The Navy's C-9Bs are assigned to its transport squadrons VR-1, VR-30 and VR-56, and the C-9As are assigned to the USAF Military Airlift Command's 375th Aeromedical Airlift Wing at Scott AFB, Illinois. These aircraft are also rotated to Europe and the Pacific for intratheater aeromedical evaluation operations. In January 1981, it was a pair of USAF C-9As that flew the

	DC-9-10	DC-9-50	DC-9 Super 80 (MD 80)
First flight	25 Feb 1965	17 Dec 1974	18 Oct 1979
First delivery	18 Sept 1965	14 Aug 1975	Summer 1980
Length	104' 4"	133' 6"	147' 10"
Wingspan	89' 4"	93' 4"	107' 10"
Height	27' 6"	28'	29' 5"
Engines	P&W JT8D-5	P&W JT8D-17	P&W JT8D-209
Engine thrust (lb)	12,250	16,000	18,500
Cargo capacity (lb)	9,000	15,510	18,975
Max gross weight (lb)	90,700	121,000	140,000
Payload (lb)	19,000-43,283 (all models)		
Cruising speed (mph)	55	542	542
Range (mi)	1,565	1,812	2,071
Operating altitude	37,000' (all models)		
Passengers	90	135	172

Above: A detail of the DC-9's Pratt & Whitney JT8D turbojet engine with its cover removed for maintenance. See also the cutaway of the engine nacelle at right.

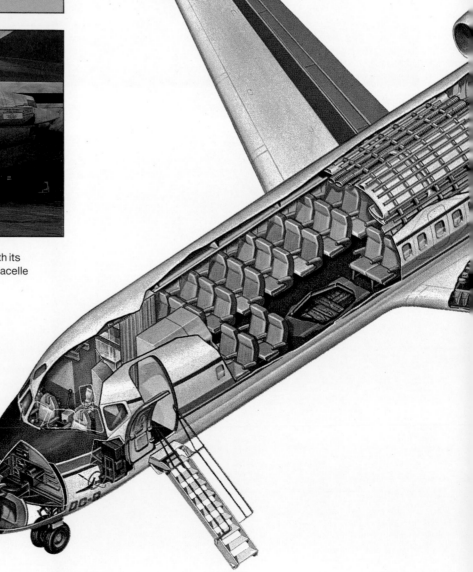

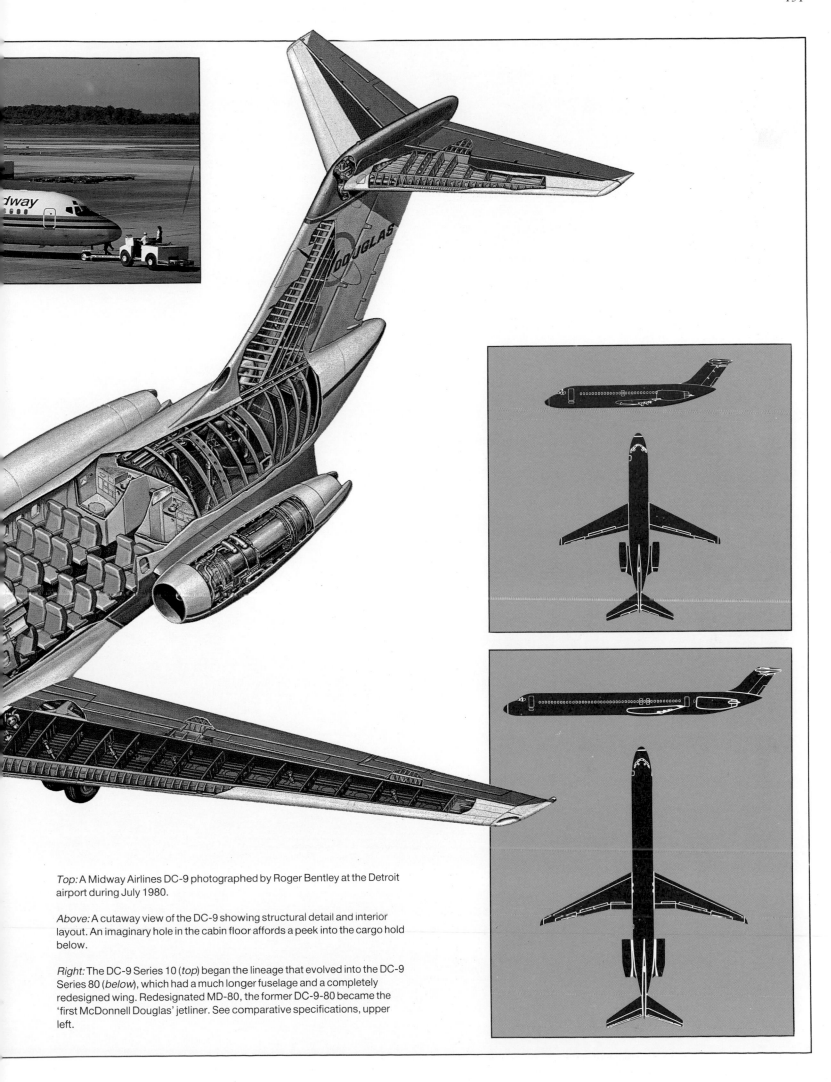

Top: A Midway Airlines DC-9 photographed by Roger Bentley at the Detroit airport during July 1980.

Above: A cutaway view of the DC-9 showing structural detail and interior layout. An imaginary hole in the cabin floor affords a peek into the cargo hold below.

Right: The DC-9 Series 10 (*top*) began the lineage that evolved into the DC-9 Series 80 (*below*), which had a much longer fuselage and a completely redesigned wing. Redesignated MD-80, the former DC-9-80 became the 'first McDonnell Douglas' jetliner. See comparative specifications, upper left.

152

American hostages seized by Iran out of Algeria where they had been sent upon their release.

The normal crew of the C-9 includes the pilot, copilot, crew chief, two flight nurses and three aeromedical technicians. While the airframe is a basic off-the-shelf DC-9-30, many specialized features have been added inside for the care of patients. These include a hydraulically operated ramp for loading and unloading litter patients and two hydraulically operated stairways. There is also an isolated special-care area with controlled humidity and built-in oxygen systems, decontamination systems and separate ventilation systems. The plane can also accommodate the medical personnel and a medical-supply work area. A self-contained auxiliary power unit (APU) provides electrical power for un-interrupted cabin power and air conditioning during enroute stops and for self-starting the two Pratt & Whitney JT8D-9 turbofans.

The DC-9 was conceived by the Douglas Aircraft Company before the merger with McDonnell and all the components (such as the wing and stretchable fuselage) of the DC-9-50, which first flew seven years after the merger, were products of the original concept. On 18 October 1979, however, a further step in the DC-9 evolution took place. This was the first flight of the DC-9 Super

80, which, with a new wing, new engines and a still longer fuselage, constituted the first 'all-McDonnell Douglas' jetliner. Because of this, the Super 80 was ultimately redesignated MD-80 and became the cornerstone in a new series of jetliners.

The DC-9 started out in the shadow of the DC-8 and faced off against Boeing's dominance of the jetliner market. Boeing had beaten Douglas into the jetliner business but Douglas beat Boeing into the business of short-haul jetliners by two years. With the DC-9, Douglas really shone. The DC-9 outsold the Boeing 737 by roughly two to one, and went on to become the biggest selling commercial airliner in Douglas history. With over a thousand

sales to commercial airlines by the early 1980s, the DC-9 outsold even the DC-3, of which only 803 units were ordered by commercial buyers. When military sales are factored in, the DC-9 still comes out second only to the DC-3/C-47/R4D and ahead of the prolific DC-4 and its C-54/R5D derivatives. Still in production in the form of the MD-80, the DC-9 might very well go on to become one of the two or three biggest selling airliners in aviation history.

Below: An All-Star DC-9 photographed in gathering twilight by Marion Pyles on a snow-spattered Cincinnati runway.

PRODUCTION CLOSE-UP
DOUGLAS, COMMERCIAL

0	500	1000	//	10,000

Model DC-1 (1933)

1

Model DC-2 (1934)

130 **DC-2** Commercial Transports

1 **C-32** (24 commandeered DC-2s later also became C-32s)

20 C-33 & C-34 (the 2 C-34s were built for the Secretary of War and had VIP interiors)

38 C-38, C-39, C-41 and C-42 (The C-38 was a modified C-33 and the prototype C-39. The C-41 and C-42 were 3 VIP versions.)

5 R2D

Model DC-3 (1935) (including **DST**, Douglas Skysleeper Transport)

803 DC-3 Commercial Transports*

9571 C-47 Skytrains

103 DC-3s ordered by commercial airlines, but built and delivered to the USAAF.**

245 C-53 Skytroopers (The paratroop version of the C-47)

17 C-117 (The staff transport version of the C-47. An additional 11 VC-47s became C-117C)

78 R4D Skytrains (12 of these were ordered by commercial airlines, but built and delivered to the US Navy.)***

2 RAF Dakota Mark IIs ****

Super DC-3 (1949) (All the Super DC-3s were converted from DC-3 airframes, none were built from scratch)

1 Prototype

3 Commercial Transports for Capital Airlines

1 C-47F/C-129 conversion for the US Air Force

100 R4D-8 conversions for the US Navy

*Only 803 of the nearly eleven thousand Model DC-3 airframes built were actually delivered by Douglas into commercial service. At the end of World War II, however, vast numbers of surplus C-47s, R4Ds and Dakotas were sold off to private and commercial operators, thus increasing the number of commercial DC-3s in service several fold. It has been estimated that over one thousand of these were in service thirty years later.

**In addition to the 103 commercial DC-3s commandeered on the assembly line, 97 of the 803 Commercial DC-3s in commercial service were commandeered between 1942 and 1944. (These included 32 that became C-48s, 58 that became C-49s, 1 that became a C-50, 1 that became a C-52, 2 that became C-68s and four that became C-84s). Six DC-3s were also impressed by Great Britain as RAF Dakota Mk IIs.

***In addition to the R4D Skytrains procured directly, the Navy also received 472 ex-USAAF C-47s and 20 ex-USAAF C-53s which were also redesignated R4D.

****While Britain purchased only two DC-3s directly, 1935 C-47s, 6 C-49s, 1 C-53 and 1 C-68 were transferred to the RAF as Dakota Mk I, Mk III and Mk IV. Many of these were in turn delivered to British Commonwealth and other air forces during World War II and/or sold on the commercial market after the war.

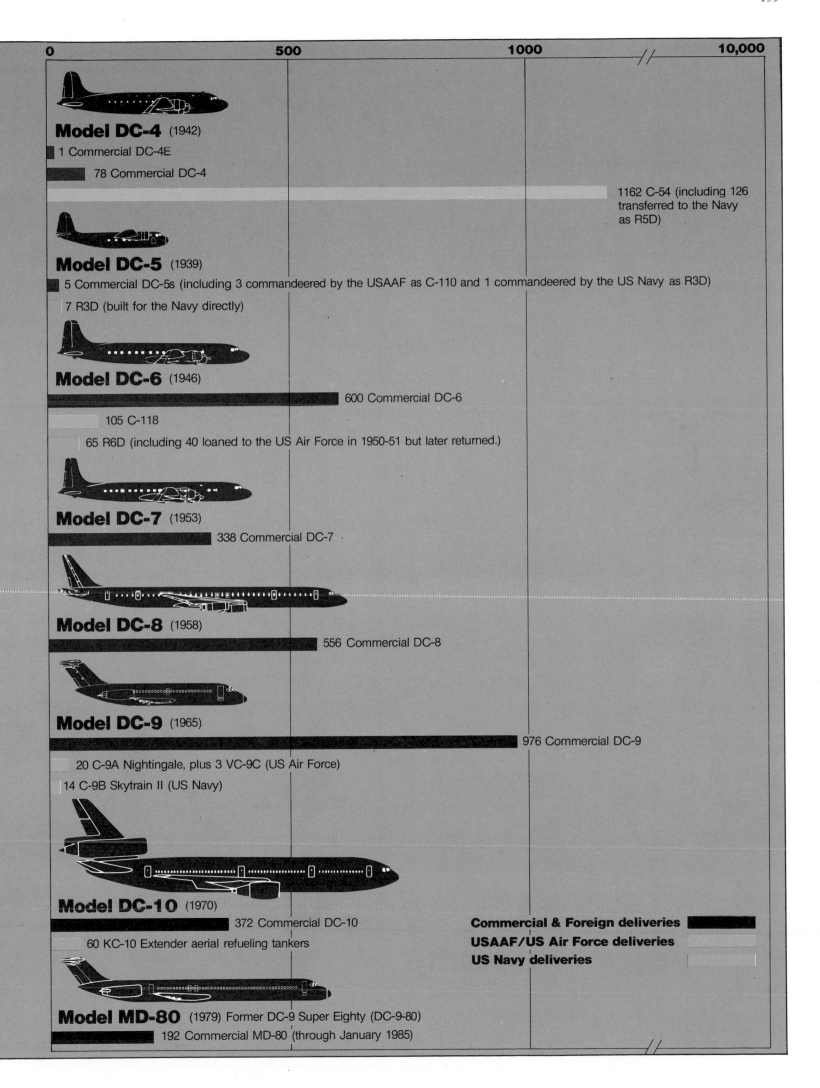

| 0 | 500 | 1000 | // | 10,000 |

Model DC-4 (1942)

1 Commercial DC-4E

78 Commercial DC-4

1162 C-54 (including 126 transferred to the Navy as R5D)

Model DC-5 (1939)

5 Commercial DC-5s (including 3 commandeered by the USAAF as C-110 and 1 commandeered by the US Navy as R3D)

7 R3D (built for the Navy directly)

Model DC-6 (1946)

600 Commercial DC-6

105 C-118

65 R6D (including 40 loaned to the US Air Force in 1950-51 but later returned.)

Model DC-7 (1953)

338 Commercial DC-7

Model DC-8 (1958)

556 Commercial DC-8

Model DC-9 (1965)

976 Commercial DC-9

20 C-9A Nightingale, plus 3 VC-9C (US Air Force)

14 C-9B Skytrain II (US Navy)

Model DC-10 (1970)

372 Commercial DC-10

60 KC-10 Extender aerial refueling tankers

Model MD-80 (1979) Former DC-9 Super Eighty (DC-9-80)

192 Commercial MD-80 (through January 1985)

Commercial & Foreign deliveries

USAAF/US Air Force deliveries

US Navy deliveries

The DC-10 Program

The era of what came to be known as the 'jumbo jets' began in May 1964 when Boeing, Douglas and Lockheed all began design studies for a US Air Force transport plane to airlift a payload weighing 60 tons. Designed under the experimental designation CX-4 (later C-5A) the new airplane was the largest plane in the world and had a range of over 8000 miles. All three companies strained to come up with extensive proposals and elaborate mock-ups. In September 1965, the winner was announced. It was Lockheed.

As Lockheed's Marietta, Georgia facility geared up for production of the C-5A, all three companies continued to investigate the feasibility of adapting designs for the commercial market. Boeing proceeded more earnestly, announcing in 1966 that it planned to build a giant airliner nearly the size of the C-5A having a payload capacity that would put it and the C-5A in a class far above any existing transport. Both Douglas and Lockheed knew that a market existed for the huge planes, and they moved quickly to finalize plans for commercial jumbo jets with which they hoped to catch Boeing's lead.

When the Boeing 747 made its first flight in September 1968, Lockheed and Douglas (now a component of McDonnell Douglas) were only a few months into their projects. Lockheed had never built a jetliner, and this was its first airliner since the turboprop L-188 Electra that had first flown in 1957. For McDonnell Douglas it was to be the largest and last of the DC series liners.

Ironically the two jetliners, the Lockheed L-1011 TriStar and the McDonnell Douglas DC-10, were so similar in appearance that to the uninitiated they looked like the same plane. They both had three engines, one under each wing and the third mounted in the tail. The major difference was that the tail-mounted engine of the L-1011 was designed with the intake above the engine and connected by an 'S-duct,' while the DC-10 had a simpler 'straight-through' design. Both planes were double-aisle widebodies of nearly the same size. They were 80 percent the size of the 747 and roughly the same length as the DC-8, although their much wider cabins accommodated a maximum passenger load of between 380 (DC-10) and 400 (L-1011), 50 percent more than could be carried by the DC-8. Aside from the 747, with a passenger capacity in the 500 range (depending on seating

Right: A DC-10 vaults the setting sun on takeoff from Los Angeles.

Below: The lights come on at the Long Beach final assembly area during the early, halcyon days of the DC-10 program.

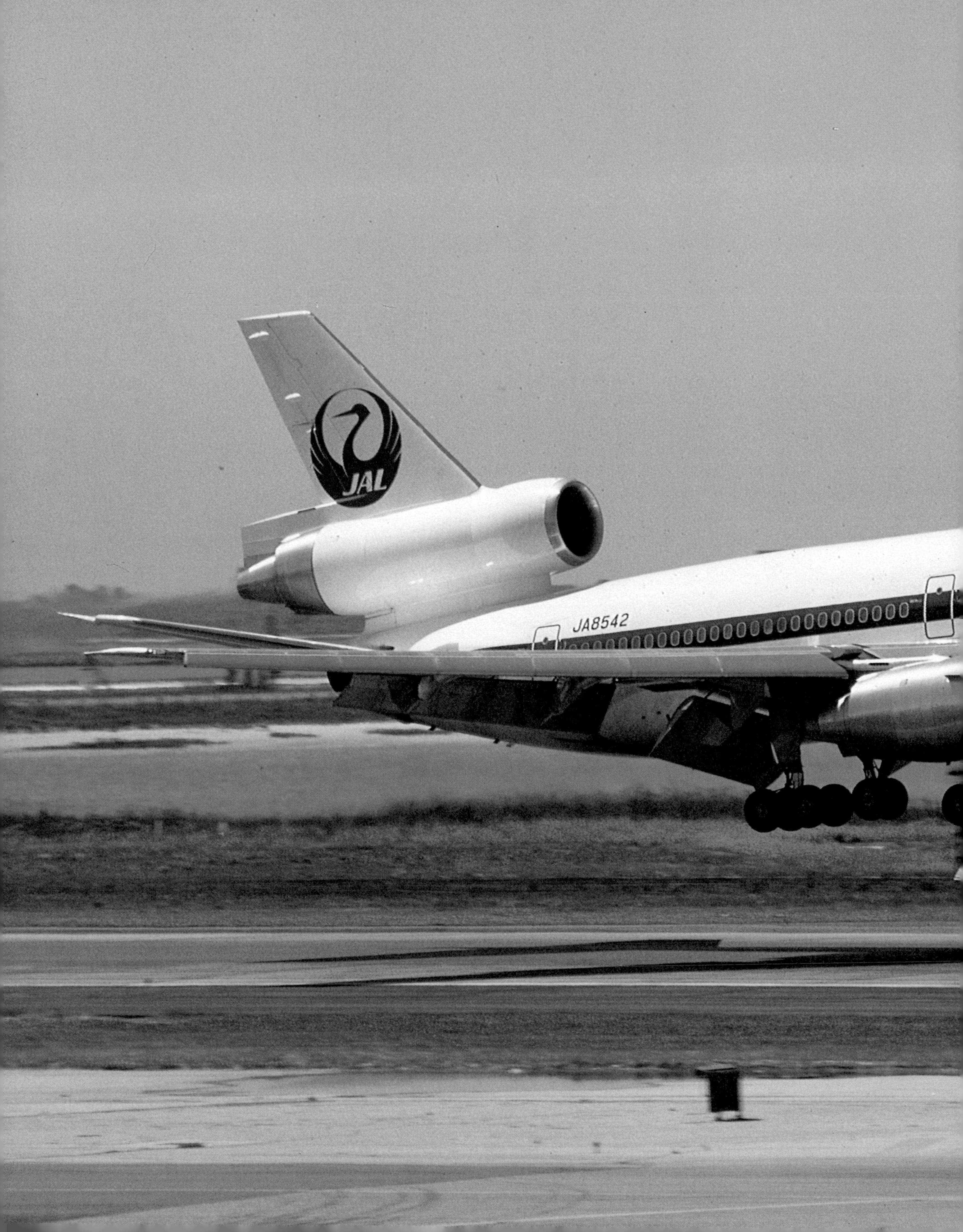
JAL
JA8542

Below: A Japan Air Lines DC-10 Series 40 on takeoff from New York's John F Kennedy Airport in June 1980. The Series 40 offered increased range, important to carriers such as JAL with route structures worldwide.

160

Above: As bands played and flags waved on 29 July 1971, United Air Lines and American Airlines took delivery of the first two DC-10s to go into regular airline service.

arrangement) the two planes had the greatest commercial passenger capacity ever to be offered to the airlines.

Market research had demonstrated a clear need for a plane the size of the L-1011 and DC-10; indeed C R Smith of American Airlines, the man who had helped launch the DC-3, had actively solicited a plane this size. The question was whether there was a need in the marketplace for two planes this size, and the answer was no. There was room for one plane in this size class to be profitable, but neither company was willing to let the other go forward alone.

The DC-10 first flew on 29 August 1970 and the L-1011 followed three months later, on 17 November. The DC-10 was powered by three 40,000-lb-thrust General Electric CF6-6D turbofans, while the TriStar was powered by a trio of 48,000-lb-thrust Rolls-Royce RB 211 turbofans. When the L-1011 first flew both Lockheed and Rolls-Royce were entangled in financial crises that were solved only by the British Government's takeover of Rolls-Royce and the United States Government's rescue of Lockheed. The DC-10 took the lead in a crowded field of two where there would be no winner.

American Airlines had picked the DC-10 and had ordered 25, with an option on a further 25. TWA had gone for the TriStar and United Air Lines was a house divided. United's engineering headquarters in San Francisco favored the L-1011, while the corporate offices in Chicago wanted the DC-10. Ultimately the corporate offices won out; an order was placed for 30 DC-10s and an option placed on a further 30. American and United took delivery of the first two production DC-10 Series 10s on 29 July 1971, and American put its new widebody in regular service just eight days later.

The DC-10-10 series was followed by a single DC-10-20 proto-type that was first flown on 28 February 1972 but redesignated and put into production as DC-10-40. The DC-10-40 was put into service by Northwest Orient Airlines with 49,400-lb-thrust Pratt & Whitney JT9D-20W turbofans (the same engine used

by Northwest's 747 fleet) and later by Japan Air Lines with Pratt & Whitney JT9D-59A turbofans delivering 53,000 lb of thrust. A major improvement in the DC-10-40 over the DC-10-10 was increased range. The range of the DC-10-10 is rated at 3753 nautical miles and the range of the DC-10-40 is rated at 4752 nautical miles with the JT9D-20 and 5292 with the JT9D-59A engines. First flown on 21 June 1972, the DC-10-30 was ordered by several European lines including Swissair and KLM. The Series 30 aircraft were powered by General Electric CF6-50C engines delivering 51,000 lb of thrust. A Series 15 aircraft was developed, based on the DC-10-10 airframe but powered by a 46,500-lb-thrust General Electric CF6-50C2-F engine similar to the CF6-50C of the Series 30. The DC-10-15 was ordered by Aeromexico and Mexicana Airlines and first placed into service in June 1981.

Though it received high marks from pilots and passengers alike, the L-1011 sold fewer than 250 units and drove Lockheed to abandon the airliner business once and for all in 1983. The DC-10, itself crippled by the competition, sold over 350, continued in production well into the 1980s but still never became a profitable item for McDonnell Douglas. Despite the competition with the TriStar, the DC-10 would probably have done even better had it not been for a series of spectacular crashes that hurt the reputation of not only the DC-10 but McDonnell Douglas as well, sounding the death knell for the DC dynasty.

The foretaste of disaster came in 1972 over Windsor, Ontario aboard an American Airlines DC-10 bound from Detroit to Buffalo. At 12,000 feet the plane's rear cargo door blew out, precipitating explosive decompression that damaged many of the control cables running through the plane. Thanks to expert handling of the situation by the pilot, the aircraft was able to

Above: A Continental Airlines DC-10 Series 30 touches down. The Series 30 aircraft were first flown in June 1972.

return to a safe landing at Detroit. The Federal Aviation Administration (FAA) of the US Government treated the matter casually, asking McDonnell Douglas to simply recommend that its customers fix what amounted to a design flaw in the cargo door locking system, rather than demanding that McDonnell Douglas actively correct the flaw. Most airlines learned about the faulty door lock. Some didn't, including Turk Hava Yollari, the national flag carrier of Turkey.

In March 1974, a Turk Hava Yollari DC-10 was 12 minutes out of Paris at 13,000 feet with an improperly latched cargo door and an inoperative warning light, when the cargo door locking system failed. Just like two years before over Windsor, explosive decompression crumpled the floor beams of the plane. This time the control cables were severed and the plane was unsalvageable. Within moments, 346 people slammed to their death at the Foret de Ermenonville in what continued to stand a decade later as the worst airplane crash in aviation history. (This excludes the downing of a Korean Air Lines 747 by Soviet interceptors in 1983, which was technically an act of war and not a crash.) Within four months of the Paris crash, McDonnell Douglas had revised the DC-10's latch actuator wiring and strengthened the floor beams. Two months later the company had developed a redundant warning-light system, which meant that if one warning light system broke down, a separate and independent system could indicate a dangerous condition.

The cloud that hung over the DC-10 in the wake of the Paris crash had begun to dissipate when American Airlines flight number 191 lifted off from Chicago's O'Hare International Airport enroute to Los Angeles five years later. American had been the first airline to put the DC-10 into service, and American had flown the first commercial flight of a DC-10 on its Los Angeles-to-Chicago run. American was as experienced with DC-10

operations as anyone, and the rear cargo door locking systems in the entire worldwide DC-10 fleet had long since been fixed. The weather was clear and the 273 passengers and crew aboard flight 181 looked forward to a reasonably uneventful flight. The pilot applied full power and the big jet lifted off the runway. Suddenly, at 300 feet, still over the runway, the port engine and pylon ripped off, rolled over the top of the wing and smashed into the runway. There is no modern jetliner that cannot fly with an engine out. It was not simply the loss of the port engine that initiated the disastrous chain of events that followed. When the engine pylon tore free of the wing, however, it ripped out the hydraulic cables located in the leading edge of the wing. This created a hydraulic imbalance, causing the port wing slats to retract, pitching the plane into a barrel roll to the left. The generator powering the warning lights was also put out of commission, so the pilot and copilot didn't know exactly what had happened. Thirty-one seconds after takeoff, the violently rolling DC-10 that was American Airlines flight 191 exploded into an Illinois trailer park. All of the 273 people aboard lost their lives in the worst air disaster ever to occur in the United States.

In the aftermath of the Chicago crash, the FAA found itself on the defensive in the face of public hysteria, much of it directed against the DC-10. For the first time in nearly three decades, the Airworthiness Certificate of a major airliner was pulled, leaving DC-10s parked idle at airports all around the country in what amounted in a public relations horror unmatched in the history of Douglas and McDonnell Douglas. The FAA investigation finally turned up the cause of the pylon failure. Cracks and metal fatigue had occurred as a result of what were determined to be faulty maintenance procedures followed by American. Instead of removing the pylon and engine separately for servicing, the two were removed as a unit to save time and money. In their final report the FAA said, 'It is unquestionable that, were it not for extensive damage to the forward flange of the pylon aft bulkhead which occurred as a result of the improper execution of a non-

	DC-10-10	DC-10-30	DC-10-40
First flight	29 Aug 1970	21 Jun 1972	28 Feb 1972
First delivery	29 Jul 1971	21 Nov 1972	10 Nov 1972
Length	182' 3"	181' 7"	182' 3"
Wingspan	155' 4"	165' 4"	165' 4"
Height	57' 6"	57' 6"	57' 6"
Engines	GE CF6-6D1	GE CF6-50C2	P&W JT9D-59A
Engine thrust (lb)	40,000	51,000	53,000
Cargo capacity (lb)	4,168	4,618	4,618
Max gross weight (lb)	444,000	572,000	572,000
Payload (lb)	103,221-156,000 (all models)		
Cruising speed (mph)	587	587	587
Range (mi)	6,325	7,414	7,033
Operating altitude	42,000' (all models)		
Passengers	250-380	250-380	250-380

Below: A cutaway drawing showing the interior detail of the US Air Force aerial-refueling version of the DC-10, which is conveniently designated KC-10 (Kerosene Refueling, Cargo, Tenth).

Fuel for aerial refueling is carried in tanks in the bottom half of the fuselage, where baggage and cargo would be carried in a commercial DC-10. The upper half of the fuselage can accommodate passengers, cargo on pallets or open cargo such as the jet engine shown in this cutaway. The refueling boom is in the rear under the tail.

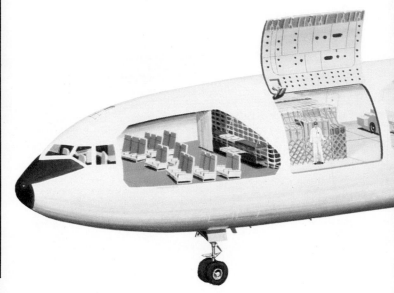

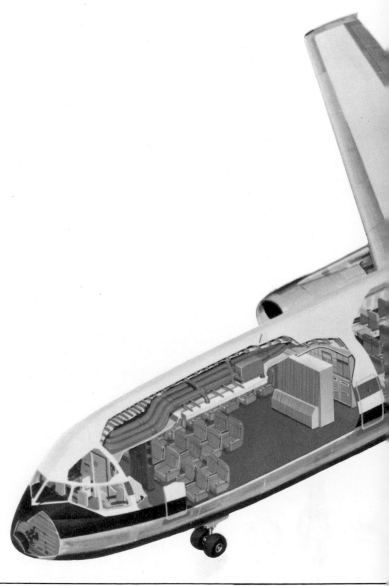

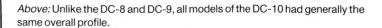
Above: Unlike the DC-8 and DC-9, all models of the DC-10 had generally the same overall profile.

83721

Above: This cutaway drawing shows the interior of a commercial DC-10 detailing the wing, tail and engine nacelle internal structure and the passenger cabin with a typical first-class/tourist layout containing two galleys. A comparison of this cutaway with the one above shows the similarity between these two variations of the same aircraft.

164

Left: A refueling exercise in which one US Air Force KC-10 Extender refueling tanker was refueled by another KC-10. Earlier aerial refueling tankers were not capable of being refueled themselves. This is one factor that makes the KC-10 unique.

Below: An Air New Zealand jet leaps into the air. Air New Zealand finds its long-range DC-10s very useful on its vast transpacific route network.

commended maintenance practice, the Chicago accident would not have occurred.' The report further stated that 'there are no fundamental shortcomings in the design of the DC-10 wing pylon. . . . The DC-10 wing pylon is of sound design, material, specification, construction and performance.'

Despite the damage done to public confidence by the crashes and the cancellation by the company of a stretched Series 60 aircraft, sales of the DC-10 continued into the 1980s. In addition to the 55 civilian airlines flying DC-10s, the US Air Force had in the meantime selected the DC-10-30CF (convertible freighter) to be adapted as its Advanced Tanker/Cargo Aircraft (ATCA) to supplement and eventually replace its aging fleet of Boeing KC-135 Stratotankers. The basic DC-10-30CF airframe has been modified with an aerial refueling boom and an internal fuel tank capacity of 53,000 gallons. In addition to the fuel capacity, the plane can handle 27 standard type 463L 7-by-9-foot cargo pallets or a cargo payload of nearly 85 tons.

Conveniently designated KC-10A, the new USAF tanker was ordered in December 1977 and first flew in July 1980. The first of 60 KC-10s was delivered to the 32d Aerial Refueling Squadron of the Strategic Air Command in March 1981. Part of the reason the DC-10 was selected for the basis of the new tanker was that the plane could use the civilian DC-10 maintenance facilities at commercial airports worldwide.

Nicknamed Extender by the Air Force, the KC-10 has a much greater capability to extend the range of American combat aircraft than has ever been available before in a single plane. This is essential for the Air Force because of the ever-increasing inventory number of aircraft which are refuelable in the air. In addition to its Advanced Aerial Refuelling Boom (AARB) the

Above from left: Two views of the KC-10 refueling boom as seen from the KC-10 being refueled and from the refueling KC-10, as well as a view of the KC-10's huge cargo bay. McDonnell Douglas designed and built the refueling boom under a separate contract, and would have built it even if the DC-10 airframe had not been chosen by the Air Force as its new tanker.

Below: The KC-10 Extender can also stow its refueling boom and refuel Navy aircraft (such as this Douglas A-4) by the hose-and-drogue method.

Extender can also refuel aircraft by the hose-and-drogue method, thus permitting it to refuel US Navy, Marine Corps and NATO aircraft as well. During the extensive tests conducted by the Air Force prior to deployment of the KC-10, the new tanker was called on to refuel a wide variety of aircraft ranging from the Air Force's big C-5s and B-52s to the small A-4 Skyhawk operated by the Navy and Marines.

The Air Force argues that the KC-10's long range will dispense with the need for forward tanker bases and the need to dip into fuel supplies in the theater of operations, as was demonstrated during American operations in Grenada during October 1983. An example of the type of operation made possible by the KC-10 was the October 1982 deployment of a flight of six McDonnell Douglas F-15 Eagles from Kadenea AB in Okinawa to Tyndall AFB, Florida. With the help of an accompanying KC-10, the Eagles made the 7000-nautical-mile flight nonstop in 15 hours. Refuelling the F-15s seven times enroute, the Extender also carried 59 of their support personnel and 55,000 lb of their supplies.

By 1983, with the last of 367 DC-10s delivered to commercial operators and KC-10s rolling out of the Long Beach factory at the rate of one per month, McDonnell Douglas and its Douglas Aircraft subsidiary turned once again to the idea of a new

Above: The winglets test flown on this Continental DC-10 were to have been an integral part of the MD-100 design.

generation DC-10. It would not be the DC-10 Series 60 concept that had been planned in the late 1970s, but rather an all-new program with an all-new designation. The DC designation that had begun with the DC-1 half a century earlier had ended quietly. The only plane from that illustrious line aside from the KC-10 still in production was the DC-9 Super 80, and it had now been redesigned MD-80. The new initials reflected the reality of the 15-year-old McDonnell Douglas merger.

With this in mind, the new advanced DC-10 program was designated MD-100, with the MD-90 designation going to a planned revival of the DC-9 Series 30. The MD-100 had a modern two-crew-member cockpit and many upgraded systems 15 years ahead of those introduced in the first DC-10s. Power was provided by three Pratt & Whitney PW4000 or General Electric CF6-80C2 high-bypass turbofan engines which could provide a substantial improvement in fuel efficiency over earlier engines, according to estimates. The outward appearance of the MD-100 was virtually identical to that of the DC-10, with the exception of 7-foot-high winglets rising from the tip of each wing and tilted outward at 15 degrees. These winglets, made of lightweight carbon composites, enhanced the aerodynamic quality of the aircraft. Initial plans called for MD-100 Series 10 and Series 20 aircraft to be available in 1987 and 1988, respectively. The MD-100-10 was 5 feet shorter than a DC-10, and was designed with a passenger capacity of 270; the MD-100-20, which was nearly 22 feet longer, seated 333. Studies were also undertaken to determine the feasibility of an MD-100-10ER with its range extended to 7000 miles, an MD-100-20 passenger/freight 'combi,' and an MD-100-30 passenger liner that would be 40 feet longer than a DC-10, all of which could be available to customers as early as 1989.

All this planning suddenly came to a halt on 11 November 1983. Faced with a profound lack of interest in the MD-100 and the MD-90, the company cancelled the two programs. The McDonnell Douglas board chairman, Sanford N ('Sandy') McDonnell, nephew of the founder of the McDonnell Aircraft Company, stepped from the board meeting to announce that the company would 'stop all work on, and investment in, the proposed MD-90 and MD-100 jetliner programs,' because, as he put it, 'the continuing depressed state of the worldwide airline industry and the absence of evidence that the market for new aircraft is likely to improve significantly in the near term. Potential customers have proved to be unable in too many cases to sign on as launch customers for these two programs.' McDonnell said, 'We, like the other manufacturers, have been waiting for an improvement in the market, but such an improvement hasn't started and is not in prospect. Under such circumstances there is no basis for confidence that a new program could be successful.'

As the first 400 project engineers were laid off, industry analysts pointed to rivalry that existed between the Douglas and McDonnell halves of the company. McDonnell had a long-developed interest in jet fighters while the Douglas heritage was closely associated with airliners. It has long been felt that McDonnell, the stronger of the two, was urging McDonnell Douglas further and further away from the jetliner market, which it saw as economically questionable. The commercial viability of the MD-80, however was not in question, and it survived the cuts. By 1 November 1983 a total of 139 had been delivered and the Long Beach factory was humming with 67 firm orders and another conditional orders, and options were on the horizon.

Also on the horizon was another twist in the evolving DC-10 story and pleasant news for Douglas. In May 1984, Federal Express, the large American small-package airfreight overnight-delivery service, placed an order for six DC-10-30s, five of them to be built from scratch. Federal Express already operated 10 DC-10s on its domestic routes and wanted the additional planes to put into service when it expanded its operations internationally in 1985. It was considering using Brussels as a European freight hub. It would use part of its DC-10 fleet to haul freight to Brussels, there breaking it down into smaller loads for other European destinations. The new DC-10 order included one

Above: The Advanced Technology Medium Range transport (*see text below*) was the plane that might have worn the DC-11 designation had it been built.

DC-10-30CF convertible freighter that McDonnell Douglas had in stock. Most important, the order breathed new life into the DC-10 production line, which was still turning out KC-10s at a rate of one per month, but which hadn't built a commercial jetliner since the delivery to Japan Air Lines in March 1983 of the 367th DC-10.

The MD-100 program had slipped away but suddenly the DC-10 program was back, albeit for a five-unit production run. Still, the Douglas Aircraft Company president, James Worsham, cautiously predicted 'additional DC-10 orders in both the passenger and freighter configurations.' Noting the lack of used DC-10s on the market, Herbert Hopkins, the DC-10/KC-10 project manager, optimistically referred to the Federal Express order as 'a first step in the re-implementation of DC-10 production.' He also went on to predict as it had been predicted before that a 'stretched, re-engined DC-10 is in the cards for the late 1980s or early 1990s.'

The DC-11 Program

The DC-10 program was destined to be the last commercial transport program to be initiated by the independent Douglas Aircraft Company, although the first aircraft didn't fly until after the 1967 merger with McDonnell. In the meantime, numerous other projects were in various states of development at Long Beach. Not the least of these was the Douglas Supersonic Transport (SST), which was rejected in favor of Boeing's Model 2707 SST in 1966. Ultimately the half-completed 2707 was killed by a withdrawal of Federal Government support in 1971 and America's planemakers turned their attention to more practical projects.

Though SST projects continued to simmer on the back burner at Douglas, the most seriously considered project came to be the Advanced Technology Medium Range transport (ATMR). The

ATMR was designed to fill an airline need for a medium-sized airliner, much smaller than a DC-10 or L-1011, but larger than a DC-9. This 180-place jet, which eventually, though tentatively, received the DC-11 designation, was among the projects inherited by James Smith McDonnell when he became chairman of the merged McDonnell Douglas Corporation.

Mr Mac was known to favor military combat jets to jetliners and he took an immediate dim view of the DC-11, remembering his own commercial jet, the Model 119 project of the late 1950s. The 119, which was redesignated Model 220 in honor of the company's twentieth anniversary in 1959, was originally developed as a military plane. The US Air Force was looking for a small utility transport, and McDonnell was among those submitting designs. Inherent in the process was the possibility of commercial sales on the business/executive jet market if the Air Force launched the project. McDonnell's first and last chance in the commercial transport market was 66 feet long with a 57-foot wingspan and a range of 2200 nautical miles. It first flew in February 1960 but lost the Air Force's UCX (Utility Transport, Experimental) competition to Lockheed's JetStar, which first went into USAF service in 1961 under the designation C-140. Despite extensive marketing efforts that followed, McDonnell was unable to make a single commercial sale for its Model 220 program.

Thus smitten, Mr Mac was expected to be wary of launching a new transport program, even if it were developed by his new subsidiary, which had one of the world's best reputations in the airliner field. The DC-11 not only had many supporters within the company, but American, Delta and United wanted it and were strongly urging him to build it. With no other plane in this size and weight class, there was, in business terminology, a 'hole in the market.' This meant that a ready market would exist for the DC-11 were it to be built. When told about this hole in the market, McDonnell is quoted as having asked why it should be him to fall into it.

In the meantime, with McDonnell Douglas failing to commit to production, Boeing moved to design a product to fill the hole.

A brilliantly colored DC-10 Series 30 in the markings of Fiji's Air Pacific, another airline serving the vast reaches of the Pacific.

In November 1980, three months after the death of James Smith McDonnell, Delta Airlines, one of the earlier supporters of the DC-11 concept, placed an order for 60 Boeing 757s. The hole no longer existed and the DC-11 joined the ranks of the planes that might have been. With the retirement of the DC nomenclature a couple of years later, no other plane would ever receive the DC-11 designation. The DC dynasty ends with an even 10.

The MD-80 Program

Though it has been marketed as a new program since the early 1980s, the MD-80 program is really an extension of the DC-9 program. The MD-80 is in fact the DC-9 Super Eighty (DC-9-80), which first flew in October 1979 and which was the first plane to be redesignated under the new MD (McDonnell Douglas) nomenclature in 1983. The DC-9-80 was made possible by the development of quieter, more powerful Pratt & Whitney JT8D-209 and 217 turbofan engines delivering up to 20,850 lb of thrust. The new engines allowed McDonnell Douglas to greatly increase the length of the Eighty to give it a cabin nearly twice as long as the original DC-10 Series 10. The MD-80 is available in three similar configurations—MD-81, MD-82 and MD-83—with the latter, launched in 1983, having the longest range.

The MD-80 family offers a redesigned cockpit with state-of-the-art digital avionics. It was the first jetliner to enter service with a digital flight-guidance system integrated with the automatic pilot.

Its increased payload and range capabilities give it the lowest per-seat-mile operating costs of any plane in its class as well as the lowest fuel consumption per passenger. The MD-80 is a quieter plane than its predecessors and it meets not only United States requirements but those of the International Civil Aviation Organization (ICAO) as well. Passenger comfort is enhanced by five-abreast seating, allowing wider seats and aisles than in traditional six-abreast airline seating.

The DC-9-80/MD-80 has proven to be extremely successful. Among the first airlines to buy it were Aeromexico, Air California, Hawaiian, Swissair and Republic (which already operated the world's largest fleet of DC-9s). In February 1984 American Airlines ordered 67 of the MD-82 variant, an order worth $1.35 billion, with an option on an additional 100 aircraft. If exercised, the option could boost the sale over the three-billion-dollar mark. The Civil Aviation Authority of the People's Republic of China (CAAC) purchased two MD-80s for delivery in 1984. China went a step further, signing an agreement with McDonnell Douglas to coproduce MD-80s in China. Under the agreement, McDonnell Douglas will supply parts and subassemblies for 25 MD-80s to the Shanghai Aircraft Industrial Corporation, which will also supply parts and carry out the final assemblies. Designed with 12 first-class and 135 coach seats, the 25 planes will be built for service with CAAC in 1986.

Despite lack of interest in the MD-90 (DC-9-30) and MD-100 (DC-10) programs, the MD-80 seemed by the mid-1980s to have

A sparkling, new Muse Air MD-80 takes off from Long Beach. The MD-80s started life as DC-9 Super 80s but are now being delivered as MD-80s. For specifications and further details, see pages 150-151.

Above: The Douglas Aircraft component of McDonnell Douglas is seriously investigating the promise of propfan technology as a means of propulsion for a new generation of commercial transports.

Below: A Pacific Southwest Airlines (PSA) MD-80 photographed by Bryant Petitt at San Francisco International. PSA is a major carrier on the San Francisco-Los Angeles commuter run, one of the world's busiest routes.

Above: A Scandinavian Airlines System (SAS) MD-80 marked with the crests of the three nations that participate in this multinational airline — Sweden, Norway and Denmark. Compare this with the SAS Douglas DC-6 on page 126.

Above: An MD-80 of the Civil Aviation Authority of China. In 1984 McDonnell Douglas struck a deal whereby MD-80s would be produced under license in China by the Shanghai Aircraft Industrial Corporation.

been the right plane at the right time for the commercial transport side of McDonnell Douglas. Plans were laid for the MD-88, which was similar to the MD-82 but powered with International Aero V2500 turbofans and available in 1989. Despite his dislike for the commercial transport business, James Smith McDonnell would have admired the MD-80. For Donald Wills Douglas, who launched the whole program with the DC-1 50 years before, the MD-80 would have been a source of pride.

The Other Douglas Transports

While the DC series was the main line of Douglas transports, serving both civilian and military customers, a parallel series of military-only transports was developing. The large four-engine Douglas transports, the DC-4 and DC-6, had their military alter egos in the C-54 Skymaster and C-118 Liftmaster, respectively. Late in World War II, with the DC-4/C-54 in service and the DC-6/C-118 under development, Douglas Long Beach turned to the idea of an even larger transport. The idea was mainly for a postwar airliner with intercontinental range, and Pan American went as far as to order 26 of them under the designation DC-7. The USAAF had also taken an early interest and the plane made its first flight under the military designation C-74 on 5 September 1945. Meanwhile Pan Am lost interest, canceled its order, and Douglas canceled the DC-7 designation to reserve it for later use.

The USAAF/USAF took delivery of 14 C-74s under the name Globemaster, a reference to the Skymaster and Liftmaster that preceded it and a commentary on the new bird's global range. In 1946 it was test flown at a gross weight of 86 tons, the greatest weight to have left the earth's surface under controlled power at that time. It was powered by four Pratt & Whitney R-4360-49 Wasp Majors delivering 3250 hp each. The C-74's range was 7250 miles, enough to circumnavigate the globe with only two stops. Self-contained electrical power units permitted crews to operate freight elevators and traveling electrical cranes inside the huge fuselage.

With the commercial version of the C-74 canceled, Douglas went to work on designing an even bigger Globemaster. There was no longer a need for pressurization (the C-74 was not pressurized though the DC-7 version would have been), and because of the canceled commercial order, huge clamshell doors were added to the front of the new Globemaster. Designated C-124, the Globemaster II had the same wingspan and almost the same length as the C-74, but its fuselage was twice as high. Its cavernous interior of over 10,000 cubic feet could swallow 200 troops and 94 percent of the Army's military vehicles, fully assembled, including tanks, field guns, bulldozers or an assortment of fully loaded vehicles. Where the C-74 had set a record with a gross weight of 86 tons, the C-124 could gross almost 100 tons.

The first C-124s (aside from a prototype rebuilt C-74) were 204 C-124As, the first of which were delivered in May 1950, a month before the start of the Korean War. Though they were not available in significant numbers until the last half of the war, the Globemaster IIs played an important role in the airlift of supplies to the Far East. They could airlift cargo of a size larger than that which could be handled by any other military transport. Beginning in the early 1950s the C-124As were retrofitted with the familiar nose radome designed to carry the APS-42 radar system. The C-124A was followed by a single YC-124B, which was experimentally fitted with four 5500-hp YT34-P-6 turboprop engines. It was considered for a time as a potential aerial tanker, but the idea was scrapped.

The C-124C, the final Globemaster II variant, was powered with four 3800-hp R-4360-63A engines, up from the 3500-hp R-4360-20s of the C-124A, but less than the power delivered to the YC-124B. There were 243 C-124Cs built, which were outwardly identical to the C-124A, but which had increased fuel and range and an AN/APS-42 nose radar. The C-124 arrived in small numbers for the Korean War, with its heyday to follow. By the time of the war in Vietnam, the Globemaster was being replaced by more modern aircraft. In the mid-1960s most of them had been transferred to Air National Guard and Air Force Reserve units, and the last of them were phased out by 1974.

Just as the C-124 had evolved from the C-74 in 1948, Douglas engineers were at work developing a successor to the C-124. The plane, which might have been called Globemaster III had it been built, combined the C-124 fuselage with swept wing and tail surfaces similar to those that would appear on the commercial DC-8. Designed to be powered by four turboprop engines, the project received the USAF designation C-132, but the program was dropped without a prototype being built.

By the time the C-132 program was passed over, Douglas had received an order for an even more advanced airlifter. Designated C-133 and called Cargomaster, the new aircraft went directly into production without building a prototype. The new plane, which first flew on 23 April 1956 under the power of four Pratt & Whitney T-34 turboprops, was roughly the same size as the C-124 but with several distinct differences. The C-133 had a circular fuselage with the wings mounted on the top rather than the bottom of the fuselage. The top-mounted wings, found on most major military transports since that time, placed the engines farther from the ground and thus farther from potential foreign-object damage (FOD) if the aircraft delivered supplies to some semi-prepared forward airfield in time of war. The C-133 could lift a bigger load than any Globemaster variant and could fly nonstop

Opposite and above: A C-124 sans radome loading a howitzer for delivery to Korea circa 1952 and a C-124 unloading a truck and trailer at Tuy Hao AB, South Vietnam in November 1966.

Below: A rare view of four C-74s during Operation Swarmer, circa 1949.

from Los Angeles to New York with a ton-mile-per-hour equivalent of 22 loaded railroad boxcars at a cost of about 5 cents per ton mile, comparable to the cost of surface transportation. The plane could accommodate over 96 percent of the items of equipment in the US Army including fully assembled tanks, and was used for delivery of the Douglas-built Thor Intermediate Range Ballistic Missile (IRBM). There were 35 C-133As built between 1954 and 1957, and 15 C-133Bs with clamshell doors built between 1959 and 1961. Ironically the C-133's service in the US Air Force ended before that of the C-124, with around six of them going into civilian service including one that was operated by NASA for many years to carry space boosters.

After the delivery of the last Cargomaster in 1961, Douglas did not design and build transports specifically for the military market for well over a decade. There had been military orders for every Douglas commercial transport from the DC-2 through the DC-6

Above: An early color view of a USAAF C-74 Globemaster I with the twin-canopy flight deck that it had in common with the B-42/B-43 and which was strongly disliked by pilots.

Below: A USAF Military Air Transport Service C-124C Globemaster II.

Opposite: A Douglas C-133B Cargomaster over San Francisco Bay with the Golden Gate Bridge, the Marin headlands and the village of Sausalito below.

but none for the DC-7 and DC-8, whose development began in the mid-1950s. Douglas made a pitch to sell the DC-8 to the Air Force as a freighter but the effort was unsuccessful. In the mid-1960s Douglas, like Boeing, lost out to Lockheed in the contest to win the Air Force contract to build the huge C-5 superairlifter. Both the losers in the C-5 sweepstakes applied the lessons learned in their C-5 programs to civilian projects, the 747 and DC-10, but there were no immediate military orders for either. Douglas (now a component of McDonnell Douglas) sold a few DC-9s to the military under the convenient C-9 designation, but the company's first all-military transport program since the Cargomaster came in 1972 in the form of the AMST. Under the Advanced Medium Short Takeoff and Landing Transport (AMST) program, the US Air Force invited both Boeing and Douglas to submit designs for a medium transport to replace the C-130 Hercules as a front-line combat-zone airlifter capable of taking off from short, unprepared runways.

Boeing and Douglas each built two prototypes, respectively designated YC-14 and YC-15. Both were high-winged aircraft with tall T-tails and wide fuselages. They were both larger than the C-130, though smaller than the heavy transports built by both

Above and opposite, from left: The evolution of Douglas military transports, the C-74 Globemaster I (Douglas Model 415A), the original C-124A Gobemaster II (Model 1129A) without radome, the C-124C (Model 1317) with AN/APS-42 radome and the C-133 Cargomaster (Douglas Model 1333).

	C-74 Globemaster I	C-124 Globemaster II	C-133 Cargomaster
Wingspan	173' 3"	174' 2"	179' 8"
Length	124' 2"	130' 5"	157' 6"
Height	43' 8"	48' 4"	48' 3"
Ceiling	21,800'	18,400'	19,000'
Range (mi)	1,200 (w/ max payload)	1,200	3,975
Gross weight (lb)	165,000	195,500	275,000
Max payload (lb)	56,000 or 200 pass.	68,500 or 200 pass.	80,000 or 200 pass.
Engine type	P&W R-4360-49	P&W R-4360-63	P&W T34-P-7WA (Turboprop)
Engine hp	3,000	3,800	6,500
Speed (mph)	325	304	359

Above: The McDonnell Douglas YC-15 Advanced Medium STOL Transport (AMST) painted in the camouflage colors it would have worn if it had been procured for service with the US Air Force.

Above: A US Air Force C-124C Globemaster II flying eastward across the city of San Francisco and San Francisco Bay on 16 February 1955.

Left: A former US Air Force C-133A after having been transferred to NASA for use during the Mercury manned-spaceflight program.

companies. The YC-15 was 123 feet 6 inches long and 42 feet 10 inches high with a wingspan of 110 feet 4 inches. The YC-14 was powered by two 51,000-lb-thrust General Electric CFG-50D turbo fans mounted above and forward of the wing, while the YC-15 had four 16,000-lb-thrust Pratt & Whitney JT8D-17 turbofans mounted in underwing pods. The YC-15, preferred by the Air Force, could take off from 2000-foot runways with a 27,000-lb payload and could make landing approaches at speeds as low as 90 mph. Testing of the four prototypes continued without a production contract issued to either company until 1979, when the Carter administration scrapped the AMST program entirely.

A year later, in October 1980, the Air Force issued a request for proposals for a new, larger transport known provisionally as CX

(Cargo, Experimental). The CX concept was for an aircraft in the DC-8/707/C-141 size class that could use the same rough forward airfields as a C-130, yet carry any of the types of equipment (though not as much of course) as the giant C-5. Thus, by utilizing inflight refueling, the CX could fly directly from the United States to a forward field anywhere in the world without the then current need to use an intermediate airfield to transfer the materiel from a C-5 to a C-130.

Proposal evaluation began in January 1981 and on 28 August 1981 the Douglas Long Beach component of McDonnell Douglas was awarded the contract to build the new transport under the designation C-17. The Douglas design met or exceeded all the Air Force design specifications. The maximum payload for the C-17 transport is 172,000 lb, with which the C-17 is able to take off from a 7600-foot airfield, fly 2400 nautical miles, and land on a small airfield in 3000 feet. The ferry range of the C-17, which also can be refueled in flight, is 5000 nautical miles. The aircraft's cargo compartment has a loadable width of 216 inches, a height of 162 inches (142 inches under the wing) and a loadable floor length of 87 feet. This length includes 19 feet of loading ramp that can be used for carrying 40,000 lb of cargo. The C-17 design includes a number of new technologies, not the least of which is a 25-degree swept wing with a supercritical airfoil, with fuel efficiency further enhanced by winglets. The four engines are new Pratt & Whitney 2037 turbofans, each producing 37,000 lb of thrust, mounted under the wings. They will be equipped with thrust reversers capable of deployment in flight. On the ground, a fully loaded aircraft can back up a 2.5 percent slope.

Using technology proven on the earlier YC-15 transport, the C-17 will use an externally blown flap system to greatly reduce final approach and landing speeds for routine short-field landings. With this powered lift system, the engine thrust is directed to double-slotted flaps to produce additional lifting force. The flaps will be made of titanium, using new-technology superplastic forming/diffusion-bonding techniques. The C-17 is designed to be operated by a cockpit crew of two and a single loadmaster. The reduced flight crew complement is made possible through the use of an advanced digital avionics system using six cathode-ray tube displays. This technology allows displayed data to be consolidated, reducing pilot eye scan requirements. In addition to normal in-flight information, the advanced displays present

Below: An R G Smith rendering of McDonnell Douglas C-17As unloading US Army hardware, including the M-1 Abrams main battle tank (center, foreground) at a remote forward landing strip. The C-17A can also haul either four UH-60 helicopters or a combination of two AH-64 and three OH-58 helicopters.

McDonnell Douglas C-17A		Gross weight (lb)	570,000
Wingspan	165'	Engine type	P&W 2037
Length	175'	Engine thrust (lb)	37,000
Height	55'	Max payload (lb)	172,200

aircraft systems status, necessary emergency procedures and normal checklists.

The C-17 combines airlift capability for outsize combat equipment that can now be carried only by the larger C-5, and short-field performance now provided only by the C-130. This means added airlift not only for direct delivery to austere forward bases, but also for high priority combat mobility within a theater of operations. Only 850 runways in the world can accommodate C-5s and C-141s, while the C-17 can utilize 19,000. In the cargo compartment, the C-17 can carry Army wheeled vehicles in two side-by-side rows, and jeeps can be carried in triple rows. The C-17 is the only aircraft that can airdrop outsize firepower such as the Army's new infantry fighting vehicle. Three of these armored vehicles comprise one deployment load for the C-17. Similarly, the Army's newest main battle tank, the M-1, can be carried in conjunction with other vehicles. The C-17, due in squadron service with the Military Airlift Command by the late 1980s, will continue in production at Long Beach into the 1990s, marking a half century of Douglas specialized military transports that began with the C-74.

184

THE TWO PATHS CROSS

A Giant in Trouble

Since the eve of World War II Douglas had been the General Motors of American aviation, the undisputed industry leader and one of the nation's industrial giants. Its founder, Donald Wills Douglas Sr had been described in 1943 by the great aviation pioneer Major Alexander de Seversky as the 'cornerstone of American airpower.' Douglas had steered a profitable course through the depression, emerging in 1939 with 7589 employees working in his southern California plants, up from 68 employees a decade before. Four years later, the Douglas payroll had increased twentyfold to 156,000 and included Betty Grable's sister, Carole Landis's mother and the famed dancer Ruth St Denis. The Douglas empire, headquartered at Clover Field in Santa Monica, California, then included operations in Chicago, Oklahoma City and Tulsa.

Don Douglas, a conservative perfectionist, took a personal interest in the day-to-day management of the company. He conducted much of his multimillion-dollar company's business by himself on the telephone. Fond of chocolate sundaes and privacy, Douglas was a man of habit and a loner. A cautious man, he shipped all his furniture to Salt Lake City at the start of World War II for fear that it might be damaged in Japanese bombing attacks. While other captains of industry might have been found on the party circuit in their off hours, Douglas would more likely have been found aboard his yacht, *Endymion*, or alone at home in his large Spanish-style house near Santa Monica, reading or playing his bagpipes.

A solid core of loyal and talented management people developed, which included long-time engineering vice-president A E Raymond, and it seemed that as long as the penny-pinching elder Douglas was at the helm the company did well. It survived the massive postwar demobilization as it had survived the depression. During the 1950s, however, Donald Douglas began to groom his heir apparent.

Born 3 July 1917, three years before his father started the company, Donald Douglas Jr was anything but a chip off the old block. Where Donald Douglas Sr was reserved, the younger Douglas was flamboyant and outgoing. He was not well liked by company old-timers. Raised in the shadow of greatness, he had been groomed all his life for only one thing. He studied engineering at Stanford and the Curtiss Wright Institute and went to work with the company in 1939, working his way to a vice-presidency

Above: Enjoying a good laugh in the Douglas executive lunchroom are Ted Conent, Donald Douglas, Earl Warren (then governor of California and later chief justice of the US Supreme Court) and A M Rochlen, who would later serve as vice president for production at Douglas.

Right: Donald Douglas in the final assembly area at the Santa Monica plant. It was from here that nearly all the Douglas commercial aircraft through the DC-7 went forth to conquer the world's airways. The heart of the Douglas empire for half a century, the huge Santa Monica facility that had grown up around Clover Field was bulldozed into the ground four years before Donald Douglas died in 1981.

after the war. In 1957, his father, heretofore president and chairman of the board, conferred the presidency upon his son and with it the burden of the family motto, *jamais arrière* (never behind).

The aggressive management style of Donald Douglas Jr came as a shock to many within the company who were used to the steady hand of his father. Between 1959 and 1962 there was a huge turnover in management, with no fewer than 10 vice-presidents abandoning ship. From the outside it was hard to tell who was steering the ship, because the older Douglas unexpectedly stepped in from time to time to veto one of his son's decisions. When the company slipped into the red in the late 1950s as a result of DC-8 development costs, it seemed as though the ship was about to flounder.

The major problem inherited by 'Junior,' as he was known throughout the company, was the failure in the early 1950s to gear up for jet transports. Boeing had seized the lead by several years and the DC-8 was Douglas's means to catch up. The DC-8 put heavy demands on the company's capital and other resources.

Above: Donald Douglas Jr (left, with foot raised) and his father (right, on lower step) after a 1958 tour of the brand-new DC-8 prototype.

Below: In 1947, Douglas took a tentative step into the business of executive jets for the general aviation market with the Model 1015. Nicknamed Cloudster, after the first Douglas airplane, only one of the little jets ever rolled off the Santa Monica assembly line. During World War II and the technology boom that accompanied it, many people were predicting widespread postwar private ownerships of small jets, but the predictions were premature.

Many millions that could be ill-afforded were poured into the project. Between 1957 and 1961 only 47 DC-8s were ordered, fewer than 10 a year, while Boeing sold 172 jet transports. But the company pulled through. This was due in part to Navy orders for the A4D Skyhawk and in large part to missiles and space programs, because by this time Douglas had the healthiest space systems divisions in the industry. Donald Douglas Jr closed the unneeded facility at El Segundo, and it began to look as though the company had successfully navigated hard times. The company's backlog of transport orders increased from $759 million in 1961 to over $2 billion in 1965—all of this on top of the space business.

In 1965 the DC-9 entered airline service. Contrasted to the DC-8 it was like a dream come true. It entered service two months ahead of schedule with 228 already on order, a total which would nearly double within a year. A short-range jetliner, the DC-9 was correctly predicted to be the most successful Douglas transport since the DC-3. Boeing had nothing in the same size and weight class and suddenly it was Boeing's turn to play catch-up. Its 737 was still two years away and the company was sent scrambling by the DC-9 phenomena.

Demand for the DC-9 was exceptional, but it was partly because of this success that serious problems arose for Douglas. The company expanded quickly to meet the demand, so fast that reserves of cash and manpower were strained to the limit. The DC-9 program took off so fast that the company lost control. The DC-9 was underpriced. When it had been planned two years earlier there had been a surplus of skilled manpower in Southern California. With an expanding economy and a war in Southeast Asia, there was a shortage of labor and expensive unbargained-for training programs had to be initiated. Because of the war, engines and subassemblies were suddenly more expensive and hard to get. In some cases, in order to get necessary parts, Douglas had to actually spend some of its dwindling cash reserves to *buy* the subcontractors. Delays in getting subassemblies caused long delays in getting DC-9s to customers and thus long delays in getting the customers' cash into the ever-draining company coffers.

Any company bringing out a new airplane has to expect to lose money on the first few units sold until costs are paid back and the new product turns a profit. In the case of the DC-9, Douglas had badly miscalculated. It figured on a unit loss of $750,000 on each of the first 20, but the company was reportedly facing a $1.25 million loss on each.

Above: Mr Mac, wearing a DC-10 tie and holding a model of his F-15, at the helm of the corporation in December 1979.

Above: Sanford McDonnell, security badge in place, on the flight line at the Douglas Aircraft component facility in Long Beach.

Another problem looming on the horizon was the $100 million in DC-9 development costs. For the 40 years that he ran the company, Donald Douglas Sr conservatively wrote off development costs as they occurred. Beginning in 1963, his freewheeling son changed this and began the practice of postponing the write-offs until the plane started to sell. Had it not been for this practice, the company would have shown a loss in 1965 when the impending storm was gathering. Instead, the DC-9 development costs were listed as an asset under deferred charges. It was hoped that the $100 million could be amortized at $200,000 per unit over 500 airplanes. With losses well above projections, this just wasn't possible.

In April 1966 the company closed its first quarter with a $4 million profit on paper due to the deferment of development costs. Its stock, which had averaged around $35 during the first half of 1965, was now up to $112. President Donald Douglas Jr said the company was 'in one of the most satisfactory phases in its history,' and his chairman-of-the-board father confidently

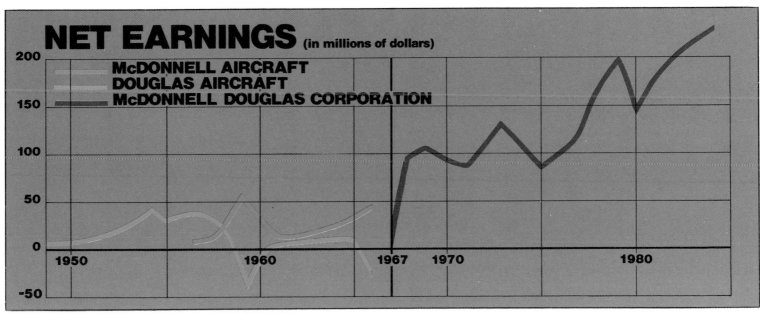

Davis–Douglas Aircraft Company

Partners
Douglas Davis and Donald Wills Douglas (1920–1921)

Douglas Aircraft Company

President
Donald Wills Douglas (1921–1928)

Douglas Aircraft Company, Incorporated

Chairman of the Board
Donald Wills Douglas (1928–1967)

President
Donald Wills Douglas (1928–1956)
Donald Wills Douglas Jr (1956–1967)

McDonnell Aircraft Corporation

President and Director
James Smith McDonnell (1939–1962)
David S Lewis (1962–1967)

Chairman and Chief Executive Officer
James Smith McDonnell (1962–1967)

McDonnell Douglas Corporation

Chairman
James Smith McDonnell (1967–1980)
Sanford McDonnell (1980–   )

Chief Executive Officer
James Smith McDonnell (1967–1971)
Sanford McDonnell (1971–   )

President
David S Lewis (1967–1970)
James Smith McDonnell (1970–1971)
Sanford McDonnell (1971–1980)
John F McDonnell (1980–   )

Honorary Chairman
Donald Wills Douglas (1967–1981)

McDonnell Douglas Corporation
(Douglas Aircraft Company component)

President
Donald Wills Douglas Jr (1967–1968)
Jackson McGowan (1968–1973)
John Brizendine (1973–1982)
James Worsham (1982–   )

McDonnell Douglas Corporation
(McDonnell Aircraft Company component)

President
Sanford McDonnell (1967–1971)
George Graff (1971–1982)
Donald Malvern (1982–   )

Above: An aerial view of the McDonnell Douglas building on Lakewood Boulevard in Long Beach. Douglas has been in Long Beach since World War II.

predicted a rosy future. The optimism was not to last. All the delivery problems that had plagued the DC-9 program were still there and, worse, the company was desperately short of cash. Investor confidence withered and the company's consortium of bankers began to tighten the strings on its line of credit. The first quarter profit turned to a $3,463,000 loss in the second quarter. The company's stock fell from $112 to $30 by October. The DC-9 was not the only problem; the company had run into trouble trying to match Boeing by bringing out too many versions of the DC-8.

The DC-9, however, was the key to any hope of salvation. If the development costs of this amazingly popular jetliner could have been overcome and the company run profitably long enough to build up cash reserves, then it would have been out of the woods. But this didn't happen until 1968 and the company needed $400 million in cash immediately to meet its commitments. A public offering was not an option. A $75 million company issue of convertible debentures wasn't selling, and advance payments from customers were out of the question. In November 1966 the Douglases flew to New York to consult with their bankers and look for investors. A few possible investors ranging from Howard Hughes to Laurence Rockefeller expressed interest but did not invest. The company's bankers insisted that the only solution that would address the long- and short-term problems would be a merger with a healthier company. Through their financial advisors, led by Stanley de Jongh Osborne of Lazard Frères, the Douglases invited merger prospects to submit proposals on 9 December 1966. North American Aviation, General Dynamics and McDonnell were invited. Lockheed and Chrysler declined and Martin Marietta asked to be included. On 12 December Signal Oil joined, through its aerospace subsidiary, Garrett, as did Fairchild.

The presentations began on 9 January 1967 and the companies with the weakest proposals gradually were weeded out. Of the three finalists, Signal was able to come up with cash, but was very weak in the management depth Douglas hoped to get from a merger. North American was a sentimental favorite. It was an established Southern California aerospace firm with many roots in common with Douglas. The facilities of the two firms were near each other and this practically invited collaboration. North American, however, was financially conservative and couldn't come up with enough cash.

The last contender was a frugal Scotsman from St Louis, who referred to himself through the entire negotiation process simply as Old Mac. James Smith McDonnell had wanted Douglas for a long time and had first suggested a merger back in 1963. By January 1967 he owned 300,000 shares of Douglas stock as against the 9000 shares owned by Donald Douglas Jr and Sr. His offer was to pay $43 cash for a million and a half shares of Douglas stock. As the bargaining went back and forth the price edged up with the final offer being $45.80 per share (the average closing price for the preceding 30 days), or $68,700,000 in cash.

At 3:30 pm on Friday the thirteenth of January 1967, Donald Douglas Jr telephoned Old Mac to tell him that the Douglas board of directors had unanimously accepted his offer.

The Scotsman from St Louis

James Smith McDonnell was once described as a man of remarkable foresight who kept an eye on the smallest details. He was a meticulous manager who built a hole-in-the-wall airplane parts factory into an industry leader. He built the biggest-selling combat aircraft since World War II as well as the capsules that carried the first dozen American astronauts into space. From a company that was expected to fold at the end of World War II, he built McDonnell into the largest employer in the state of Missouri by the time of the merger with Douglas. When it came time for the merger, the frugal Mr Mac did not have to borrow to put up the $68,700,000 and was easily able to arrange a $350 million line of credit for McDonnell Douglas from St Louis area banks.

Like Donald Douglas, Mac was a creature of habit, including working late at the office long after most of his employees had gone home. He was very active in the US Committee for the United Nations from 1953 and was its national chairman during 1955, its tenth anniversary year. A big promoter of both NATO and the UN, he was also chairman of the United Nations Association for two years, between 1975 and 1977. Active in civic affairs, he was founder and chairman of the McDonnell Foundation from 1949 until his death, and a member of many St Louis area councils throughout his career. He was recipient of the 1963 Guggenheim Medal and the 1966 Collier Trophy for superior achievement in aeronautics and astronautics.

The Aftermath of the Merger

The McDonnell Douglas merger became official on 28 April 1967 with James Smith McDonnell, 68, assuming the place at the head of the table as chairman of the board of directors and chief executive officer of the new McDonnell Douglas Corporation. The 74-year-old Donald Douglas Sr stayed on as honorary chairman of the board of the merged corporation. The McDonnell Aircraft Company and the Douglas Aircraft Company remained separate operating entities within the McDonnell Douglas corporation. Known briefly as divisions, they officially retained the suffix 'Company' though they are known informally and more descriptively within the company as

Above: McDonnell and Douglas together in the first-class section of a DC-10 during the May 1969 board meeting in Long Beach. This was a marriage of convenience and the relationship was frequently a tense one.

components. The space-related activities of the new corporation were combined into the McDonnell Douglas Astronautics Company with centers in Huntington Beach at St Louis.

Donald Douglas Jr, the 47-year-old son of the legendary plane-builder who ruled the Douglas Company for a decade, continued as president of the Douglas component until he was replaced a year later by Jackson McGowan, the former head of the Douglas Aircraft Division at Long Beach. The younger Douglas was vice-president for administration from 1968 to 1972 and served as corporate vice-president for a year after that. Though he continued on the board of directors of McDonnell Douglas, he had no position with the corporation after 1973.

The presidency of the McDonnell Douglas Corporation went to Mr Mac's heir apparent, David Lewis, from 1967 to 1970, after which Mac assumed the role as well as that of chairman and chief executive officer for a year. The first president of the McDonnell Aircraft component was nephew Sanford McDonnell. The son of Mac's banker brother (former chairman of the First National Bank of St Louis), William A McDonnell, Sandy was born in 1922 and joined his uncle's company in 1948. In 1957, after two years with the F-101 program, he became project manager, and in 1961 he became vice-president and general manager at the F4H (later F-4) Phantom program. Sandy McDonnell served as president of the McDonnell component for four years, and became corporate president in 1971.

On Friday, 22 August 1980, James Smith McDonnell died in St Louis and was succeeded as chairman of the board by Sanford McDonnell. Donald Wills Douglas Sr died five months later on 1 February 1981 and was not replaced. The two giants with over a century of aerospace leadership between them had folded their wings within half a year of one another.

DIVERSIFICATION

Missile Systems

Paralleling the development of their aircraft systems, both Douglas and McDonnell had been deeply involved in missile systems for 25 years before their merger. The first Douglas activities in the area of guided missiles began in 1940 with the development of the Roc I, an air-launched missile designed to fly down a radar beam. At the time, both the Roc and the radar that guided it were closely guarded secrets. Development of the 1000-lb Roc I continued into 1941 with an electric eye being used to guide the missile to light sources. The Roc II, which first appeared by 1943, was a television-guided air-to-ground missile and designed for use on a wide variety of bombers. Despite the early lead taken by Douglas in the guided-missile field, neither Roc was used in combat.

In the meanwhile, half a continent away in St Louis, McDonnell was developing a series of glide bombs known as Gargoyles. The McDonnell Gargoyle, which appeared in 1944, was cigar shaped, with short straight wings and a V-tail. By 1945, it evolved into a sleeker, powered version called Katydid, which was used as a target drone. A third development in this McDonnell lineage was the Kingfisher, which appeared in 1949. Like its two predecessors, the Kingfisher had short wings and a V-tail, but it was even longer and sleeker and, like the Douglas Roc, intended for an air-to-surface attack mission. It was designed for use against ships, and was air-launched with detonation underwater near the target. A fourth type of McDonnell air-launched missile was the Quail (US Air Force designation GAM-72), which appeared in 1958. Unlike its predecessors, the Quail was designed to be anything but sleek. It was about the size of a large refrigerator with a shape to match. Its flat sides and angular shape gave the Quail a prominent radar signature. The plump little birds were carried by Strategic Air Command B-52s and could theoretically be released by them to confuse enemy radar and to draw anti-aircraft fire away from the target-bound bombers.

After its initial experience with the Roc, most of the missile and rocket activity at Douglas was directed to the area of surface-launched missiles. A couple of notable exceptions were the development work on the airframe of the Sparrow 1 air-to-air missile in the early 1950s and production of the MB-1 (later AIR-2) Genie. The Genie, which first appeared in 1954, was an air-launched rocket designed to be carried by interceptor aircraft. The Genie had a 1.5-kiloton nuclear warhead and was the first nuclear-armed air-intercept rocket to be tested on 19 July 1957 over Yucca Flat, Nevada. The AIR-2 was 9 feet 7 inches long, weighed 820 lb, had a speed of Mach 3 and a range of 6 miles. Thousands of Genies came off the production line before it closed in 1962, with the durable rocket equipping both American and Canadian interceptor forces well into the 1980s.

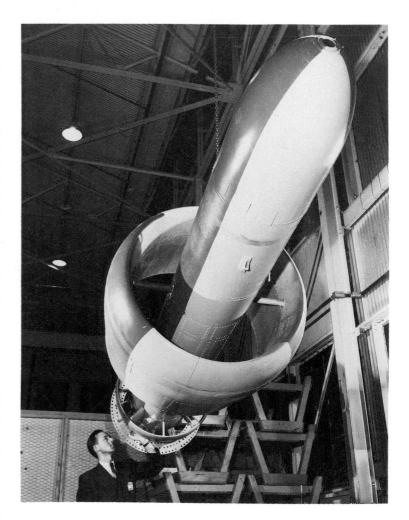

Above and opposite bottom: The Douglas Roc was the United State's first air-launched cruise missile, but it arrived too late for combat in World War II.

During World War II, Germany built and deployed the first real long-range surface-to-surface rocket in the IRBM/ICBM (Intercontinental Ballistic Missile) class, placing itself well ahead of the rest of the world. This system was the supersonic solid-fuel A-4IRBM, popularly known as V2 (Vengence Weapon, Second), which caused considerable damage during the war's final year. Though the United States did not have a comparable system ready for action for another decade, Douglas had an experimental system, the WAC corporal, ready for testing in 1948. Captured German V2s were also shipped to the New Mexico desert after the war and incorporated into American tests. On 24 January 1949 a German V2 was combined with a Douglas WAC Corporal in a two-stage unit known as a 'Bumper WAC' and launched high (250 miles) and faster (5000 mph) than any man-made vehicle before it.

Above: An early test launch of the Douglas Nike Ajax surface-to-air missile at White Sands Proving Ground in New Mexico.

Other experimental programs aside, the first major operational Douglas missile program was the Nike series. The idea of the Nike, which originated during World War II, was for a guided surface-to-air missile (SAM) that could shoot down an enemy aircraft with a higher degree of accuracy than antiaircraft artillery. The Army contracted with the Bell Telephone Laboratories of Western Electric in 1944 to build such a system. Bell Labs, which designed the radar and guidance systems, turned to Douglas, at the time the country's largest maker of aircraft, to build the missile and launching equipment. The first Nike Ajax missile site became operational in December 1953 at Fort George Meade, Maryland. Shortly thereafter Douglas undertook to open a plant at Charlotte, North Carolina specifically for building the Nike, and the first Charlotte-built Nike Ajax was delivered in July 1956. Named for the Greek winged goddess of victory, the

Left: The Douglas WAC Corporal atop a huge, finned German V-2 as the two-stage 'Bumper WAC,' and alone.

Right: The Douglas Thor IRBM went directly into production at Santa Monica without the prior delivery of a prototype.

Nike was 20 feet long in two stages with two sets of fins to provide stability in flight and permit steering to counteract evasive maneuvers of targeted enemy aircraft. The Nike was capable of supersonic speeds sufficient to catch any potential bombers of the era and destroy them with its high explosive warhead. The Nike Ajax, like the second generation Nike Hercules that Douglas first delivered in 1955, was managed by the US Army and was designed to be launched from highly mobile and air transportable batteries. The batteries were established near military bases and around major American cities for two decades until the American Government perceived that risk of attack by enemy bombers was no longer a threat, and scrapped the country's entire Nike system. They were still, however, in place in Europe and Japan into the mid-1980s.

To protect the nation against enemy missile attack, Douglas developed the Zeus (later Nike Zeus) three-stage nuclear-armed antiballistic missile (ABM). First tested in 1959, the system successfully knocked down California-launched Atlas ICBMs from sites on Kwajalein Atoll in the mid-Pacific. The Nike Zeus had been an important step in the development of the Safeguard ABM system that would have helped protect the country from ICBM attack. Development of the Safeguard program was, however, halted in the wake of the signing of the SALT I treaty of 1972.

At the same time the Nike Ajax SAM program was getting underway, the Army asked Douglas to build a surface-to-surface missile that could be used in lieu of conventional artillery. The resulting single-stage missile, called Honest John, was first test-fired in 1950. It was designed for use with either high-explosive or nuclear warheads and could be launched from a self-propelled mobile launcher.

While development of short-range missiles like the Genie, Nike and Honest John continued, Douglas and the Air Force were secretly developing America's first long-range missile, and the first IRBM to be deployed since the V2. Called Thor, this IRBM

was designed in the space of only eight months in 1956, and the first missile was delivered straight off the Santa Monica assembly line without a prototype having been produced. The rush was due to the fact that the Russians were building long-range missiles and the deployment of American ICBMs was still several years away. The Thor IRBM gave the US Air Force some breathing space until the advent of the ICBM, but it became a major part of the strategic nuclear arsenal of the Royal Air Force for a longer term. The first of the RAF's 60 Thor IRBMs arrived in England during the summer of 1958, along with Douglas-built support equipment. The Thor's 1500-mile range provided a more realistic deterrent force for Great Britain with its proximity to the Eastern Bloc than it did for the United States.

In 1959 Douglas was named prime contractor for another missile system that was intended to be shared by both the USAF and the RAF. Called Skybolt, the new missile was an air-launched strategic nuclear weapon with a 1000-mile range and thus an ancestor of the Air Launched Cruise Missile that was to enter the USAF arsenal 20 years later. The Skybolt was designed to be carried by both the USAF B-52 and RAF Vulcan bomber. In December 1962, however, the successfully tested Skybolt system was dropped by the US Government, with the British accepting the Polaris submarine-launched missile as a substitute.

While Douglas was expanding into the missile field, McDonnell's missile activities after development of the Quail were more limited. The McDonnell Alpha Draco in 1959 experimentally demonstrated lifting body flight previously unattainable at Mach 5 within the atmosphere. In 1963 McDonnell's ASSET re-entry research vehicle tested advanced metals and materials in gliding flights up to 18 times the speed of sound. Meanwhile McDonnell was producing airframes and integrated ramjet engines for the US Navy's Talos missile system. The Talos was a shipboard surface-to-air missile designed to protect the fleet from enemy aircraft. On 9 May 1972, during the wartime mine-laying operations at the approaches to North Vietnam's Haiphong Harbor, a Talos fired from a US Navy guided missile cruiser (CG-11) brought down a North Vietnamese MiG. This was the only North Vietnamese aircraft to be shot down by American ground fire during the war.

Subsequently, McDonnell Douglas had been involved in two other important missile programs which started out primarily as US Navy systems, but which are gradually becoming part of the Air Force as well. The McDonnell Douglas Astronautics Company is the prime contractor for the Harpoon antiship cruise missile. As of 1984 well over 2800 of 3440 Harpoons on order had been produced, and most of them were delivered to the US Navy as its basic fleetwide antiship missile. Harpoons have also been ordered by 12 allied navies and by the Air Force for use from B-52 bombers under the designation AGM-84. The Harpoon's re-usable canister launcher allows it to be launched from shore-based installations as well as virtually any type of ship. The US Navy has it deployed aboard 223 battleships (BB), guided missile cruisers (CG/CGN), destroyers (DD/DDG), frigates (FF/FFG), patrol hydrofoils (PHM) as well as below the surface aboard Nuclear attack submarines. Both the Navy and Air Force have deployed the Harpoon aboard aircraft, and the Navy used it with both the A-6 attack bomber and the P-3 antisubmarine patrol plane. The Harpoon's low-level sea-skimming cruise trajectory, counter-countermeasures, active radar guidance and effective

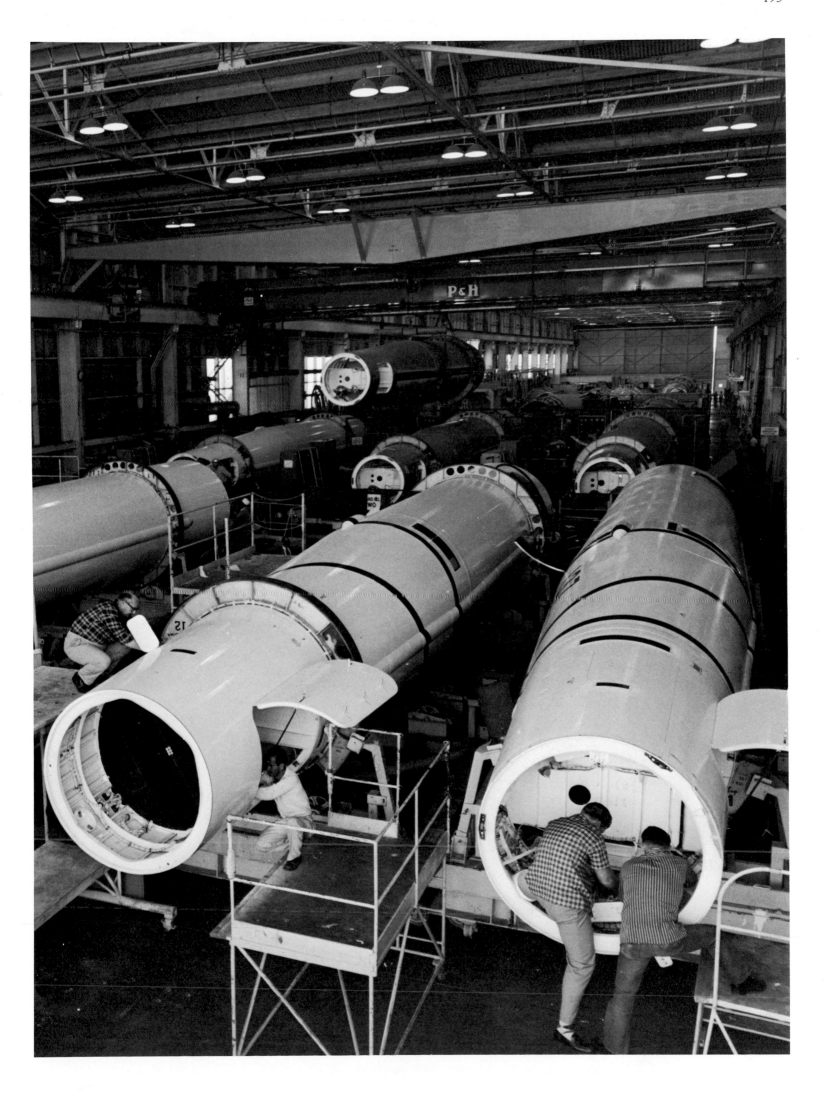

194

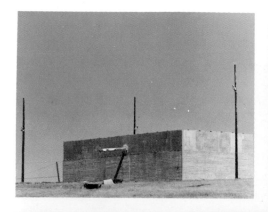
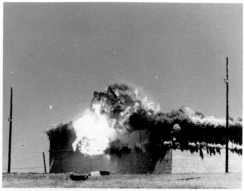

Top: A Tomahawk cruise missile impacts and destroys a concrete block house.

Above and opposite: McDonnell Douglas Astronautics Harpoon antiship missiles during tests from US Navy ships (including the USS *Fletcher* at right) off the Pacific Missile Test Center in California.

warhead design assure high survivability and kill probability. One of the most successful and widely deployed missiles in the Navy arsenal, the Harpoon demonstrated flight reliability greater than 95 percent. It was delivered under warranty by McDonnell Douglas.

The BGM-109 Tomahawk Cruise Missile project is actually a joint venture of McDonnell Douglas (Astronautics Division) and General Dynamics (Convair Division). McDonnell Douglas produces complete missiles at its Titusville, Florida facility. The Tomahawk is designed to fly at high subsonic speeds and low altitude, striking land targets at a range of up to 1550 miles and ship targets at a somewhat shorter range.

Separate guidance systems have been designed for antiship attack, land attack and airfield attack missions. The antiship guidance system is a development of the McDonnell Douglas Harpoon guidance system that includes longer radar search range, more computer memory and a passive target identification system.

The land-attack guidance system for Tomahawk uses a Digital Scene Matching Area Correlation System (DSMAC) using look-down radar to construct terrain-altitude profiles along a pre-selected path that it can match to computer-stored terrain profile data to keep the missile on its flight path. McDonnell Douglas has also developed and deployed the Theater Mission Planning System for the missile. It consists of computer and display equipment and application software with the capability to plan land-attack missions, generate and verify detailed route data and provide it to the DSMAC in the Tomahawk when a mission is to be flown.

In addition to major large-missile systems, McDonnell Douglas has been involved with lighter one-man missile systems. One example is the M-47 Dragon, of which the company built 50,000 units for the US Army and Marine Corps and a dozen other armies before 1977. The Dragon is an antitank assault weapon that can be carried by one man and be used to knock out tanks and other such armored vehicles at distances of nearly a mile. The 28.5-inch, 14-lb Dragon was packaged in its launch tube at the factory with the final unit still measuring a manageable 44 inches and weighing 31 lb. Five years after the last Dragon was produced, McDonnell Douglas was still at work, upgrading the first M-47s to extend their shelf life. The company also builds night sights and simulators for the Dragon.

The Shoulder-Launched Multipurpose Assault Weapon (SMAW) is a one-man recoilless rocket system very similar in appearance to the bazooka of World War II. Like the bazooka, it is designed for use during military operations in built-up areas and for attacking tanks and fortified positions. Based on the Israeli Military Industries B-300 (which is produced in the US under license by McDonnell Douglas), the SMAW uses a reusable smooth-bore fiberglass epoxy launching tube that can be operated for up to 100 rounds.

Douglas Experimental

By the end of World War II, aviation technology had developed to a point where it seemed possible to mount an attack on the mysterious and seemingly insurmountable sound barrier. In June 1945, with much valuable technical data flowing in from captured German files and the end of the war in sight, the US Navy contracted with Douglas to build a research aircraft to explore speeds just short of the speed of sound (Mach 1). With a project team including Leo Devlin, Bob Donovan and Ed Heinemann, Douglas began work in 1946 on its Model 558, a jet-powered aircraft designed to fly at speeds in the Mach .85 range and under pressures of 18 times the pull of gravity. The D-558, called Skystreak by the company, had short straight wings and a tail something like that of the Skyraider. Painted bright

red, the plane was occasionally referred to as the Crimson Test Tube, a commentary on the plane's function as a purely research aircraft and on its shape. Powered by a General Electric GE T-6-180 turbojet, the Skystreak first flew at what is now Edwards AFB on 28 May 1947. The Navy's plan was for a series of test flights, increasing the speed with each flight as data for the previous flights was evaluated. On 20 August 1947 the Crimson Test Tube captured the world's official speed record with a speed of 640.77 mph. Four days later Marine ace Major Marion Carl set a new speed record of 650.6 mph. Despite landing gear problems that delayed the program, the Douglas Skystreak had managed to get up to speeds of Mach .99, just short of the sound barrier. In October 1947, however, Chuck Yeager finally broke the elusive sound barrier in the US Air Force X-1 research plane built by Bell Aircraft.

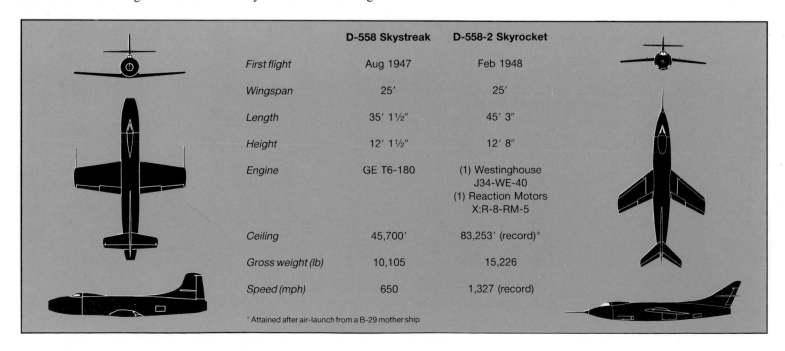

	D-558 Skystreak	**D-558-2 Skyrocket**
First flight	Aug 1947	Feb 1948
Wingspan	25'	25'
Length	35' 1½"	45' 3"
Height	12' 1½"	12' 8"
Engine	GE T6-180	(1) Westinghouse J34-WE-40 (1) Reaction Motors X:R-8-RM-5
Ceiling	45,700'	83,253' (record)*
Gross weight (lb)	10,105	15,226
Speed (mph)	650	1,327 (record)

* Attained after air-launch from a B-29 mother ship

Above left: The Douglas D-558-2 Skyrocket is dropped from a B-29 mother ship for its record-breaking supersonic flight.

Above: The Douglas X-3 Stiletto looked fast, but never achieved supersonic speeds because it was underpowered.

As tests continued with the D-558 Skystreak, Douglas went to work on its successor, the D-558-2 Skyrocket. Though the two research planes shared a Douglas model number, they had very little else in common. Where the Skystreak had been a stocky straight-winged bird, the Skyrocket was sleek with a swept wing. Painted white where the Skystreak had been red, the Skyrocket was powered by a combination of jet and rocket propulsion. The rocket was a Reaction Motors XLR-8-RM-5 and the jet (which was deleted midway through flight testing) was a 3000-lb-thrust Westinghouse JE34 WE-40. Despite bad relations between the two companies, Reaction Motors produced a rocket engine that put a Douglas plane through the sound barrier for the first time.

The Skyrocket flight testing, in which Ed Heinemann described the plane as sluggish, began in February 1948. It was not until the summer of 1949, with its jet removed, that the plane finally broke the sound barrier, but having done that, it went on to set a speed record of 1238 mph and an altitude record of 79,494 feet. In the beginning, the Skyrocket took off under its own power but on its record-breaking flights it was carried aloft aboard a B-29, like the Air Force X-1, and released at about 35,000 feet. The D-558-2 program helped the image of Douglas as a company on the leading edge of aviation technology and prompted the El Segundo engineers to come up with a design for a D-558-3. Presented as a proposal in May 1954, the D-558-3 could be released at 40,000 feet, climb into the ionosphere to altitudes in the range of 700,000

	Model 120	XV-1 Convertiplane
Rotor diameter	31'	31'
Wingspan	N/A	26'
Height	9'	10' 6"
Ceiling	N/A	17,500'
Range (mi)	6,300	5,391
Engine type	(3) AirResearch GTC-85-35 gas turbine compressors (3) McDonnell rotortip jet burners	(1) Continental R-975-19 radial (3) McDonnell pressure jets
Engine thrust (lb)	N/A	550 170
Speed (mph)	127	200

Above: The Douglas D-558 Skystreak was called the Crimson Test Tube because of its shape and because of its research mission.

Right: The Douglas D-558-2 Skyrocket turned in disappointing results when it took off from the ground, but became a supersonic success when air launched.

feet and reach a velocity many times the speed of sound. After purchasing three Skystreaks and three Skyrockets, the Navy declined the D-558-3 proposal. The US Air Force picked up the thread of hypersonic research aircraft a few years later, giving North American the contract for the X-15 rocket plane, the craft that accomplished what had been planned for the D-558-3.

In the meantime, Douglas had received a contract from the Air Force in 1949 to build a pair of supersonic research aircraft. Designated X-3 (Air Force Experimental, Third) by the Air Force and called Stiletto because of its knife-like shape, the plane first rolled out in 1952. If anything, the X-3 looked faster than either the Air Force's X-1 or the Douglas/Navy Skyrocket. Ultimately, however, the sleek ship with its pair of Westinghouse J34-WE-17 jet engines proved underpowered and barely able to reach Mach .98. Of two Stilettos that were ordered only one was built.

McDonnell Experimental

While Douglas, the builder of transports and attack planes, was researching supersonic flight, McDonnell, the builder of fast fighter planes, was researching the slowest of all heavier-than-air aircraft, helicopters. Though they never built a production helicopter, McDonnell made several important research helicopters in the years before it merged with Douglas. James McDonnell's interest in helicopters began in the spring of 1942 when his newborn company had yet to build its first aircraft. He bought an interest in Platt-Le Page Helicopters of Eddystone, Pennsylvania. A year later the McDonnell Helicopter Research Division, headed by long-time McDonnell associate Costia Zakhartchenko, was moved to St Louis and put to work on its first project, an experimental helicopter given the US Navy designation XHJD-1 (later XHJH-1 for Experimental Utility Helicopter, McDonnell). Nicknamed Whirlaway, the XHJH-1

had two main rotors mounted at the ends of short wings, like the German Focke Achgelis Fa 223 of World War II fame. When the single Whirlaway was completed in 1946, it was the largest helicopter ever flown—about 12 feet longer rotortip to rotortip than the Fa 223. It continued in service until 1951.

McDonnell's second helicopter venture was the tiny Little Henry (McDonnell Model 38), built for the US Air Force under the designation XH-20. Little Henry was only 12.5 feet long, 7 feet high and 5 feet wide. First flown in 1947, it weighed in at only 250 pounds, but it could lift 500 pounds and travel at speeds of 50 mph under the power of two 12-lb ramjet engines on the rotortips. Only one Model 38 was built and a two-seat Model 79 (USAF designation XH-29) was canceled without being built.

McDonnell's next excursion into the world of vertical flight was the company's Model 82, built for the US Air Force under the designation first of L-25 (since it was intended as a liaison aircraft), then later the helicopter designation of H-35 and finally XV-1 (for USAF, Experimental Vertical Takeoff Aircraft, First). The XV-1 was actually designed to have characteristics of both helicopter and airplane, thus was more appropriately described as a 'convertiplane.' Its first flight as a helicopter came on 14 July 1954; its first flight converting inflight from helicopter to

Above: The much modified McDonnell 188 STOL Demonstrator during tests in November 1968. It later wore airline colors, but never saw commercial service.

Left: The McDonnell 188 STOL prototype, a Breguet Model 941, as photographed over France in June 1964.

aircraft was in April 1955. Each of its three rotor blades had a ramjet engine located in the tip, permitting the blades to be shorter than if they had not been so equipped. A pusher prop was used for forward speeds over 100 mph. Two Model 82s were built, each designed to carry three passengers in addition to pilot and copilot. Though all flight tests were successful and the XV-1 managed to break a world helicopter speed record with a 200-mph forward speed, the engine was deemed underpowered in the face of advancing helicopter technology and the program was canceled in the summer of 1957.

As its other helicopter projects were being toyed with by the Navy and Air Force, McDonnell in 1951 proposed its Model 120 ship-to-shore flying crane to the US Marine Corps. Ordered under the Navy/Marine Corps designation XHCH-1 (Experimental Helicopter Crane, McDonnell, First), the government program was canceled before the prototype was built. The project was revived a few years later by McDonnell as a commercial venture and a prototype Model 120 was carried to completion. It was a small craft with a fuselage weighing only 171 lb but with powerful engines capable of lifting a 4500-lb load with either a cable winch or specially designed modular cargo pods. The Model 120 was really just a frame with an engine on top and a pilot on the front

fitted around the cargo module that could carry 12 people or 2 tons of cargo. Simplicity was the order of the day with the McDonnell 120. Engines could be charged in 5 minutes without tools. The three main engines, as well as the McDonnell designed rotortip ramjets could accommodate a variety of fuels. In one instance 13 pilots were checked out in just two days and in another eight Marine Corps pilots learned to fly the 120 in two hours.

Not all of McDonnell's activities in the field of vertical and short takeoff and landing (V/STOL) aircraft revolved around helicopters. In 1961 McDonnell approached the French firm Breguet Aviation with the idea of participating in the latter's STOL aircraft program. Breguet's Model 941 had been developed as a successful STOL aircraft, and McDonnell could see a potential market for such an aircraft in the United States. In June 1962 McDonnell obtained a license to manufacture and sell a Breguet 941 variant, the McDonnell Model 188, in the Western Hemisphere. The Model 188 was powered by four 1500-hp turboprop engines (the later 188H had 3400-hp turboprops) and could operate from rough unprepared landing strips of 500 feet and lift loads of over 12 tons. Successful tests of the Model 188 continued for several years, accompanied by an equally unsuccessful attempt by McDonnell to sell the STOL transport to either the US Army or Air Force. A secondary sales possibility, the commercial airlines, also proved fruitless. There was and is considerable talk about short-runway airports close to city centers served by STOL transports, but existing airports are too well established, and they are in areas that don't require STOL aircraft. Though the Model 188 operated in the colors of both Eastern and American Airlines as a demonstrator, it was never integrated into an airline fleet. It remained simply another in a long line of research aircraft that represented good ideas whose time had not yet arrived.

Spacecraft Systems

A decade before they merged, McDonnell and Douglas were moving toward cooperation of a totally different kind. Out of its experience with missiles in the 1950s Douglas was moving into the development of the huge launch vehicles that were to put America's spacecraft and her astronauts into space in the 1960s and later. Meanwhile, even before the launch of Russia's Sputnik in 1957, McDonnell was conducting research into the manned spacecraft. On 12 January 1959 McDonnell was selected by NASA to build America's first manned spaceship. The contract, issued on 13 February 1959, called for the construction of 12 one-crew-member space capsules (the total was later increased to 20) under Project Mercury. Just over two years later, on 5 May 1961, Navy Commander Alan Shepard made the first American manned space flight in a Mercury capsule. The 15-minute flight was followed on 21 July by a 16-minute flight with astronaut Virgil ('Gus') Grissom. A successful unmanned Mercury orbital flight took place in September, and on 20 February 1962, astronaut John Glenn became the first American to orbit the earth in space aboard a McDonnell Mercury capsule.

McDonnell had accepted an extraordinary challenge in tackling the Mercury program. Even though the company had long experience in the development of aircraft and missiles, space capsule development was in large part a new frontier. The company designed new methods of fusion-welding titanium and pushed beyond the state of the art in miniaturization. A super-clean 'white room' was established for the manufacturing of the capsules to prevent dust or corrosion from damaging the delicate components of America's first manned space ships. The 9000-square-foot white room, which incorporated an air-conditioning filtration system that removed dust particles down to a size of .3 micron, maintained a steady temperature of 74 degrees F with a relative humidity of not over 50 percent (to control perspiration and provide for dimensional control of materials). McDonnell assigned 125 quality-control personnel to the Mercury program and established a continuous quality audit. The result of McDonnell's desire for perfection was a series of capsules in which the first six American manned space flights took place, all of them successful. The bell-shaped Mercury capsules were 9 feet high with a width of 74 inches at the base and a weight of about 2000 lb. It was constructed of titanium, beryllium and nickel-based alloys with a beryllium heat shield to withstand the tremendous heat created by the friction of re-entry into the earth's atmosphere.

Even before the third of the six manned Mercury missions took place, NASA announced on 7 December 1961 that it had contracted with McDonnell for a second generation of manned space capsules. Called Gemini, the new two-man capsules were 11 feet high, 7.5 feet in diameter and weighed 3.5 tons. The cabin area of Gemini was 50 percent greater than the volume of Mercury. Where Mercury had been a research vehicle flown for the most part by automatic ground control with only secondary manual override from the astronaut, Gemini was a spacecraft designed primarily to be flown by its crew. An important part of the Gemini mission was to train astronauts to maneuver in space and to rendezvous and dock one spacecraft with another. All this was in anticipation of President Kennedy's announced goal of putting an American on the moon by the end of the 1960s. McDonnell had the first Gemini mock-up available for NASA inspection on 29 March 1962 and on 2 April 1963 NASA officially ordered 13 flight-rated Gemini spacecraft, two mission simulator trainers and eight nonflying spacecraft for ground tests. The first of the flight-rated spacecraft (Gemini 1) was delivered to Cape

Above: A McDonnell two-place Gemini space capsule being hoisted into place atop a Titan launch vehicle during tests in May 1964.

Above right: Four of the first seven Mercury capsules under construction at the McDonnell 'white room' in St Louis.

Canaveral by McDonnell on 4 October 1963 and the first simulator was delivered on 13 December. The first unmanned Gemini test was successfully conducted on 8 April 1964.

The first manned Gemini mission, Gemini 3, came on 23 March 1965 and Virgil Grissom and John Young were the first space crewmen to change the orbit of a spacecraft from on board. There were five Gemini missions flown during 1965, culminating with the flights of Gemini 6 and Gemini 7, which resulted the first rendezvous between manned spacecraft in history. Gemini 7 was launched first, on 4 December, with Frank Borman and James Lovell aboard, and Gemini 6 was launched 11 days later, with Walter Schirra and Tom Stafford flying it to a rendezvous the

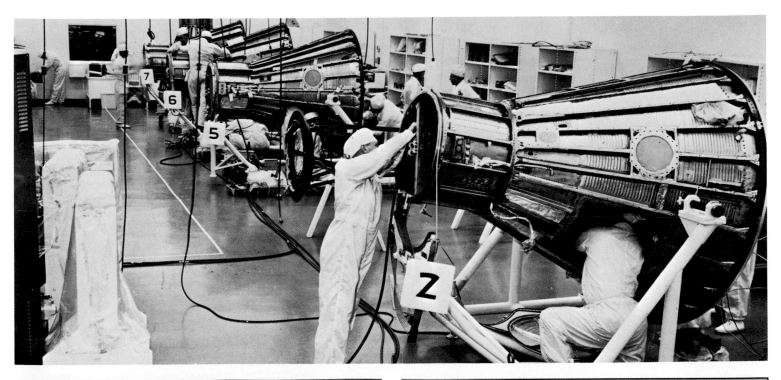

Manned Flights of McDonnell Douglas Spacecraft

Spacecraft	Launch Date	Astronauts	Flight Duration
Mercury 3	5 May 1961	Alan Shepard	15 min
Mercury 4	27 July 1961	Virgil Grissom	16 min
Mercury 6	20 Feb 1962	John Glenn	4 hrs 55 min
Mercury 7	24 May 1962	Scott Carpenter	4 hrs 56 min
Mercury 8	3 Oct 1962	Walter Schirra	9 hrs 13 min
Mercury 9	15 May 1963	L Gordon Cooper	1 day 10 hrs 20 min
Gemini 3	23 Mar 1965	Virgil Grissom John Young	4 hrs 53 min
Gemini 4	3 June 1965	James McDivitt Edward White	4 days 1 hr 56 min
Gemini 5	21 Aug 1965	L Gordon Cooper Charles Conrad	7 days 22 hrs 56 min
Gemini 7	4 Dec 1965	Frank Borman James Lovell	13 days 18 hrs 35 min
Gemini 6	15 Dec 1965	Walter Schirra Thomas Stafford	1 day 1 hr 51 min
Gemini 8	16 Mar 1966	Neil Armstrong David Scott	10 hrs 41 min
Gemini 9	3 June 1966	Thomas Stafford Eugene Cernan	3 days 21 min
Gemini 10	18 July 1966	John Young Michael Collins	2 days 22 hrs 47 min
Gemini 11	12 Sept 1966	Charles Conrad Richard Gordon	2 days 23 hrs 17 min
Gemini 12	11 Nov 1966	James Lovell Edwin Aldrin	3 days 22 hrs 34 min

Mercury Spacecraft

Spacecraft height (Mercury Atlas 3-4, Mercury Redstone 3-4)	9'
Spacecraft height (Mercury Atlas 5-9)	9' 6"
Escape tower height	16'
Base diameter	6'
Weight (lb)	Variable (2000-3000)
Material	.01" titanium skin with an ablative fiberglass heat shield

Gemini Spacecraft

Height (Manned Re-entry Module)	18.4'
Height (Aft Adapter Module)	19'
Diameter (Adapter Module Base)	10'
Diameter (Adapter/Re-entry Module Junction)	90"
Diameter (Top of Re-entry Module)	39"
Weight (lb) (Re-entry Module)	Variable (7,000-8,374)
Weight (lb) (Adapter Module)	4,400
Material (Re-enttry Module)	Titanium structure with forward section skin of beryllium and cabin section hatch covered with nickel alloy
Material (Adapter Module)	Frame of magnesium, aluminum and titanium with magnesium skin

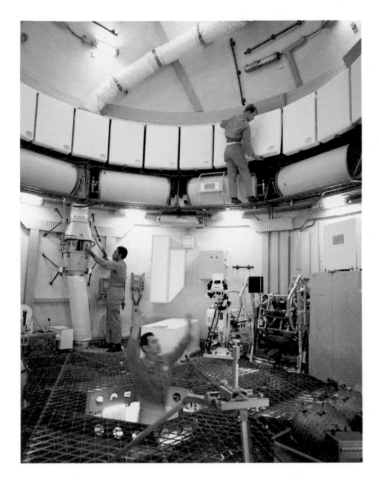

same day. Gemini 6 promptly returned to earth after six orbits, but Gemini 7 stayed in orbit for nearly two weeks, making a record 206 orbits around the globe. It was a record of 330 hours 30 minutes that was not equalled for five years. It was a McDonnell spacecraft that supported Americans in space longer than any of the Apollo moon missions (the longest of these was Apollo 17, which lasted 302 hours). The next time Americans were in space for longer than 300 hours was in 1973 aboard the Skylab space station, also a McDonnell Douglas product.

Skylab, America's First Space Station

McDonnell Douglas had a good record in space going into the Skylab program. The Mercury program had been successful and the Gemini program put 20 astronauts into space in 20 months and brought them back safely. The Skylab program demonstrated that mankind could live and work in space for extended periods of time.

Designed and built by McDonnell Douglas Astronautics, Skylab was placed into earth orbit on 14 May 1973. It was a cluster of four units, three of them habitable. These included the Orbital Workshop (OWS), containing the principal crew quarters and work areas; the Airlock Module (AM), containing the station's control and monitoring center as well as access to the outside for extravehicular activity; the Apollo Telescope Mount (ATM), a solar observatory; and the Multiple Docking Adapter (MDA), which contained docking ports for the Apollo spacecraft that brought astronauts to Skylab as well as controls for the ATM and other scientific equipment. The OWS was a converted McDonnell Douglas Saturn IVB rocket stage 21.6 feet in diameter and 48.1 feet long, divided into two stories. The upper of these was equipped with such items as foodlockers, refrigerators, water tanks and space-suit lockers. The lower story contained crew quarters and an experiment station. The habitable volume of the OWS was more than 10,000 cubic feet.

Facing page: Two astronauts enter a Gemini capsule at Cape Kennedy.

Above left: McDonnell Douglas Astronautics engineers simulate astronaut activity within the Skylab space station's orbital workshop.

Above: The McDonnell Mercury capsule *Freedom 7,* America's first spacecraft.

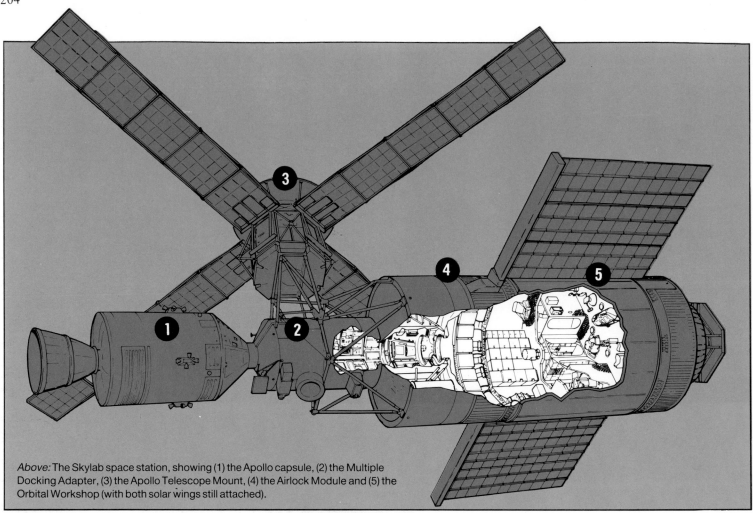

Above: The Skylab space station, showing (1) the Apollo capsule, (2) the Multiple Docking Adapter, (3) the Apollo Telescope Mount, (4) the Airlock Module and (5) the Orbital Workshop (with both solar wings still attached).

The AM, with a volume of 622 cubic feet, was 17.6 feet long, 10 feet in diameter and permitted access to the exterior without the need to depressurize the entire station. The MDA, just a few inches shorter than the AM, was the control center for the ATM, the first orbiting solar observatory controlled by men in outer space, although ground control was exercised during crew sleep periods and when the station was not staffed.

The objectives of the Skylab program were to evaluate the long-term effects of spaceflight on people and equipment, to conduct scientific observations of both the earth and sun, and to provide information for the development of future space stations. Scientific equipment included instruments for White Light Coronagraphy, an Ultraviolet Scanning Polychromator-Spectroheliometer, an Extreme Ultraviolet and X-ray Telescope, an X-ray Spectrographic Telescope, and a Chromospheric Extreme Ultraviolet Spectrograph—all to fit in the ATM alongside the cameras and film. The MDA contained equipment for space-manufacturing experiments and externally mounted Earth Resources cameras and experiments, including a Multispectral Photography Facility, Earth Terrain Camera, Infrared Spectrometer, Multispectral Scanner, Microwave Radiometer/Scatterometer and Altimeter, and an L-Band Microwave Radiometer.

During the unmanned launch of the station, a meteoroid/thermal shield ripped loose from the OWS, severing one of the two major solar 'wings,' or power-generating panels. Temperatures inside the station were raised to uninhabitable levels and electrical power was cut drastically.

The first crew of astronauts arrived at Skylab on 25 May 1973, 10 days after it was put into space. They were able to repair the durable space station so that it would be habitable not only for them, but for two Skylab crews that followed them. The first crew to man Skylab, Charles Conrad, Joseph Kerwin and Paul Weitz, lived in the station for 28 days. The second group, Alan Bean,

Owen Garriott and Jack Lousma, arrived on 28 July 1973 and stayed for nearly 60 days, while Gerald Carr, Edward Gibson and William Pogue arrived on 16 November 1973 and stayed for 84 days.

The McDonnell Douglas Skylab, even though severely damaged at launch, proved that it had the systems to support human beings in outer space for 172 days in relative comfort. Had the original three manned Skylab missions been followed by more, and had Skylab not been allowed to re-enter the earth's atmosphere in July 1979, the station could have been resupplied to support even more crews.

Launch Vehicles

While McDonnell was building the Mercury and Gemini spacecraft that would take the first Americans into outer space, Douglas was at work on the other end of the mission, developing the launch vehicles that would put the spacecraft into space. The launch vehicle program developed out of the Douglas Thor IRBM project and became the cornerstone of not only the McDonnell Douglas aerospace effort but of the whole American space program.

The two major McDonnell Douglas launch vehicle programs have been Saturn and Thor/Delta. The Saturn launch vehicles were developed during the middle to late 1960s when NASA was working to put an American on the moon and deploy its first space station, Skylab. The Saturn program began with the Saturn S-1 launch vehicle for which Douglas built the upper stage, designated Saturn S-4. Ten S-1s with Douglas S-4 upper stages were launched between October 1961 and July 1965, with a then unprecedented 100 percent success rate. They were used to place both satellites and unmanned 'boilerplate' test replicas of the Apollo spacecraft into earth orbit.

The Skylab space station as it was seen by the first Skylab crew as they departed in June 1973.

Above: A McDonnell Douglas Saturn 1B lifts off from Kennedy Space Center on 25 May 1973 carrying the manned Apollo/Skylab 2 spacecraft into space.

The Saturn 1 program was followed by the Saturn 1B program, which utilized upgraded elements of the Saturn 1 vehicle and offered 50 percent greater payload capacity than the Saturn 1. The Saturn 1B had a Chrysler first stage and a Douglas S-4B upper stage, and was first used on 26 February 1966 to place an unmanned Apollo test capsule into orbit. The Saturn 1B was used throughout the early Apollo tests and for the first manned Apollo mission (Apollo 7) in October 1968. Overshadowed by the Saturn 5 through the height of the Apollo program, the Saturn 1B made a comeback in 1973 as the launch vehicle that took all three Skylab crews to the space station. The ninth and last flight of the 100 percent successful Saturn 1B and of the whole Saturn program came in July 1975 with the launch of the Apollo component of the historic US/USSR Apollo/Soyuz rendezvous in space.

The Saturn 5 was the successor to the Saturn 1B launch vehicle and was the vehicle used for all of the Apollo lunar missions. It was much larger than the Saturn 1B by twice the height and six times the weight. Boeing was the prime contractor for the first stage and Rockwell for the second; McDonnell Douglas supplied the S-4B third stage, which was basically the same as the S-4B used in the Saturn 1B. Development of the Saturn B began in January 1962, and it was first used on 9 November 1967 to launch the unmanned Apollo 4 test capsule. A total of 15 Saturn 5s with Huntington Beach-built S-4B third stages were produced, and 13 were used for 13 successful missions, including all Apollo lunar landing missions.

The S-4B third stage was fired approximately 8 minutes and 30 seconds after lift-off of the Saturn 5 vehicle, when the first two stages had dropped off. It was fired for about 150 seconds, with its initial task to place the Apollo spacecraft into earth orbit. After one or two earth orbits, the S-4B (which could be stopped and restarted in space), was firing up a second time for about 5 minutes to send the Apollo on its way to the moon. Having established the necessary velocity to reach the moon, the Apollo jetisoned the S-4B and the two continued to the moon separately. The last use of Saturn 5 came with the launch of the Skylab space station in May 1973.

One of the most successful American launch vehicle programs, Delta, developed out of the Douglas Thor IRBM. The Thor itself was used as a launch vehicle and was used as a first stage, with a USAF Able second stage, to put NASA's first (and America's fifth) satellite, Pioneer I, into orbit on 11 October 1958. The Thor-Delta combination was first successfully tested in May 1960 and used operationally in August of that year to

Saturn IB Second Stage (Saturn V Third Stage)	
Height	58' 5"
Diameter	21' 8"
Launch weight (lb)	230,000
Empty weight (lb)	24,800
Propulsion engine type	Rocketdyne J-2 restartable engine
Propellants	Lox/liquid hydrogen
Thrust (lb)	215,000
Burn time (secs)	294
Guidance and control	Three-axis thrusters

put the Echo 1 satellite into orbit. Though Thor was discontinued as an IRBM in 1963, it continued to be used as a launch vehicle, primarily by the US Air Force, until 1981. During this time it was used for 500 launches, a record number for an American launch vehicle. The Delta series of launch vehicles, originally Thor Delta, grew out of a Thor first stage with nine Thiokol Castor 'strap-on' solid fuel boosters attached to the base. The first NASA use of Thor Delta was in August 1960, the Thor-Augmented Delta (TAD) in 1964 and Delta (DSV-3C) in 1966. Since then the Delta 1914, 2914 and 3914 series have been among the most important launch vehicles in use by the US Air Force and NASA.

McDonnell Douglas in Space

With a legacy of spacecraft that includes Mercury and Gemini and a heritage of launch vehicles like Saturn and Delta, it is only natural that McDonnell Douglas continues to be a cornerstone of the American space program. While the centerpiece of that space program is the space shuttle, for which Rockwell is the prime contractor, McDonnell Douglas is involved in many of the systems used in conjunction with the shuttle. As a subcontractor to Rockwell, McDonnell Douglas has supplied a number of important subsystems for the space shuttle Orbiter Vehicles themselves. These include the Orbital Maneuvering Subsystems (OMS) that provide thrust for putting the shuttle into orbit, for circulation, orbit transfer, rendezvous and re-entry. Another McDonnell Douglas component is the Aft Reaction Control Subsystem (ARCS) that operates with a Forward Subsystem (FRCS) to provide attitude control for the Shuttle during orbital flight and re-entry. The company has provided a variety of systems for the shuttle launch vehicle as well.

McDonnell Douglas has also developed a line of Payload Assist Modules (PAM), a special type of upper stage, to boost satellites into higher orbit from the space shuttle or from launch vehicles such as the McDonnell Douglas Delta. The PAM-A was developed for use with the Atlas Centaur class launch vehicle, while the PAM-D was developed for the Delta. A special PAM-D2 was developed for use aboard the space shuttle, raising geosynchronous orbit capability for satellites to 4160 lb.

In 1977 McDonnell Douglas established the Electrophoresis Operations in Space (EOS) project to explore the processing of materials in the weightlessness of space. The effort centers around the separation of materials in solution by subjecting them to an electrical field. A continuous stream of biological material is injected into a liquid buffer solution flowing through a thin rectangular chamber. When an electrical field is established, the desired materials are pulled apart into separate streams that flow to the top of the chamber for collection. The reason for the EOS project is that scientists had determined that cures or improved treatment of some diseases might be possible using certain natural human cells, enzymes, hormones or proteins. Although these materials can be separated from other biological materials on earth, the separation process is impeded by gravity. If done in the weightlessness of space, it is theoretically possible to separate larger quantities with greater purity.

The first EOS separation experiment device went into space aboard the space shuttle in July 1982. After four flights it was determined that the EOS could produce the desired pharmaceuticals in much larger quantities than on earth and with four times the purity. Initially, NASA furnished space-shuttle flight time for the experimental and precommercial prototype operations of the EOS device under terms of the Joint Endeavour Policy. Under this agreement McDonnell Douglas processed

Above: McDonnell Douglas technician Charles Walker closing the biological sample container of the EOS experiment aboard space-shuttle mission 41-D in September 1984.

samples of interest to NASA researchers. Initially, on the sixth shuttle flight, EOS separated a quantity of hemoglobins for NASA scientists in a study of the fundamentals of fluid dynamics in space.

Beginning in 1984, with commercial production imminent, McDonnell Douglas and the EOS project became paying customers of NASA's space-shuttle program. By the end of 1985, EOS pharmaceutical processing capacity had grown from the initial 500-lb prototype to a 5000-lb unit capable of processing 24 times the capacity of the prototype. The ultimate outcome of the EOS project, if it continues to demonstrate its practicality, will be a full-scale production plant in earth orbit by the early 1990s. On 30 August 1984, McDonnell Douglas engineer Charles Walker became the first ticket-holding passenger in the 25 years of manned spaceflight. He was sent by McDonnell Douglas into space aboard the maiden flight of the shuttle *Discovery* to operate the EOS separation device for McDonnell Douglas. Walker was the first astronaut ever to represent a private company in space.

A Myriad of Other Products

Both Douglas and McDonnell are known first and foremost for their aircraft. Secondly, they are known for their missile and space systems, but also of importance is a vast array of other products for which they are less well known. For example, Harry Gann of Long Beach, who probably knows

McDONNELL DOUGLAS SYSTEMS IN THE NASA SPACE SHUTTLE

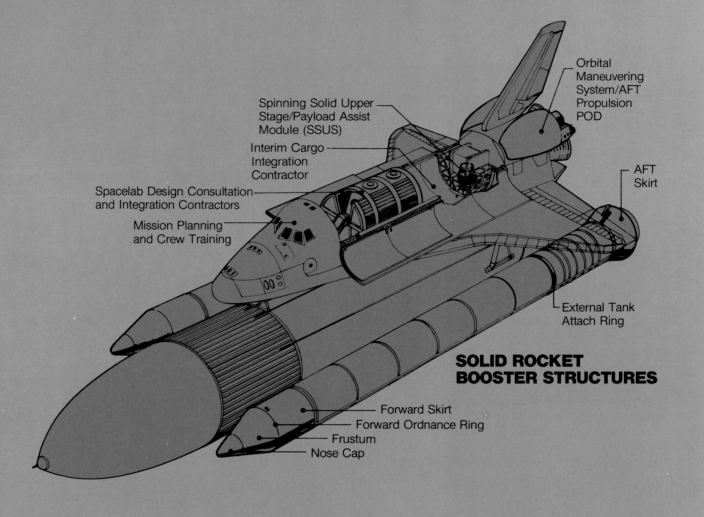

Orbital Maneuvering System/AFT Propulsion POD

Spinning Solid Upper Stage/Payload Assist Module (SSUS)

Interim Cargo Integration Contractor

AFT Skirt

Spacelab Design Consultation and Integration Contractors

Mission Planning and Crew Training

External Tank Attach Ring

SOLID ROCKET BOOSTER STRUCTURES

Forward Skirt
Forward Ordnance Ring
Frustum
Nose Cap

MDAC PAYLOAD ASSIST MODULE PROGRAMS

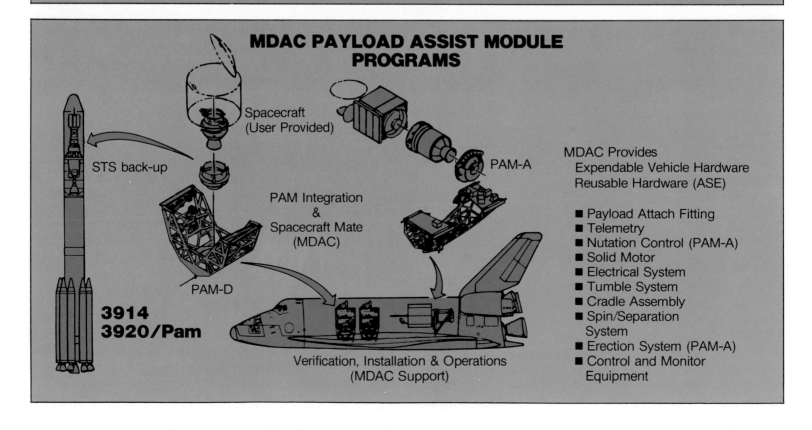

Spacecraft (User Provided)

STS back-up

PAM-A

PAM Integration & Spacecraft Mate (MDAC)

PAM-D

3914 3920/Pam

Verification, Installation & Operations (MDAC Support)

MDAC Provides
Expendable Vehicle Hardware
Reusable Hardware (ASE)

- Payload Attach Fitting
- Telemetry
- Nutation Control (PAM-A)
- Solid Motor
- Electrical System
- Tumble System
- Cradle Assembly
- Spin/Separation System
- Erection System (PAM-A)
- Control and Monitor Equipment

as much about Douglas as anyone now living, reckons that Douglas built more bomb racks than any other company ever.

Toward the end of World War II, the Navy sought to develop a supplier other than Goodyear to build some of its patrol dirigibles. Douglas was asked to submit a design. Douglas didn't really want to get into the airship business, but its engineers worked up a design anyway. Much to their surprise, the design was accepted over the design submitted by Goodyear. Still not wanting to be in the airship business, Douglas turned the blueprints and Navy contract over to Goodyear for production.

A good early example of a Douglas nonhardware activity is the Rand Corporation. Rand Corporation, known for its work as a strategic policy think tank, began during World War II as Project RAND. It is named not for a person called Rand but is an acronym for Research and Development. The project began with General Henry ('Hap') Arnold, wartime commander of the US Army Air Forces, who was a strong believer in the integration of advanced scientific thought into strategic policy and weapon systems development. Arnold asked his friend Donald Douglas to set up and operate the supersecret Project RAND under the umbrella of the Douglas Aircraft Company, which he did. RAND began by developing long-term strategic policy and weapons systems by entering economic, political and social factors as well as military factors into the equation.

In May 1946, RAND issued a report calling for development of an 'experimental earth orbiting spaceship.' In the mid-1940s such an idea raised a lot of eyebrows in official circles, but it was also taken seriously. Ten years and seven months later the United States put its first experimental spaceship into space. Another early RAND study called for basing strategic bombers in the United States rather than overseas and developing aerial refueling. These ideas were somewhat unorthodox at the time, but have proven themselves over the years.

By 1948, however, RAND had evolved into such an important institution that the Air Force decided to set it up as an independent entity to avoid any accusation of a conflict of interest. Thus RAND and its staff were transferred from Douglas to the independent Rand Corporation, which still has its headquarters in Santa Monica.

During the next two decades both Douglas and McDonnell developed and produced a wide variety of products and services, ranging from tiny isotope batteries to the EROS Airborne Collision Avoidance System. After the 1967 merger the company continued to diversify its product line. Its Hycon subsidiary produced the cameras that the Apollo spacecraft used to photo-map the moon's surface, while on the earth's surface McDonnell Douglas Astronautics was developing its Cryo-Anchor arctic soil stabilizer for use with the structural supports on the Alaska pipeline. The product, based on heat-pipe technology, stabilizes the temperature of the ground in which the pipeline is anchored to prevent the expansion and contraction produced by freezing and thawing from breaking the pipeline.

The EOS project for developing pharmaceuticals outside the earth's gravity is another example of the diversification of the activities and interests of McDonnell Douglas.

Flight Simulators

Out of the design of aircraft came the design of an aircraft flightdeck simulator for pilot training. McDonnell Douglas built simulators for the Douglas DC-8, DC-9, DC-10 and MD-80 as well as the Boeing 727, 737, and 747 and Lockheed C-5. With the McDonnell Mercury and Gemini spacecraft came cockpit simulators for both. Ultimately the company found

itself building locomotive cab simulators for the Southern Pacific Railroad.

McDonnell Douglas has developed the Vital visual flight simulation system which gives the pilot of the simulator a realistic computer-generated video replica of the view he would have from a real aircraft. Day, night, dawn and dusk are produced to meet operational training requirements. Features such as airport and area lighting, fog, clouds, lighting, terrain features, military targets and weapons effects are created in color with very high resolution. More than 200 Vital systems are in service with more than 30 commercial airlines and military services of 21 countries. The McDonnell component at St Louis has developed the Air Combat Maneuvering Simulator (ACMS) for training F-4 and F-14 pilots and the Manned Air Combat Simulators (MACS) system in support of training for the F-15, F-18, A-18 and AV-8B combat-aircraft programs. Five MACS simulators can be flown simultaneously as combatants in a simulated air battle. In one MACS, as many as 12 aircraft can be visually simulated for the battle along with terrain and weather features. Four of the MACS are located in domed rooms, where the interior surface serves as a projection screen. In simulated flight the earth, sky and other aircraft recede from or approach the simulator cockpit in concert with the pilot's movement of the controls. An advanced computer insures that all scenes and images match what the pilot would see if he were actually airborne.

Commercial Financing and Leasing

In 1962 A V ('Vic') Leslie came to Douglas as chief financial officer, having served as such for both Hughes Tool and Trans World Airlines. Vic Leslie was instrumental in setting up the Douglas Finance Corporation to help potential commercial aircraft buyers finance their purchases. Known as McDonnell Douglas Finance Corporation (MDFC) since 1967, this subsidiary is still an important part of the McDonnell Douglas Corporation and the only subsidiary issuing its own separate annual report. In 1983 MDFC earned a total of $20.3 million, with investments in receivables and leases of $999.3 million. Roughly 43 percent of the total financing portfolio was related to financing McDonnell Douglas aircraft, with the balance consisting of other commercial and industrial financing. The diversification of MDFC itself resulted in its 1983 purchase of Brind Leasing, a Philadelphia full-service truck-leasing company that in turn bought Riteway Rentals, a New Jersey-based truck lessor.

Computer Services

Starting with punch-card computing systems in the 1930s, up through the establishment of the McDonnell Automation Center in 1960 and the subsequent McDonnell (McDonnell Douglas after 1967) Automation Company, this has been a corporation and industry where computer support has been vital. McDonnell Douglas Automation Company, generally known by its registered trade name McAuto, is one of the largest commercial data-processing companies in the world, with over 7700 employees in data centers and offices worldwide. For example, one out of five hospitals in the United States uses its services. McAuto's repertoire includes computer processing, software, professional services and turnkey systems that combine hardware purchased from other companies with McAuto-developed software. Among the services provided by McAuto are inventory control and distribution for the Hartford Insurance Group, computer-aided design and manufacturing for Britain's Cranfield

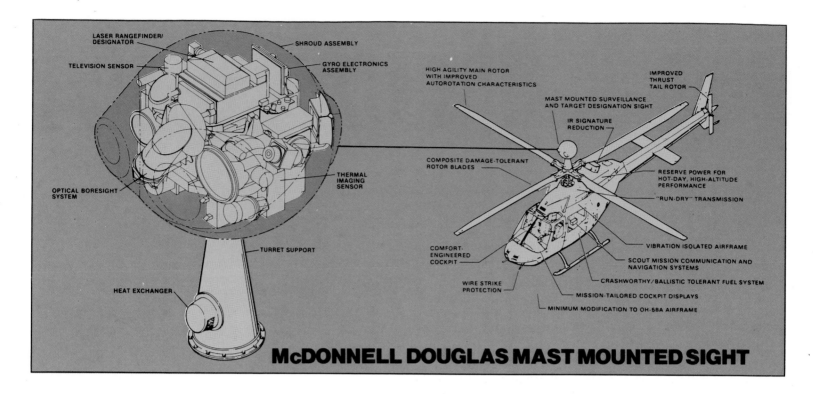

McDONNELL DOUGLAS MAST MOUNTED SIGHT

Institute of Technology, automated labor scheduling for the Mountain Bell Telephone Company, transportation rating and routing for Chevron Chemical's consumer products, project management for the Gulf States Utilities Company of Beaumont, Texas and Medicaid claims for the US Government, state and local governments—including New York State, the largest system in the country.

Microdata, a wholly owned subsidiary also specializing in information systems, sells hardware and software based on its REALITY small-business hardware, SEQUEL large-business system and SOVEREIGN distributed data-processing system. Microdata's RESULTS application program software products combined with REALITY/SOVEREIGN SYSTEMS provide a comprehensive business system for management solution and control. The ALL (Application Language Liberator) virtually eliminates programing by allowing users to tell the computer what they need by responding to prompts or questions displayed on the terminal screen. The Wordmate system offers both word and data processing with superior information storage, processing speed and versatility.

Laboratory Testing

The Electrophoresis Operations in Space (EOS) project is not the only McDonnell Douglas activity that supports the medical industry. The company's VITEK subsidiary is also involved in the development of its successful AutoMicrobic System (AMS), an automated instrument for both the clinical and industrial microbiology laboratory. Including both test kits and instrumentation, the AMS system offers streamlined sample testing and faster results. In use, samples or organisms are placed in the wells of a small card that is diluted in a saline solution and placed in an AMS reader/incubator, where they are scanned. After the proper time the results are seen on the AMS terminal screen.

Alternative Energy

The McDonnell Douglas subsidiary CoaLiquid, based in Louisville, Kentucky, manufactures a liquid fuel called COM (coal/oil mixture) that is seen as a relatively inex-

pensive alternative to fuel oil. It is usable in conventional oil-burning equipment and oil-fired boilers or burners with relatively little modification to the equipment and with 90 percent of the Btu output of oil. The COM fuel is a mixture of roughly 50 percent pulverized coal, 40 percent Number Six residual oil and 10 percent water, made into a stable emulsion by a patented ultrasonic treatment process. The original plant at Shelbyville, Kentucky, which began operation in August 1979, can produce up to 2500 gallons of fuel per hour. The fuel is then shipped to the McDonnell Douglas plant in St Louis and to an Ohio steel producer. A second plant in Mulberry, Florida, supplies its 3600 barrels per day output to the area's phosphate industry.

CoaLiquid International BV has been established in the Netherlands and is involved in a joint venture with Impala Securities, Ltd of Australia and in ventures in Belgium, France, Spain, Israel and Korea. The Israeli plant will produce 11,500 gallons daily and the Korean plant will produce 34,000 gallons per day. The CoaLiquid approach is attractive because the capital cost is approximately one percent of the cost of a coal liquefaction or gasification plant of similar size.

On the solar energy front, McDonnell Douglas engineers have been involved with the 10-megawatt Solar One power tower near Barstow, California, a joint venture of the US Department of Energy and California utilities companies. The power tower, a central receiver solar-thermal power system, uses a circular field of 1818 heliostats (giant movable mirrors) to reflect the suns rays to the central receiver located on top of a 240-foot tower. The receiver is actually a boiler, producing super-heated (950 degrees F) pressurized steam that is used to drive a turbine, which generates electricity.

In Guntersville, Alabama, at the Continental Grain Corporation facility, McDonnell Douglas and Aeroglide Corporation have teamed up to develop a commercial-scale microwave/vacuum drying system called Mivac. The Mivac system is demonstrating significant reductions in the energy required to process soybeans into high protein animal feed and vegetable oil. The Mivac commercial prototype (based on a 1974 experimental prototype) is capable of processing a minimum of 5 tons of soybeans per hour, demonstrating its commercial potential as a technology base for larger and varied applications.

211

Hardware for Military Aircraft

Almost from the beginning, both McDonnell and Douglas were developing vast varieties of aircraft parts. Indeed, these made up the bread and butter of McDonnell's first decade. From the tens of thousands of bomb rocks produced by Douglas during the war years, the subsystems business has led today to a range of specialized aerospace hardware. These include electromechanical actuating equipment such as high voltage brushless DC motors (270 VDC), high-temperature motors, high torque gearboxes, high-reliability clutches, digitally controlled direct-drive servo actuators and high-torque permanent magnet DC motors. The McDonnell Douglas Electronics Company supplies this equipment for DC-9, DC-10, MD-80, KC-10, F-4, F-15, F-18 and AV-8B aircraft built by McDonnell Douglas as well as to other companies like Boeing and General Dynamics for their aircraft.

McDonnell and Douglas engineers first began developing emergency escape systems for their aircraft in the 1940s, and over the years the companies have produced more than 11,000 ejection seats. The number includes over 3500 of the advanced McDonnell Douglas ACES II ejection seat, developed not only for the McDonnell Douglas F-15 but for the General Dynamics F-16 and Fairchild A-10 as well. The ACES II, designed for maximum reliability and maintainability, is so effective that it permits escape, when inverted, at only 155 feet above the ground. The system includes a high-speed drogue chute and a self-contained gyro-controlled rocket system to stabilize the person in the seat during ejection.

One of the US Army's more pressing needs has been to improve the capabilities of its scout helicopters. As McDonnell Douglas points out, 'the scout system used in the field today differs only in the mode of transportation from that used during the Civil War. Then the scout was mounted on a horse and used binoculars for "seeing" the enemy. Today the scout rides in a helicopter but still uses binoculars to find the enemy.'

The point is that if a scout in a helicopter can see the enemy, then the enemy can probably see him and shoot at him. Thus came the need for a periscope of some sort so that the helicopter could hide behind a terrain feature, such as a grove of trees, and look over them at the enemy. Because of the helicopter's rotor, the only place for such a periscope was on the rotor hub. In 1981, McDonnell Douglas Astronautics won the Army contract to build a mast-mounted internal-bearing surveillance and target designation sight. The McDonnell Douglas Mast Mounted Sight (MMS) consists of a sphere 25 inches in diameter mounted atop a conical pylon that positions the sensor line of sight 32 inches above the rotor. This sphere contains a stabilized platform on which direct view sensors and a laser range finder/designator are mounted. Because of the internal bearing stabilization there is low vibration and high reliability. Testing of the MMS prototype began aboard five Bell OH-58A helicopters in 1983, and deliveries of production MMS-equipped helicopters began in 1985.

A Helicopter Subsidiary

The merger of McDonnell and Douglas brought together two of the nation's most important aircraft manufacturers, but with the exception of a handful of prototypes built by McDonnell in the 1950s, neither company had any experience with helicopters. On 6 January 1984 McDonnell Douglas purchased Hughes Helicopters, Inc from the estate of the reclusive late billionaire Howard Hughes for $470 million. With much of its successful diversification coming about through the acquisition

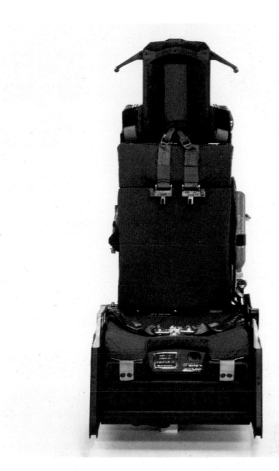

The McDonnell Douglas ACES II ejection seat for the F-15 fighter.

of subsidiaries, the addition of Hughes to the McDonnell Douglas family rounds out its product line with the addition of a mature helicopter company. The Hughes operation had 5800 employees, with major facilities at Mesa, Arizona and Culver City in Southern California near the Douglas facilities.

Hughes is a leader in the manufacture of light single-turbine helicopters, used by both military and commercial customers, having delivered 6000 units since 1952 when it separated from the Hughes Aircraft Company. Among its major products are the Model 500 helicopters, of which the 500E executive version was the official helicopter of the 1984 Los Angeles Olympics, and the AH-64 Apache helicopter. The Apache, built appropriately at the Arizona facility, was developed for the US Army as an advanced attack helicopter and first delivered in 1984. The Army initially ordered 515 Apaches, but the total inventory could surpass 1000. The AH-64 is a fast two-place, heavily armed helicopter gunship equipped with infrared viewing systems that make it capable of destroying enemy armored vehicles with operations at night and under adverse weather conditions. The most advanced helicopter gunship yet produced in the West, the Apache, in service with antiarmor forces, has been said to represent the most revolutionary tactical concept since the Germans introduced the Blitzkrieg in World War II. Its armament consists of four weapons pylons capable of carrying up to 16 Rockwell Hellfire laser-seeking antiarmor missiles, up to 76 unguided rockets in four pods or a combination of these weapons. The Apache also carries a Hughes M230A1 30-mm Chain Gun automatic cannon in a turret beneath the forward fuselage.

The 30-mm Chain Gun is only one of three such weapons in the Hughes ordnance line. The company also produces 25-mm and 7.62-mm guns. These three cannons are in use aboard Navy ships, armored vehicles (such as the Army's Bradley Fighting vehicle) and the Hughes Model 500 (military designation H-6) light helicopter.

THE FIGHTER MAKERS

The F-4 Phantom II

She started out as a fighter redesigned as an attack bomber, a decidedly ugly duckling by comparison to the Navy's graceful Skyrays and the Air Force's sleek Century Series. Before she was through she would be regarded as the greatest American fighter since the Sabre Jet and would serve in the first line of more western air forces than any other fighter. The F-4 first came off the McDonnell drawing boards in 1953 as a single seat twin-engined fighter bomber for the Navy's carriers. The design lost to Chance Vought's design, which became the F8U Crusader, but McDonnell was undaunted. A year later, revised drawings were accepted by the Navy as an attack-bomber project under the designation AH-1 (First McDonnell Attack, Model One). Before the first two prototypes were completed, however, the Navy decided that the plane should be an interceptor fighter and the designation was changed to F4H-1 (Fourth McDonnell Fighter, Model One).

After extensive redesign, the US Navy accepted its F4H-1 in 1955. Of the 47 F4H-1s built, 21 were assigned to the first Phantom squadrons, VF-101 and VF-121, while the remainder continued in testing. The testing led in 1961 to the production fighter version, designated F4H-1F and the production photo-reconnaissance version for the Marines designated F4H-1P. The F4H-1 was powered by a pair of 16,150-lb-thrust General Electric J79-GE-2 turbojets, the F4H-1F and P by 17,000-lb-thrust J79-GE-8 turbojets. Both were equipped with APQ-72 fire-control intercept radar and provision for four Sparrow air-to-air missiles under the fuselage with the latter Phantom able to carry four Sidewinder air-to-air missiles on its wing pylons.

The success of the Phantom in Navy service drew a good deal of interest from the US Air Force, which borrowed 29 F4H-1s from the Navy in January 1962 under the designation F-110. Two months later the Air Force announced that it would buy its own Phantoms. In August 1962 the independent Navy and Air Force designation systems were merged into a common system, with the numbering restarting at 1. The F-1, F-2 and F-3 designations went to existing Navy fighters (F-2 and F-3 were assigned to the McDonnell Banshee and Demon). F-4 became the new designation for the F4H/F-110 programs for both the Navy and Air Force. The F4H-1 became F-4A, the F4A-1F became F-4B and the F4H-1P became RF-4B. The new Air Force version, originally designated F-110A, was redesignated F-4C. The first

Above: The US Navy's F4H-1 (F-4A after 1962) was the first production model of the legendary Phantom II.

Right: Britain's Royal Air Force received 118 F-4Ms under the designation Phantom FGR Mk II.

flight of the F-4C on 27 May 1963 resulted in speeds in excess of twice the speed of sound, and the first of 635 F-4C were accepted immediately more than two months ahead of schedule. Operational service began on 20 November. The F-4C was powered by J79-GE-15 engines and had provision for a wide variety of air-to-air missiles, including Genie and Falcon as well as Sparrow and Sidewinder. Air-to-ground ordnance included both AGM-12 Bullpup and AGM-45 Shrike antiradar missiles.

The appearance of both the F-4B and F-4C came on the eve of the war in Southeast Asia and the Navy F-4B went into combat as a fighter escort on the first raid against North Vietnam in August 1964. The first Air Force F-4C squadron arrived in the Far East in December with deployment to South Vietnam early in 1965. It was not until April that North Vietnamese interceptors began to challenge the American aircraft and on 17 July 1965

their first encounter with Navy F-4Bs resulted in the loss of two MiG-17s. On 10 July, the Air Force claimed a pair of MiG-17s and the air battle for the skies over Southeast Asia was on. As air-combat tactics evolved, several shortcomings in the Phantom became obvious. A critical shortage of spare F-4C parts developed and was solved by concentrating the F-4s at certain bases. A major deficiency in armament also became apparent. McDonnell had designed the Phantom as an interceptor to catch bombers, not as a dogfighter. Air-to-air missiles developed for use against bombers were frequently found to be inadequate in close-in maneuvering. The problem was provisionally corrected by fitting the F-4Cs with SUU-16 gun pods containing a 20-mm Gatling gun. The guns helped make up for the lack of an internal gun but the externally mounted pods created drag and degraded the plane's performance. It was not until the F-4E, with its internally mounted gun, was deployed to Southeast Asia in 1968, that the problem was finally corrected.

The reconnaissance version of the F-4C, the RF-4C, first flew in May 1964 and the first nine-plane contingent arrived in South Vietnam, at Tan Son Nhut AB, on 31 October 1965. By October 1967 four RF-4C squadrons were in Southeast Asia, including the one at Udorn RTAFB in Thailand that had been operating McDonnell RF-101 Voodoos. The RF-4C had a nose 33 inches longer than the F-4C, containing AN/AAS-18 (later AN/AAS-18A) infrared sensors and KS-72 cameras. In combat, several shortcomings were detected. The cameras required photoflash cartridges ejected from the side of the fuselage for lighting at night, which alerted the enemy. In-flight film processing proved impractical and was replaced by photoprocessing vans parked

on the runways to provide processing immediately after the flight. Despite their short range and other problems, RF-4Cs posted an impressive record during the most intense years of the war. Fierce North Vietnamese defense accounted for many losses, but compared to the number of sorties flown, the losses were low.

The F-4D, which first flew in June 1965 and first entered operational service with the USAF in April 1966, was simply an advanced F-4C. Both the F-4C and D were powered by two 17,000-lb-thrust General Electric J79-GE-15 turbojets. To the basic F-4C McDonnell added an improved bombing capability with the ASQ-91 bombing computer. Better air-to-air combat range was derived from an ASG-22 stabilized lead computing gunsight. From the beginning the F-4D featured AIM-4 Falcon

Above: Four USAF 388th TFW F-4E Phantoms return to Korat RTAFB, Thailand after a 1972 combat mission over North Vietnam.

Above left: A pair of Navy F-4B Phantoms from Fighter Squadron 41 (VF-41) attached to the aircraft carrier USS *Franklin D Roosevelt* (CVA-42).

Left: US Air Force F-4E Phantoms flying out of Clark AB in the Philippines, headquarters of the USAF Thirteenth Air Force.

air-to-air missiles that replaced AIM-9 Sidewinders featured on the F-4C. Sidewinders continued to arm the C, however, and were carried by F-4Ds after June 1969. Both missiles complemented four AIM-7 Sparrows carried by all Phantoms through F-4E. The first F-4Ds arrived in Southeast Asia in May 1967, and were supplied to the 555th Tactical Fighter Squadron at Ubon RTAFB. The 555th, known as the 'Triple Nickel,' was destined to be the American fighter squadron to shoot down the greatest number of enemy aircraft during the war.

As a war-rushed product (almost 800 were built in less than two years) the F-4D proved successful. Nonetheless, it bore many failings in common with the F-4C and received similar modifications. The most significant improvements came during the second half of 1969. In July, 90 were programed for the new Wild Weasel (antisurface-to-air missile) APR-38 advanced avionics system. During 1967 the F-4D replaced the F-4C as the first-line American fighter in Southeast Asia. Four years later, in October 1971, they were the first F-4s to be withdrawn from the war zone as part of the de-escalation process. In May 1972, however, in light of the communist spring offensive, four F-4D squadrons were rushed back to Southeast Asia to take part in Linebacker I,

during which they succeeded in destroying the Thanh Hoa Bridge, long a symbol of North Vietnamese resistance.

Results of the first year of the Phantom's combat career in Vietnam resulted in the Air Force ordering what to many was the ultimate Phantom. Ordered in July 1966, the F-4E was powered by two General Electric J79-GE-17 turbojets delivering 17,900 lb of thrust with afterburner. The first Phantom designed by McDonnell to carry internal guns, the F-4E was armed with a 20-mm General Electric Vulcan multibarrel Gatling gun mounted under the nose and directed by the AN/APQ-120 fire-control system. The F-4E also introduced leading-edge maneuvering slats and armor plating for the rear fuselage and other systems.

The F-4E, like all the earlier USAF Phantoms, was actually ordered by the Navy on behalf of the Air Force. It first flew on 30 June 1967 and was accepted immediately as a production aircraft. Because of what the Air Force perceived as an 'urgent need' for F-4Es in Southeast Asia, flight testing (combat evaluation) was accelerated. A reconnaissance version of the F-4E was also developed, but solely for the export market. Designated RF-4E, it was actually as much a development of the RF-4C as it was of the F-4E.

The F-4E first arrived in Southeast Asia on 13 November 1968, with its first two air-to-air victories chalked up on 23 May 1972 by Lieutenant Colonel Lyle Beckers and Captain John Nuwe against a MiG-19 and by Captain James Beatty and Lieutenant James Summer against a MiG-21. The latter victory was achieved with the internally mounted Vulcan cannon. Over the next five months air-to-air combat reached its most intense level of the war. During that time the US Air Force shot down 32 enemy

Above: The cockpit canopy and nose probe of the earliest Navy F4H-1s was decidedly different from those of the later Phantoms.

Below: A munitions crew of the 431st TFS loads bombs aboard an F-4C at a Southeast Asia base in November 1965. The F-4C was the first US Air Force Phantom to go to war.

Above: The first US Air Force Phantoms bore the designation F-110A, but this nomenclature changed to F-4C in 1962 at the same time that the Navy's operational F4H-1s became F-4Bs. These Air Force Phantoms were originally ordered from McDonnell under a Navy contract.

aircraft, 22 of them claimed by F-4Es. The remaining MiGs were also downed by Phantoms, F-4Ds.

During the war, 78 percent of the enemy aircraft destroyed by the US Air Force were shot down by Phantoms. The F-4C claimed 42, the F-4D 44, and the F-4E achieved all 22 of its victories in just those five months of 1972. The US Navy, like the Air Force, achieved most of its air-to-air kills with Phantoms. Of the 58 enemy aircraft downed by the Navy, 66 percent of them were by Phantoms, 21 by F-4Bs and 15 by the upgraded F-4Js. The Navy's F-4J bore roughly the same relationship to its F-4B as the Air Force F-4D did to its F-4C. The F-4J was powered by two 17,859-lb-thrust General Electric J79-GE-10 turbojets and equipped with upgraded fire-control, bombing and navigational systems. Like earlier Navy and Air Force Phantoms, the F-4J carried no internal guns. The F-4J first flew on 27 May 1966, entering operational service in December of the same year and claiming its first probable MiG kill in June 1968. On 10 May 1972 Navy Lieutenants Randy Cunningham and Willie Driscoll, flying as a team in an F-4J, shot down three MiG-17s. Added to their previous two MiG kills, the events of that date made Cunningham and Driscoll the first American aces of the war. By the end of the summer, the Air Force had three aces of its own, Captains Chuck DeBellvue, Jeff Feinstein and Steve Ritchie. Like the two Navy aces, all three scored their victories with F-4 Phantoms. The last two MiG kills came in the war's last month and are also both credited to Phantoms. On 8 January 1973, Captain Paul Howman and Lieutenant Lawrence Kullman downed a MiG-21 in an Air Force F-4D. Four days later Lieutenants Vic Kovaleski and Jim Wise flew from the carrier USS *Midway* in a Navy F-4B and downed a MiG-17. More F-4s were built for the Air Force than any other airplane since the F-86.

By the time the war ended, McDonnell, then a component of McDonnell Douglas, had built over 4300 Phantoms, not only for the US Air Force and Navy, but for foreign customers as well. The F-4D had been delivered to the Shah's Imperial Iranian Air Force in September 1968 and to South Korea under the Military Assistance Program in 1969. Beginning in September 1969 Israel received F-4Es that formed an integral part of the Israeli counteroffensive in the Yom Kippur War four years later. McDonnell also sold F-4Fs to Iran, Greece and Turkey, with export-only RF-4E reconnaissance aircraft going to Israel, Iran and Germany. The German Luftwaffe ordered 175 specially designed F-4E-type fighters under the designation F-4F. Like the F-4E, the F-4F carried a Vulcan-nose cannon, but unlike the

Above: Sharkfaced USAF F-4Es line up behind a KC-135 tanker to top off their fuel tanks before heading into combat over North Vietnam.

Right: Two F-4Ds, wingtips folded, photographed by the author in the US Air Force maintenance facility at Hill AFB, Utah in January 1979.

F-4E and earlier Phantoms, it carried Sidewinder air-to-air missiles with no provision for Sparrows. Unlike most other exported Phantoms, the F-4Fs were coproduced, in this case by McDonnell Douglas in the United States and Messerschmitt Bolkow-Blohm in Germany. First flown in May 1973, the F-4F first entered Luftwaffe service in February 1976.

Meanwhile McDonnell Douglas also struck a similar deal with Mitsubishi of Japan. Two St Louis-built F-4Es were acquired by the Japan Air Self Defense Force in 1971 and the balance of 136 Phantoms were built in Japan by Mitsubishi under a McDonnell Douglas license. Designated F-4E(J), the Japanese Phantoms were very similar to the McDonnell Douglas F-4E, but had provisions for specialized avionics and Mitsubishi AAM-2 missiles.

Great Britain was among those McDonnell Douglas customers that ordered specialized versions of the Phantom. First came the F-4K, developed for the Royal Navy and similar to the US Navy's F-4J. The F-4K was powered by a pair of British-built Rolls-Royce RB168-25R Spey turbofans. Delivering 20,515 lb of thrust, they were the most powerful yet seen on a Phantom. Known under the British designation Phantom FG Mark 1, the F-4K was slightly smaller to accommodate the hangar-deck elevators of the last of the Royal Navy's conventional aircraft carriers. In 1982, during the Falklands War, the Royal Navy bitterly regretted not having its then long-gone conventional carriers and powerful Phantoms.

The first flight of the Royal Navy's F-4K in June 1966 was followed in February 1967 by the first flight of the F-4M destined for Britain's Royal Air Force. Known under the RAF designation

Above: A US Air Force F-4G 'Wild Weasel' of the 52d Tactical Fighter Wing at Spangdahlem AB, West Germany, armed with Shrike AGM-45 antiradar missiles.

Phantom FGR Mark 2, the F-4M was similar to the F-4K but designed for operation from land bases. The F-4K was built in St Louis by McDonnell, but half the subassemblies were British made.

By the mid-1980s, as the Phantom entered its third decade of service, a number of changes had been made to the original McDonnell product. The first major modification came in 1965, when 12 Navy F-4Bs were retrofitted with AN/ASW-21 data link communications for operations off North Vietnam. Briefly redesignated F-4G, these USS *Kitty Hawk*-based fleet interceptors were later designated back to F-4B.

The F-4G designation was reassigned in October 1978 to former US Air Force F-4Es modified to seek out and destroy enemy radar and surface-to-air missile sites. Called Advanced Wild Weasels, the F-4Gs are equipped with AGM-45 Shrike and AGM-78 (Standard ARM) and AGM-88 HARM antiradar missiles. They can also carry AGM-65 Maverick air-to-ground missiles and Rockeye Cluster Bomb Units. They were deployed to Europe to spearhead an Allied counteroffensive in the event of war.

Starting in 1971 the Navy began upgrading the avionics systems and structural integrity of 228 F-4Bs to extend their service life. Redesignated F-4N, these Phantoms are being joined by 302 F-4Js, which are being retrofitted with leading edge maneuvering slats and upgraded avionics, and redesignated F-4S.

By late 1983, Pratt & Whitney, a world leader in the manufacture of aircraft engines, had developed an ambitious plan to upgrade a substantial part of the worldwide inventory of F-4s, which then stood at 3500. Noting a potential market they calculated at $14.4 billion, Pratt & Whitney contacted McDonnell Douglas about a joint venture under which the two companies

A US Marine Corps RF-4B reconnaissance version of the Phantom attached to VMFP-3 aboard the Navy's carrier USS *Midway* (CV-41). The unarmed RF-4B Phantom is actually more like the US Air Force RF-4C or RF-4E reconnaissance aircraft than like the Navy's F-4B fighter.

PRODUCTION CLOSE-UP
F-4 PHANTOM II

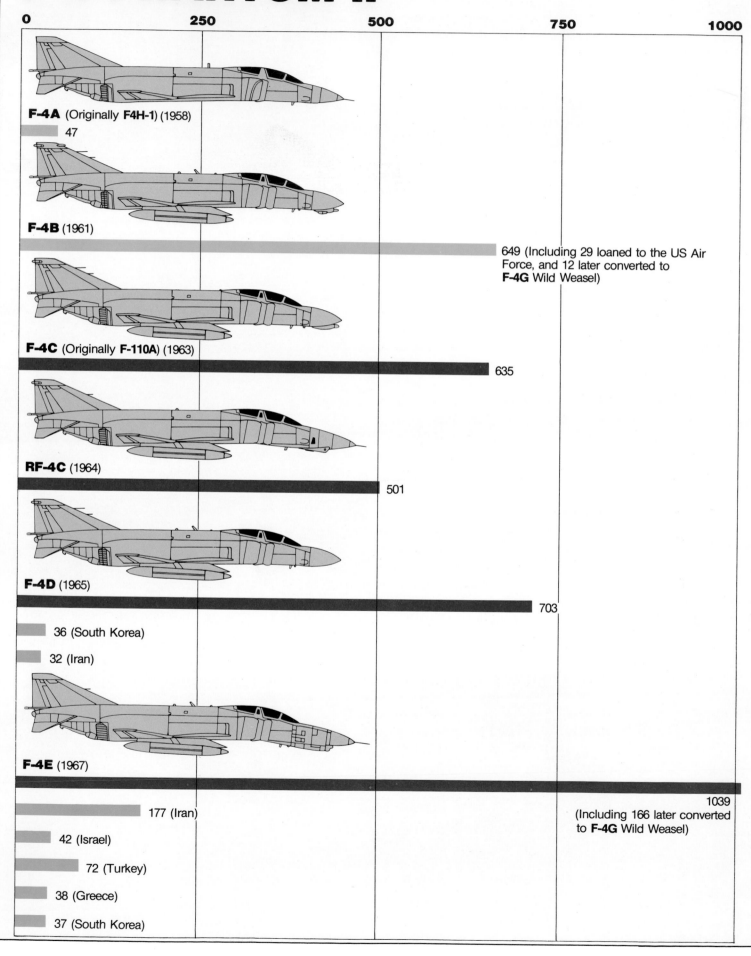

0   250   500   750   1000

F-4A (Originally **F4H-1**) (1958)

47

F-4B (1961)

649 (Including 29 loaned to the US Air Force, and 12 later converted to **F-4G** Wild Weasel)

F-4C (Originally **F-110A**) (1963)

635

RF-4C (1964)

501

F-4D (1965)

703

36 (South Korea)

32 (Iran)

F-4E (1967)

1039
(Including 166 later converted to **F-4G** Wild Weasel)

177 (Iran)

42 (Israel)

72 (Turkey)

38 (Greece)

37 (South Korea)

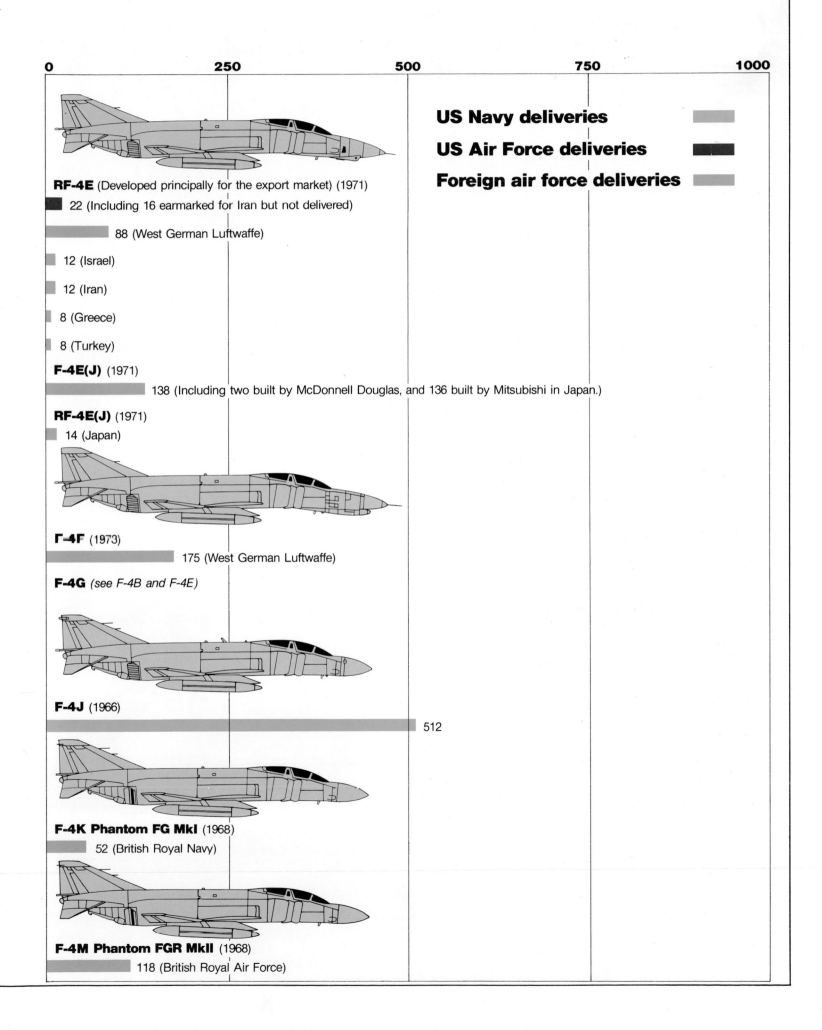

0   250   500   750   1000

US Navy deliveries

US Air Force deliveries

Foreign air force deliveries

RF-4E (Developed principally for the export market) (1971)

22 (Including 16 earmarked for Iran but not delivered)

88 (West German Luftwaffe)

12 (Israel)

12 (Iran)

8 (Greece)

8 (Turkey)

F-4E(J) (1971)

138 (Including two built by McDonnell Douglas, and 136 built by Mitsubishi in Japan.)

RF-4E(J) (1971)

14 (Japan)

Г-4F (1973)

175 (West German Luftwaffe)

F-4G *(see F-4B and F-4E)*

F-4J (1966)

512

F-4K Phantom FG MkI (1968)

52 (British Royal Navy)

F-4M Phantom FGR MkII (1968)

118 (British Royal Air Force)

	F-4B	F-4C	RF-4C
Wingspan	38' 5"	38' 5"	38' 5"
Length	58'3"	58' 3"	62' 11"
Height	16' 4"	16' 6"	16' 6"
Wing area (sq ft)	530	530	530
Service ceiling (ft)	N/A	56,100	56,220
Combat ceiling (ft)	56,850	56,100	55,790
Combat radius (mi)	885/Mk 28 530/12-500 lb bombs	538/Mk 28 323/11-750 lb bombs 1,926 ferry	838 506/Mk 28 1,750 ferry
Weight (lb)			
Empty	27,897	28,496	28,104
Gross	34,907	51,441	52,346
Maximum	55,948	59,064	52,450
Combat	38,505/4 Sparrow	38,328	39,788
Engine type	GE J79-GE-8	GE J79-GE-15	GE J79-GE-1
Engine thrust (lb)	17,000	10,900-17,000	10,900-17,000
Speed (mph)			
Top (at 40,000')	1,490	1,433	1,460
Sea level	845	826	834
Cruising	580	587	587
Stalling	195	165	167
Climb	40,800'/1 min.	40,550'/1 min.	38,950'/1 min.

would provide new engines and rebuild the airframes to turn Phantoms into Super Phantoms. McDonnell Douglas declined, seeing the suggested program as competitive with its efforts to sell new F-15s and F-18s. Boeing, the old competitor in the commercial transport market, recognizing that the F-4 was one of of the best combat planes in service in the world, saw the value of the program and joined with Pratt & Whitney.

Under the program Boeing will upgrade the airframes and redesign external fuel tanks and weapons pylons to reduce drag. Pratt & Whitney will supply its 20,000-lb-thrust 1120 engine, both lighter and more powerful than earlier F-4 engines. Together, the two modifications would increase the sustained turn rate by 17 percent, acceleration by 18 percent, the climb rate by 25 percent and the thrust-to-weight ratio by 55 percent. The program is intended to be a cost-effective means for countries to obtain 'new' aircraft. It is particularly enticing for Israel, who is using the Pratt & Whitney 1120 engine in its domestically produced Lavi fighter.

In September 1984, McDonnell Douglas announced at last that it too would be developing an F-4 enhancement program. The USAF, West Germany's Luftwaffe and the British RAF and Royal Navy received company presentations in September, and presentations to Egypt, Korea and Turkey were made in October. Though interest in the program from the US Air Force was reported in *Aviation Week* as being 'lukewarm,' other countries seemed to be ready for the program, which included a

Left: The Navy's F-4J (like this one from the USS *Saratoga*) is the newest factory-built Phantom, but some are being further enhanced to F-4S standard.

Below: A US Air Force RF-4C reconnaissance Phantom out of Shaw AFB, South Carolina is readied for a 1981 mission.

new higher visibility single-piece birdstrike-resistant windshield and upgraded avionics. The latter included modern pulse-doppler radar and an ARU-118 Tacan adapter, a flight-director computer and radar-warning processor. Also included in the McDonnell Douglas proposal were airframe improvements such as a new forward-landing-gear actuator rib, new inboard slat actuator supports and a new upper-engine mount. The engines themselves will be improved General Electric J79 turbojets with reduced smoke signature and an optional increase in the available thrust.

Rolling off the assembly line at St Louis for two decades, over 5000 Phantoms were produced, more than any other combat aircraft since World War II. In the combined history of Mc-Donnell and Douglas, only the ubiquitous DC-3 was a bigger seller. Just over half the total was purchased by the US Air Force, with about 27 percent going to the US Navy and Marine Corps. After 25 years, those services still retain them as an integral part of their arsenals.

Germany still had 273 by 1984, Israel had 252, Great Britain had 185 (including 15 ex-US Navy F-4Js), Japan had 154, Turkey had 100, South Korea had 73, Greece had 64 and Iran had about 40 that remained in flyable condition half a decade after the fall of the Shah and the American embargo on spare parts. Spain had meanwhile received 44 F-4Cs and RF-4C from the US Air Force and Egypt had gotten 35 F-4Es from the USAF. Australia operated two dozen F-4Es under a lease arrangement with the US Air Force.

If Pentagon estimates are correct, 2000 Phantoms will still be in service worldwide at the turn of the century. A plane uncertain of its identity through its preflight development, the fabulous F-4 Phantom proved itself early, then went on to become one of only a handful of airplanes to join the ranks of the legendary.

	F-4D	FE-4	F-4J
Wingspan	38' 5"	38' 5"	30' 5"
Length	58' 3"	63'	58' 3½"
Height	16' 6"	16' 6"	15' 10"
Wing area (sq ft)	530	530	530
Service ceiling (ft)	55,400	59,200	54,700
Combat ceiling (ft)	55,850	59,600	54,700
Combat radius (mi)	502 1,844 (ferry)	533 1,885 (ferry)	596/ 1,956 (ferry)
Weight (lb)			
Empty	28,958	29,535	30,770
Gross	51,557	53,848	46,833
Maximum	59,380	61,651	55,896
Combat	38,781	38,019/4 Sparrows	41,399
Engine type	GE J79-GE-15	GE J79-17	GE J79-GE-10
Engine thrust (lb)	10,900-17,000	11,870-17,900	17,859
Speed (mph)			
Top (at 40,000')	1,432	1,485	1,416 (at 36,089')
Sea level	826	914	875
Cruising	587	586	580
Stalling	165	158	195
Climb	40,100'/1 min.	54,200'/1 min.	41,250'/1 min.

Above: A British Royal Air Force Phantom FGR Mark II (F-4M). The RAF Phantoms, like those of the Royal Navy, have a large number of British-built subassemblies, notably their Rolls-Royce engines.

Below: An F-4E Phantom in the colors and markings of the Imperial Iranian Air Force just prior to its delivery in July 1977. The Shah's air arm took delivery of over 200 Phantoms before his downfall in 1979, of which a handful still remained in service five years later.

Right: The F-4F Phantoms, such as this one from Fighter Wing 71 (JG-71 'Richthofen') based at Wittmundhafen, were produced exclusively for West Germany's Luftwaffe, with deliveries beginning in 1973. This Phantom, number 37+01, was the first F-4F delivered. Its wing, Jagdgeschwader 71, is named for the World War I ace Baron Manfred von Richthofen.

The F-15 Eagle

When McDonnell and Douglas merged in 1967 both companies were involved in diverse aerospace activities, but each had a single very strong speciality. For Douglas, swamped with orders for the DC-9 and the DC-10, the speciality was commercial transports. For McDonnell, then well into the F-4 program, the speciality had always been fighters.

It was at about the time of the McDonnell Douglas merger that the US Air Force began actively to think about a successor to the F-4. When the F-4 was being developed a decade earlier, the theory of fighter design held that a fighter should be designed for a variety of roles. It should be useful as an interceptor, an air superiority fighter or a fighter bomber. This meant compromise. No plane could be designed to do all three and at the same time be designed to be extremely good at any one. While the F-4 did a very good job, better than most, the handwriting was on the wall at the Pentagon.

There were really two major factors that caused the Air Force to change its mind about fighters in the late 1960s. First, there was the evaluation of F-4 performance in Southeast Asia. The Phantom did well in air combat, shooting down two enemy aircraft for the loss of a single Phantom; but, while this was good, F-86 Sabre Jets in Korea a generation before had shot down 14 enemy MiGs for the loss of a single Sabre. Part of this had to do with pilot training, part of it with severe restrictions placed on American pilots in Southeast Asia, and part of it was that the F-4 was a very complicated airplane designed for a variety of roles. The second factor to change the idea that the Air Force had about fighters was the advent of a new generation of Russian fighters, notably the MiG-25 Foxbat. Flying at three times the speed of sound, the Foxbat could fly reconnaissance or strike

missions without fear of being intercepted by a missile-armed Phantom.

In December 1967 the Air Force awarded concept formulation study contracts to General Dynamics and McDonnell Douglas under a program called FX (Fighter, Experimental) for a high performance all-weather single-seat jet fighter with a high thrust-to-weight ratio that was capable of speeds up to Mach 2.5. Two years later, on 31 December 1969, the Air Force signed a developmental contract with McDonnell Douglas for the new fighter under the designation YF-15. The plane rolled out of the St Louis factory on 26 June 1972, at which time it was christened Eagle. The first flight at the hands of McDonnell chief test pilot Irv Burrows took place at Edwards AFB on 17 July, lasting nearly an hour and demonstrating the Eagle's potential. The production go-ahead came in February 1973, followed by the first deliveries in November 1974.

In January 1975, the nineteenth F-15 was stripped down and rechristened Streak Eagle for the purpose of breaking a number of world speed records. In just over two weeks of flying out of Grand Forks AFB, North Dakota, the Streak Eagle broke eight time-to-altitude records, three of them held by the notorious MiG-25 Foxbat, and in doing so demonstrated the F-15's ability to accelerate to supersonic speeds while climbing straight up. The margins by which the Streak Eagle shattered existing records ranged from 15 percent to 33 percent, with the latter record being a climb to 49,212 feet (15,000 meters) in 77 seconds compared to almost two minutes taken by the previous record holder, an F-4 Phantom.

Right: A pair of F-15Cs from MacDill AFB, Florida in June 1983.

Below: The first F-15 prototype in the final stages of production at the McDonnell Douglas St Louis factory in June 1972.

230

Above: An F-15A from the USAF Tactical Air Command's 555th Tactical Fighter Squadron based at Luke AFB, over Arizona's Painted Desert.

Above right: One of the McDonnell Douglas-built F-15Js ordered by Japan's Air Self-Defense Force under Peace Eagle I.

Below: A cutaway rendering the internal structure of a single-seat F-15. Note the armament of AIM-7 Sparrow air-to-air missiles and the 20-mm multibarreled cannon in the right wing root. The pink areas are fuel tanks and fuel lines.

	YF-15 Eagle	F-15A Eagle	F-15C Eagle
Wingspan	42' 8"	42' 10"	42' 10"
Length	64' 11"	63' 9"	63' 9"
Height	18' 5"	18' 5"	18' 5"
Ceiling	65,000' (all models)		
Range (mi)	2,000	2,400	2,878
Weight (lb)	40,000 takeoff	41,500 gross	68,000 gross
Engine type	P&W F100-PW-100	P&W F100-PW-100	P&W F100-PW-100
Engine thrust (lb)	23,000	23,820	23,930
Speed (mph)	Mach 2.5 (all models)		

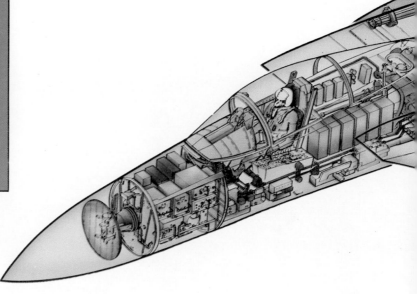

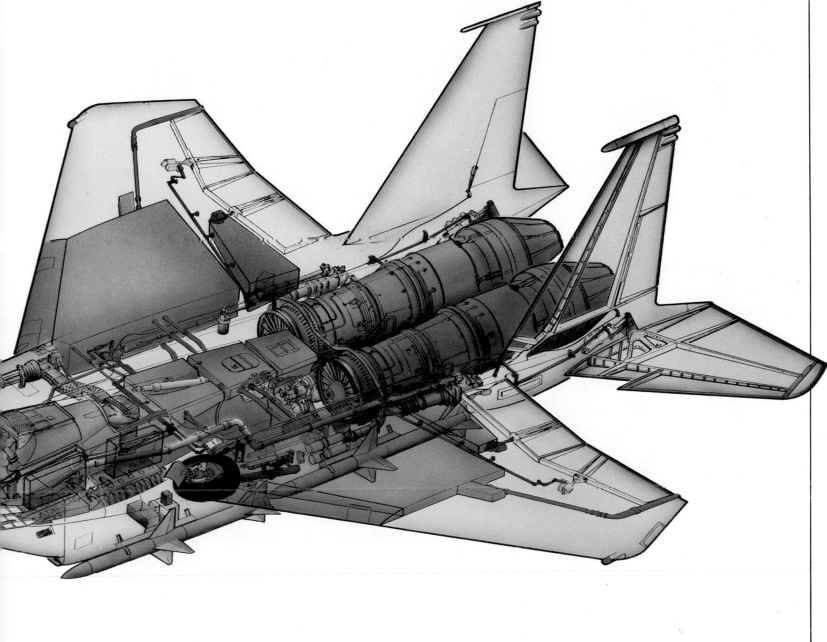

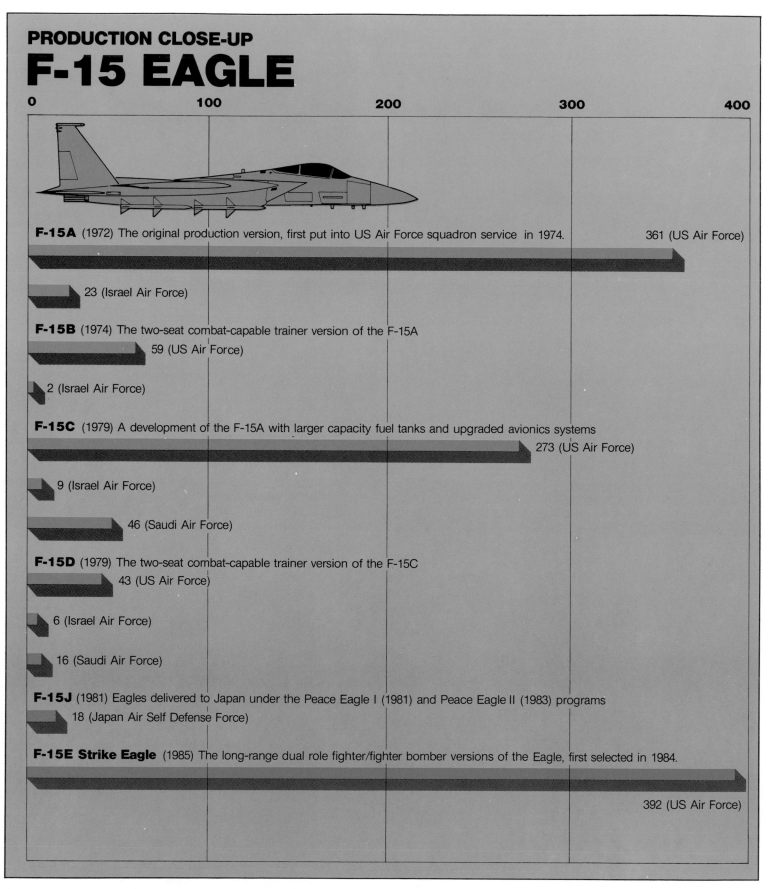

PRODUCTION CLOSE-UP
F-15 EAGLE

| 0 | 100 | 200 | 300 | 400 |

F-15A (1972) The original production version, first put into US Air Force squadron service in 1974.

361 (US Air Force)

23 (Israel Air Force)

F-15B (1974) The two-seat combat-capable trainer version of the F-15A

59 (US Air Force)

2 (Israel Air Force)

F-15C (1979) A development of the F-15A with larger capacity fuel tanks and upgraded avionics systems

273 (US Air Force)

9 (Israel Air Force)

46 (Saudi Air Force)

F-15D (1979) The two-seat combat-capable trainer version of the F-15C

43 (US Air Force)

6 (Israel Air Force)

16 (Saudi Air Force)

F-15J (1981) Eagles delivered to Japan under the Peace Eagle I (1981) and Peace Eagle II (1983) programs

18 (Japan Air Self Defense Force)

F-15E Strike Eagle (1985) The long-range dual role fighter/fighter bomber versions of the Eagle, first selected in 1984.

392 (US Air Force)

For all its speed and power, the Eagle was designed to be an easy plane to fly. It is a highly automated weapons system that a pilot can fly instinctively. Perched high in his bubble canopy, the pilot has a 360-degree field of vision. He need not even look down at his instrument panel because all the data he needs, such as speed, altitude and target range, are projected onto the canopy by a system called a head-up display (HUD). Fighter pilots love the Eagle because it is designed to serve its pilots, not vice versa. While the F-4 Phantom, like many planes of its era, had been developed under the multirole theory, the Eagle was designed as a fighter, a fighter-pilot's fighter.

The Eagle's pylons carry much of the same armament proven aboard the F-4 and more, including the 20-mm multibarrelled cannon and provision for four AIM-7 Sparrow air-to-air missiles semirecessed into the fuselage. Underwing pylons can accommodate other types of stores ranging from Sidewinder missiles and bombs to electronic countermeasures (ECM) pods. The Eagle's offensive avionics systems are designed to easily

accommodate new missiles and weapons that might be developed, such as the AIM-120 AMRAAM air-to-air missile. In January 1984, an F-15 successfully testfired the ALMV two-stage anti-satellite (ASAT) missile. The F-15 is powered by two Pratt & Whitney F100 turbofans delivering an aggregate of 47,640 lb of thrust, more than 33 percent more than that available to the F-4E, which has a gross weight 6 tons heavier than the F-15.

The first US Air Force unit to become fully operational with the Eagle was the First Tactical Fighter Wing at Langley AFB (Tactical Air Command Headquarters) in January 1976. The first overseas deployment of USAF Eagles, to Bitburg AB in Germany, followed later in the year. The initial deliveries consisted primarily of the F-15A, but these were supplemented with a small number of fully combat-capable F-15B two-seat trainers. By the end of September 1977 there had been deliveries of 245 F-15s to the Air Force and by April 1980 the total had more than doubled to 504. Eagles were assigned to both training and operational bases in the United States as well as overseas to Germany and to Kadena AB on Okinawa. Twelve F-15s were temporarily deployed to Khmis Mishayt RSAFB in Saudi Arabia in January 1979 at the request of the Saudi Government, which had coincidentally placed an order for 60 F-15s of their own.

In June 1979 the second series of Eagles made its appearance under the designations F-15C and F-15D, with the F-15D being the two-seat trainer version of the F-15C. Outwardly identical to the F-15A/B, the new Eagles had greatly upgraded avionics, centerline FAST Pack (Fuel and Sensor, Tactical) drop tanks, additional internal fuel capacity and structural enhancement to permit heavier loads. Under the 1983 Multi-Stage Improvement Program (MSIP II) even more upgrading is being introduced into the F-15D program. Under MSIP II (MSIP I upgrades existing F-15A/Bs), the Eagles' weapons systems are being improved and their APG-63 radar is having its memory increased from 96K to 1000K. It will now be possible for the APG-63 to process information at a rate of 1.4 million operations per second, three times

Above: A Luke AFB-based Tactical Air Command F-15 Eagle. Luke AFB was the first home of operational USAF Eagles.

Below: US Air Force F-15s over Neuschwanstein Castle in West Germany.

Overleaf: The F-15 Eagles of Israel's air force have an outstanding record of success in combat against Soviet-built aircraft. In 1982 they shot down 81 Syrian fighters without a loss.

faster than before. The plane's central computer will be able to store four times the data and process it three times as fast. The Armament Control System control panel in the cockpit is being replaced by a multipurpose color video screen. Meanwhile, an equally potent though less sophisticated unofficial addition has been a six-power rifle scope adjacent to the HUD on the plane's centerline, which has greatly aided in the identification of opposing aircraft in simulated air-combat exercises.

The first foreign delivery of F-15s included eight aircraft to Japan under the Peace Eagle I program. This was followed by the sales to Israel under the Peace Fox program and to Saudi Arabia under Peace Sun. An additional four McDonnell-built F-15s were delivered to Japan in 1983, where 86 Eagles are being built by Mitsubishi under the designation F-15J.

The Eagle's first taste of combat came in June 1979 when six Israeli F-15s and two Kfirs were jumped by a similar number of Syrian MiG-21s. Within three minutes six of the attackers had been shot down, five of them by F-15s. On 24 September of the

Left: The 'Strike Eagle,' first demonstrated by McDonnell Douglas in 1980, became a USAF fighter bomber under the designation F-15E five years later.

Below: F-15s in the USAF Warner Robins Air Logistics Center maintenance hangar.

same year, Israeli F-15s engaged four more MiG-21s, shooting them all down without a loss to their own number. In June 1982 Syria had moved mobile SA-6 surface-to-air missile launchers into the Bekaa Valley to intimidate Israel Air Force reconnaissance flights over Lebanon. When Israeli aircraft attacked the SA-6 sites, they were in turn attacked by Russian-built MiGs in Syrian markings and presumably flown by Syrian pilots. Two major air battles and several small skirmishes during the first week of June resulted in the MiGs facing off against American-built F-15s and F-16s. At the end, 55 MiGs had been shot down without the loss of a single Israeli fighter. Because the Israel Air Force only recognizes kills that can be proven by gun-camera footage, the total may actually have been higher. An Israeli A-4 Skyhawk attack plane had been shot down, but by a SAM and not a Syrian fighter. At the end of a month of air-to-air combat over Lebanon, 81 Syrian fighters had been downed, with no losses recorded on the Israeli side. Of the total victories, 60 percent are credited to the F-15, with at least three of these kills coming in combat with the sinister MiG-25 Foxbat. Even if the Israelis had lost an Eagle to the Syrians, the kill ratio for the F-15 still would have been 28 times better than for the F-4 in Vietnam and four times better than the F-86 in Korea. Some of this probably has to do with circumstances and with training (Israeli as well as

Above: The McDonnell Douglas 'Strike Eagle' over a central Wisconsin lake during a low-level bomb run demonstration.

Left: F-15A Eagles are readied for a dawn patrol on the Holloman AFB, New Mexico flight line.

American fighter pilots of the 1980s are far better trained for air combat than USAF pilots of the 1960s), but a lot of it has to do with the Eagle.

During 1983, US Air Force F-15s were sent to the Sudan to counter a possible threat by Libya, but they deployed back to their bases, having perhaps caused Libyan dictator Qaddafi to think twice. In June 1984 Saudi Arabia became the second nation whose Eagles were involved in air combat. The war between Iran and Iraq, then in its fourth year of bloody stalemate, had spilled over into the Persian Gulf with Iranian aircraft bombing oil tankers in international waters. A pair of Saudi F-15s intercepted one of these aircraft, ironically a McDonnell Douglas F-4 Phantom, and blew it out of the sky.

Though they developed the Eagle strictly as an air-superiority fighter, the people of McDonnell Douglas had continued to keep alive the notion of the F-15s potential as a fighter bomber. The potential was originally demonstrated in the 1970s with a specially prepared bomb-carrying F-15 they called the Strike Eagle. The Strike Eagle idea was still alive and well in the halls at St Louis in 1983 when the USAF Tactical Air Command went looking for a dual-role fighter/fighter bomber to replace its aging fleet of F-111s in the long-range deep interdiction mission. The Air Force compared the Strike Eagle, now known at McDonnell as the Dual Role Fighter Demonstrator (DRFD), to General Dynamics' F-16XL, a delta-winged, bomb-carrying development of its F-16 Fighting Falcon fighter.

On 25 February 1984, Chief of Staff General Charles Gabriel announced that the USAF had picked the DRFD and would spend $1.5 billion to procure it as a fighter bomber under the designation F-15E. The F-15E would essentially be a modified F-15D with 96 percent of its systems in common with other Eagles. The two-man cockpit would be modified to accommodate a weapons system operator in the back seat, and the F-15E would be capable of carrying bomb loads up to 12 tons, including

nuclear weapons, with a gross weight 19 percent greater than an F-15C. It could also carry air-to-air missiles and could convert to the air-superiority role.

The F-15 is a plane that matured quickly, winning high praise from the pilots who fly it and racking up an incredible record in air-to-air-combat. Still at the threshold of its career, the Eagle is already on the verge of becoming as big a legend as its older brother the Phantom.

The AV-8B Harrier II

The capability of an operational nonhelicopter combat aircraft to take off vertically had stood as the answer to many an air tactician's dreams since the beginning of tactical air combat. It was not until 1960, however, that the first step was made toward a practical VTOL (Vertical Take-Off and Landing) combat jet. In that year Hawker Aircraft in Great Britain began testing its P1127 VTOL experimental aircraft. By the late 1960s the design had matured into the Hawker (then Hawker Siddeley) Kestrel Mk1 being evaluated by the air arms of several nations including the United States. Britain's RAF began receiving the unique VTOL 'jump jet' from Hawker Siddeley in 1969 under the name Harrier. A year later Harriers began service with the US Marine Corps under the designation AV-8A (Attack, VTOL, variant A of the Eighth US attack plane since the start of the 1962 nomenclature system). There were 110 AV-8A Harriers delivered to the USMC by Hawker Siddeley, including eight TAV-8A trainers.

In 1975 McDonnell Douglas and the USMC jointly began development of an advanced Harrier to be built by the McDon-

Opposite: A brace of McDonnell Douglas F-15 Eagles from Holloman AFB, New Mexico during a training mission.

Above and below: McDonnell Douglas Harriers: the brightly colored AV-8B prototype at St Louis and a gray AV-8B for the Spanish Navy.

nell component of McDonnell Douglas at St Louis under the designation AV-8B. The AV-8B Harrier II differed from the Hawker Siddeley (now part of British Aerospace) version by the addition of a graphite epoxy wing with a supercritical airfoil for greater lift, better cruise characteristics and much greater fuel capacity. Redesigned engine inlets and new fuselage-mounted lift-improvement devices result in greater lift for improved take-off, landing and cruise performance. The avionics systems for the AV-8B have been completely revised. The AV-8B first flew on 9 November 1978 and the first of 328 production Harrier IIs reached the USMC in 1983.

While Royal Air Force and Royal Navy Harriers proved themselves outstanding interceptors and air superiority aircraft during the 1982 Falklands conflict, the Harrier's primary role is that of a ground-support attack bomber. It is uniquely suited for this

PRODUCTION CLOSE-UP
AV-8 HARRIER

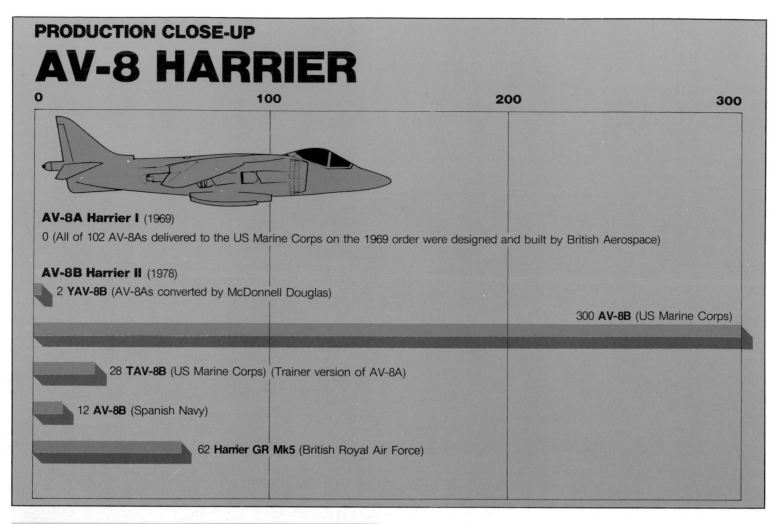

0	100	200	300

AV-8A Harrier I (1969)

0 (All of 102 AV-8As delivered to the US Marine Corps on the 1969 order were designed and built by British Aerospace)

AV-8B Harrier II (1978)

2 **YAV-8B** (AV-8As converted by McDonnell Douglas)

300 **AV-8B** (US Marine Corps)

28 **TAV-8B** (US Marine Corps) (Trainer version of AV-8A)

12 **AV-8B** (Spanish Navy)

62 **Harrier GR Mk5** (British Royal Air Force)

Right: US Marine Corps AV-8B Harriers aboard the Navy's light assault carrier USS *Tarawa* (LHA-1).

Left: Marine Harriers make small carriers potent and practical, and permit flexibility in Marine assault operations.

mission and as such it is the right type of plane for the Marines. Powered by a Rolls-Royce Pegasus turbofan engine, the thrust can be vectored down as well as back, allowing the Harrier to make conventional, short-distance (STOL) or straight-up (VTOL) takeoffs and landings. Short-distance takeoffs permit greatly increased attack payloads. The Harrier can conduct takeoffs and landings from the decks of assault ships, from fields, roads, parking lots and runways that have been made unusable by conventional aircraft through bomb damage. The plane can operate from just about any patch of level ground near the front, quickly jumping up to attack a target, then returning to its hiding place. Because of this dispersal capability and basing flexibility, an AV-8B force would be hard for an enemy to find and destroy.

In flight, the same thrust-vectoring capability that makes the Harrier able to takeoff vertically makes it just about the most maneuverable combat aircraft in service. This characteristic is what made the Harrier such an outstanding fighter in the Falklands and what makes it an extremely difficult aircraft to shoot down in air-to-air combat, and such an exceptional military aircraft.

Ironically, the American-designed Harrier II is being purchased by the country that originated the first Harrier. British Aerospace is building 62 Harrier IIs for the RAF, with McDonnell Douglas acting as principal subcontractor. Meanwhile the Spanish Government, which had earlier purchased 13 Harrier Is (called AV-8S Matador by Spain) through the US Government, decided in 1983 to buy a dozen AV-8Bs from McDonnell Douglas.

Left from top: A McDonnell Douglas CF-18 Hornet delivered to the Canadian Armed Forces in July 1982, and a pair of McDonnell Douglas T-45 Hawk US Navy strike trainers.

Below: US Marine Corps F-18 Hornet fighters during a low-level mission in January 1983.

The T-45 Hawk

With the McDonnell component of McDonnell Douglas successfully developing the Harrier that was originated by Hawker Siddeley, the Douglas component in 1983 began to develop an American version of another aircraft that began with Hawker Siddeley. The British Aerospace Hawk trainer first began service with the RAF in 1976. An efficient aircraft with a secondary ground-attack training capability, the Hawk caught the eye of the US Navy, which selected it as the basis for a new aircraft-carrier trainer. McDonnell Douglas was in turn selected to develop the Hawk from a shore trainer to an aircraft capable of operating from carriers under the designation T-45. The McDonnell Douglas T-45 Strike Training System (STS) is being developed as a totally integrated system to improve training effectiveness and lower training costs. Students will begin undergraduate jet flight training in late 1988 with the T-45 STS. The system is designed to remain an advanced training system until after the turn of the century.

The F/A-18 Hornet

At the same time that McDonnell Douglas was developing the F-15 air superiority fighter for the US Air Force, the latter was conducting a competition for a lightweight fighter under a program called, appropriately, LWF. The competition boiled down to the General Dynamics F-16 and the Northrop F-17, which were flown for the first time in February and June of 1974. The winner, announced in January 1975, was

the single-engined F-16. Meanwhile, the US Navy had been developing a lightweight fighter/attack aircraft under its VFAX program. When Congress cut VFAX funding, the Navy took a look at the Air Force LWF program prototypes. The McDonnell component of McDonnell Douglas, which had built the F-4 Phantom that the new plane would replace, proposed a McDonnell-modified version of the Northrop F-17, and in May 1975 it received a Navy contract to develop the new plane. McDonnell Douglas was the prime contractor and Northrop was the 'major airframe subcontractor.' Hughes Aircraft produced the APG-65 long-range radar and General Electric built the plane's two 16000-lb-thrust F404 turbofan engines. The new aircraft, nicknamed Hornet, was procured by the Marine Corps as a fighter under the designation F-18 and by the Navy as an attack aircraft under the designation A-18. The program is generally referred to as the F/A-18 program because the two aircraft are actually identical (except for markings and whatever armament might be hanging on a plane at a given moment). The planes can be easily converted from one role to the other, and thus from one designation to the other. The Hornet is also being modified to permit rapid conversion for photoreconnaissance, which replaces a more expensive earlier proposal to develop an RF-18 reconnaissance version.

The Hornet first flew on 18 November 1978 and entered operational squadron service with both the Navy and Marine Corps as well as the Canadian Armed Forces in 1983. In addition to the 24 CF-18s delivered to Canada, 75 F/A-18s have been ordered by the Royal Australian Air Force, with final assembly of all but two of these to take place in Australia. In May 1983 Spain signed a contract to purchase 72 EF-18s for delivery in 1986.

For its variety of roles, the Hornet has been equipped to carry an assortment of armament. In the fighter mode, the plane carries wingtip-mounted Sidewinder air-to-air missiles with Sparrow missiles mounted on the fuselage. Four wing pylons can carry either Sidewinders and Sparrows or, in the attack role, bombs or air to ground missiles. A fuselage centerline pylon can accommodate either a fuel tank or strike weapons. All of these weapons, as well as the nose-mounted MG1 20-mm cannon, are controlled via an all-weather multimode radar and fire-control system. The total ordnance load that can be carried on the Hornet's nine weapons stations can exceed 17,000 lb.

In November 1983 cracks began to turn up in the F/A-18 engine mounts, and by July 1984 other cracks were also found in

Above and below: US Navy F/A-18 Hornets of Fighter Attack Squadron 125 at NAS Lemoore in California.

Left: A Marine F-18 of the Third Marine Air Wing at El Toro, California test fires an AIM-9L Sidewinder air-to-air missile.

Above: A Marine Corps F-18 Hornet is prepared for action while a second one screams overhead.

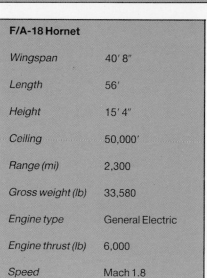

F/A-18 Hornet

Wingspan	40' 8"
Length	56'
Height	15' 4"
Ceiling	50,000'
Range (mi)	2,300
Gross weight (lb)	33,580
Engine type	General Electric
Engine thrust (lb)	6,000
Speed	Mach 1.8

Above: A cutaway view of a McDonnell Douglas F-18 Hornet showing internal detail and armament. The latter includes fuselage-mounted AIM-7 Sparrow air-to-air missiles, wingtip mounted AIM-9 Sidewinder air-to-air missiles and the multibarreled 20-mm cannon directly ahead of the cockpit.

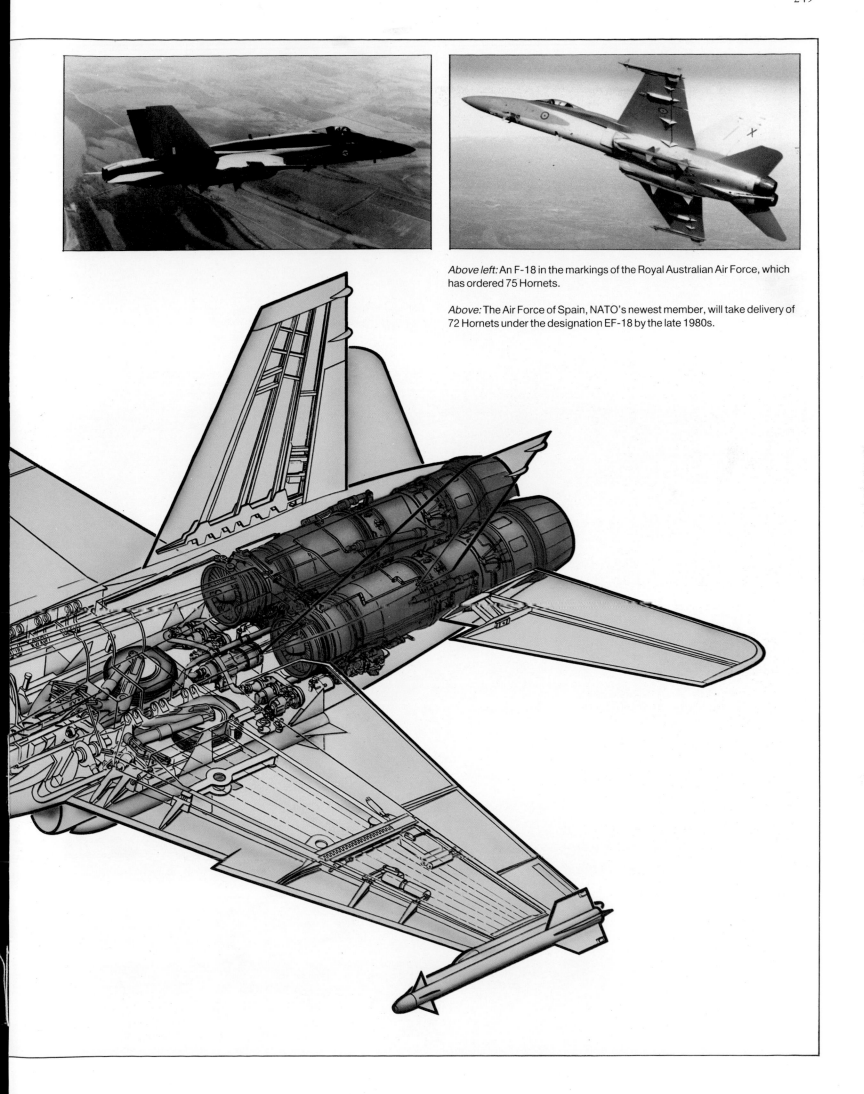

Above left: An F-18 in the markings of the Royal Australian Air Force, which has ordered 75 Hornets.

Above: The Air Force of Spain, NATO's newest member, will take delivery of 72 Hornets under the designation EF-18 by the late 1980s.

Above: An F-18A Hornet from the US Navy's Fighter/AEW Wing Pacific Squadron (VX-4), an air-test and evaluation squadron. It was armed with both Sparrow and Sidewinder air-to-air missiles for this February 1981 mission.

Left and below: One of the US Navy's first F-18s is catapult launched for a 1979 test flight from the carrier USS *Amorioa.*

the plane's tail section. Turbulent airflow produced by the leading edge extension of the tail was determined a probable cause. Though at first the cracks were not regarded as a safety issue, the Navy told the company on 27 July that it would accept no more aircraft until the problem had been rectified. As for the earlier Hornets, those delivered after January 1984 would be retrofitted by McDonnell Douglas under terms of the warranty. Those delivered prior to that time would be fixed for the Navy at cost. The repairs began in September 1984 and took roughly two weeks for each aircraft.

Ironically the problems with the F-18 arose in large part because it is capable of doing what no other plane could do. The Hornet can operate at a higher angle of attack than any other aircraft, and consequently the effects of the turbulent airflow have not been previously encountered by any other plane.

The Fighter Makers

Despite problems with the F/A-18 program, the McDonnell component of McDonnell Douglas has earned a reputation for fighter aircraft shared by few companies in the history of military aviation. Development of the F-4 Phantom alone would have earned the company a place in history, but the amazing unprecedented success of the F-15 Eagle in the hands of the Israeli Air Force assures a place for McDonnell in the pantheon of the truly legendary. The tactical-combat aircraft engineers at McDonnell have in a real sense charted the course of McDonnell and subsequently of McDonnell Douglas. As the US Air Force plans the generation of fighters that will fill its squadrons at the turn of the century, the fighter makers from St Louis will be there.

INDEX

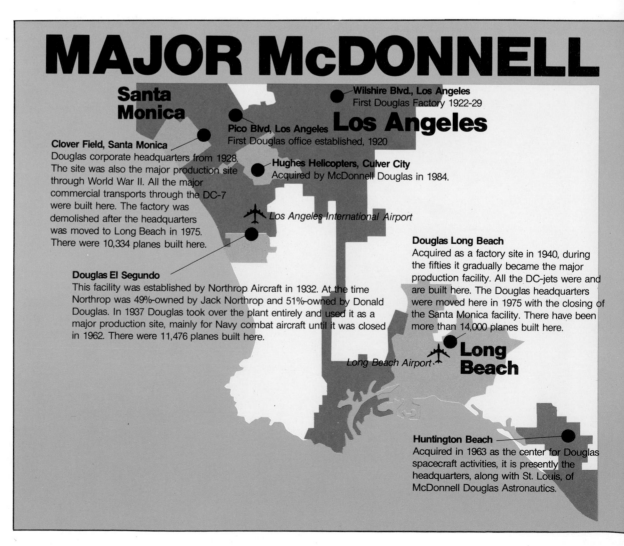

DOUGLAS LOCATIONS

*Chicago, Illinois (wartime transport production, 655 planes built)

Lambert Field, St. Louis , Missouri. Headquarters of McDonnell Aircraft Company since 1939 and the McDonnell Douglas Corporation since 1967, it is the major McDonnell production facility and also the headquarters of McDonnell Douglas Automation, McDonnell Douglas Electronics and VITEK.

Brooklyn, New York Donald Wills Douglas born, April 6, 1892

*Sacramento, California (missile testing)

Denver, Colorado James Smith McDonnell, Jr. born, April 9, 1899

St. Louis

*Culver City

Area enlarged at left

Louisville, Kentucky Headquarters of the CoaLiquid subsidiary

Mesa, Arizona Hughes Helicopters production facility acquired by McDonnell Douglas in 1984.

*Charlotte, NC (missile production)

*Tucson, Arizona (B-66 production)

Tulsa, Oklahoma Acquired by Douglas in 1941 as a bomber production facility, it was closed after the war and reopened in 1950. There were 3267 planes built here.

*Oklahoma City, Oklahoma (wartime transport production, 5381 planes built)

Titusville, Florida Production facility for the Tomahawk Cruise Missile.

Former Douglas Aircraft Company facilities no longer extant.

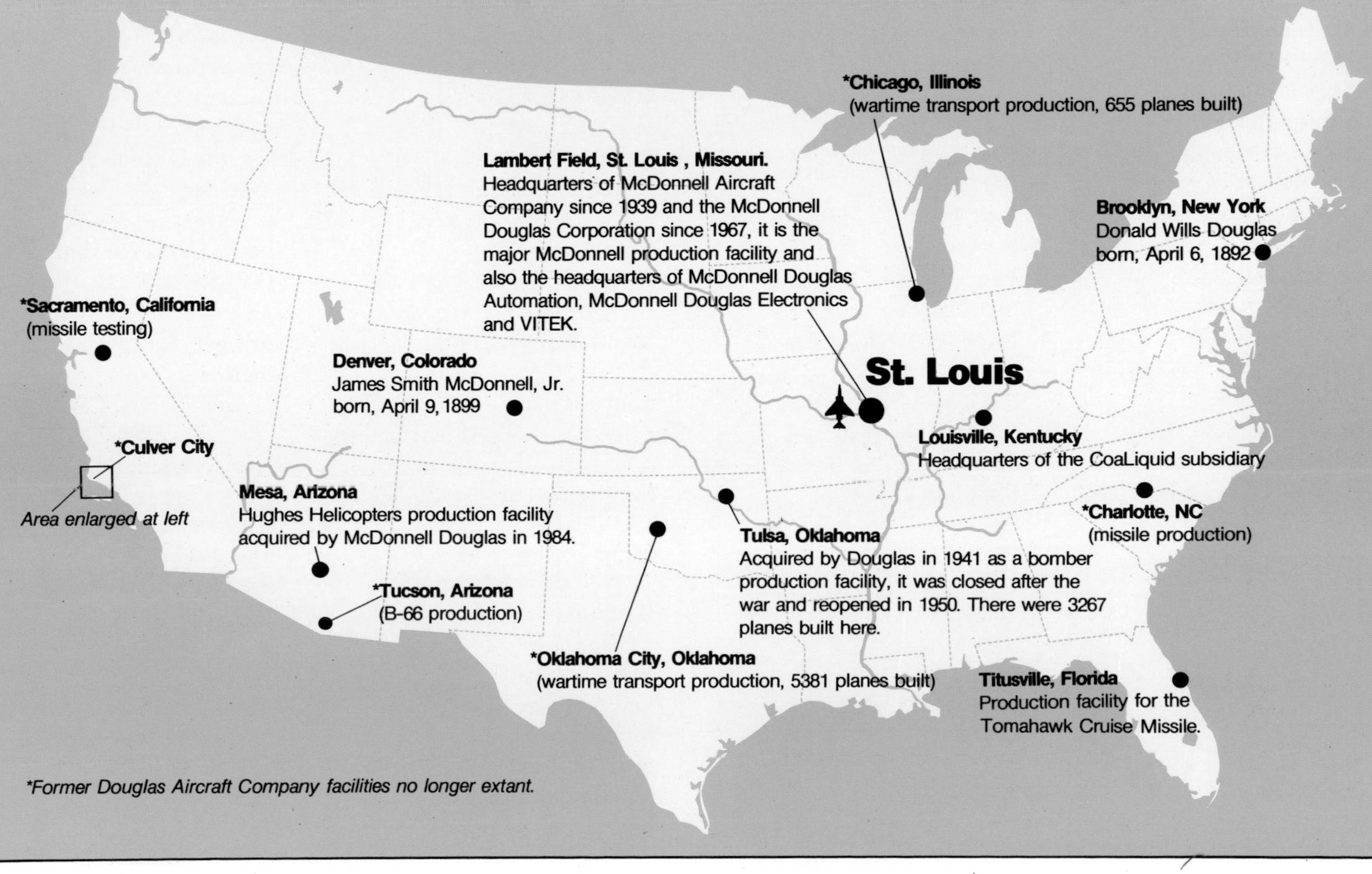

Above: A group of six DC-9s destined for airlines on three continents undergo finishing touches in the final assembly area of the McDonnell Douglas Long Beach plant.

Above left: An aerial view of the Douglas plant at Clover Field, Santa Monica at the time of the XB-19 rollout in 1941. The aircraft on the field are (left to right) a pair of DC-3s, the XB-19, a DC-3, two TBD Devastators (one with wings folded) amid 14 RAF-bound A-20s and another DC-3. Immediately beyond the A-20s are a pair of TBDs, two DC-3 fuselages and five more A-20s.

Note: In military nomenclature, the common designations of experimental and service test aircraft have the prefixes X or Y (respectively) added. For the purpose of clarity this index lists all the aircraft of a given type under their common designations..

The Douglas Transports

Douglas Commercial Model	USAAF/USAF Designation	US Navy Designation	First Military Use
DC-1	None	None	(None)
DC-2	C-32, C-33, C-34, C-38, C-39, C-41, C-42	R2D	(1900)
DC-3	C-47 Skytrain, C-48, C-50, C-51, C-52, C-53 Skytrooper C-68C-84, C-117	R4D Skytrain	(1941)
Super DC-3	C-47F Skytrain, C-129	R4D Skytrain	(1951)
DC-4	C-54 Skymaster, C112	R5D Skymaster	(1942)
DC-5	C-110	R3D	(1940)
DC-6	C-118 Liftmaster	R6D Liftmaster	(1950)
None	C-74 Globemaster I	None	(1942)
None	C-124 Globemaster II	None	(1949)
None	C-132	None	(Never built)
None	C-133 Cargomaster	None	(1954)
DC-7	None	None	(None)
DC-8	None	None	(None)
DC-9	C-9A Nightingale	C-9B Skytrain II	(1967)
DC-10	KC-10 Extender	None	(1978)
MD-80	None	None	(None)

A group of McDonnell Douglas F-15 Eagles from the USAF Tactical Air Command's 555th Tactical Fighter Squadron out of Luke AFB, over an enormous meteor crater in northwestern Arizona. The 555th TFS, the 'Triple Nickel,' had the best USAF air-to-air combat record during the war in Southeast Asia and was the first squadron to receive Eagles, perhaps the best fighter jet ever to fly in combat.